SECURITIES LAW

FIFTH EDITION

by

LARRY D. SODERQUIST
Late Professor of Law
Vanderbilt University

THERESA A. GABALDON
Lyle T. Alverson Professor of Law
George Washington University

CONCEPTS AND INSIGHTS SERIES®

FOUNDATION
PRESS

Concepts and Insights Series is a trademark registered in the U.S. Patent and Trademark Office.

© 1998, 2004 FOUNDATION PRESS
© 2007, 2011 THOMSON REUTERS/FOUNDATION PRESS
© 2014 LEG, Inc. d/b/a West Academic

    444 Cedar Street, Suite 700
    St. Paul, MN 55101
    1-877-888-1330

Printed in the United States of America

ISBN: 978-1-60930-469-0
Mat. #41552362

*

In Memoriam

Larry D. Soderquist

———————

For Bob and Will

*

PREFACE

The aim of this book is to make securities regulation classes fun—or at least not painfully confusing. There is no reason why a student shouldn't enjoy a class on securities law. As described in the Introduction, securities law is a puzzle, and most people can have fun working with a puzzle. The trick is to be properly prepared.

Studying the Securities Act of 1933 or the Securities Exchange Act of 1934 can be miserable if a student is not adequately prepared, because it means trying to put together a puzzle without knowing the rules. Or, picking up on an analogy used in the Introduction, it is like trying to figure out a Houdini illusion without having been shown the mirrors and trap doors.

For some students, reading a casebook and going to class is all the preparation needed. Others find that they get behind, or get lost on some point, and thereafter can't get back on track on their own. And, in the case of securities law, once one is lost, finding one's own way back is extremely difficult. One object of this book is to get a student on track and keep him or her there. Another is to help in reviewing material and preparing for examinations.

What about the student who keeps up—and doesn't have to miss classes for, say, job interviews? Will this book be of much value for that student? Almost certainly. For such a student, this book can be a great aid at exam time because of the quickly understandable synthesis it will provide. In addition, reading about a subject in this book before doing a class assignment likely will make the assignment easier, quicker, and more understandable.

Securities law cases often are filled with material extraneous to the subject being studied, and they often throw a student in over his or her head by discussing material that has not yet been introduced in class. This alone can make a securities regulation class difficult and an assignment tedious. Often, too, cases are not as well written as one would like, making them needlessly hard to understand. No student can protect himself or herself from these problems without help.

In this book, I have followed the example of the founding author, Larry Soderquist, in taking pains to make securities law more accessible to all students. I believe that the material is broken down in easily digestible chunks. In addition, I have tried to be very careful not to get students in over their heads, for example by not using terms or discussing concepts without adequate explanation. Most important, I have tried hard to make the book easy to read.

PREFACE

There is no excuse for turgid prose. Not ever. And certainly not in discussing securities law.

My wish is that you will enjoy your study of securities regulation and find it readily understandable, and I hope that you find this book helpful.

THERESA A. GABALDON

February 2014

SUMMARY OF CONTENTS

TABLE OF CONTENTS

TABLE OF CONTENTS

SECURITIES LAW

FIFTH EDITION

INTRODUCTION

Securities law has a reputation for being difficult. And it is, especially the Securities Act of 1933. This act is so difficult, in fact, that a student, or lawyer, cannot learn it on his or her own. *Gustafson v. Alloyd Co., Inc.*,[1] which is discussed in Chapters 4 and 8, provides a good example. In that case, some very bright Supreme Court justices, and their equally intelligent clerks, evidently attempted to figure out the Securities Act on their own and they failed miserably. From the careful reasoning of the case, it is clear that the problem was not a lack of diligence. The problem, rather, was that the Securities Act is a puzzle that can be put together in many ways that look right, but only one of them is. The justices and their clerks seemed simply to have picked the wrong way to put the puzzle together.

Those attempting to learn securities law should take heart, however. Thankfully, securities law is not conceptually difficult in the way that, say, quantum physics is. Its difficulty is more akin to the difficulty of seeing through one of Houdini's illusions. Although doing that is almost impossible on one's own, it is easy when someone points out the mirrors and trap doors. That is what this book attempts to do—point out the mirrors and trap doors of securities law, or more correctly put, of the most often encountered provisions of the Securities Act of 1933 and the Securities Exchange Act of 1934. These are the parts of those acts that students typically study in a securities regulation course and that corporate and securities lawyers generally encounter in their practices.

In doing this, the book covers such other topics as (i) the workings of the Securities and Exchange Commission, (ii) the rules and other pronouncements of the Commission, (iii) many of the more significant securities law cases, (iv) how securities law actually works (which one cannot learn from the statutes, rules, and cases), (v) the business context in which securities law is practiced, (vi) the special position of securities lawyers with respect to professional responsibility, (vii) the Sarbanes–Oxley Act of 2002, and (viii) some of the responses to the panic and subsequent recession afflicting the financial markets beginning in 2008. These topics are all part of the mirrors and trap doors of securities law.

---

[1] 513 U.S. 561 (1995).

Chapter 1

WHAT IS A SECURITY

The issue of what is a security is one of the most interesting in securities law. Everyone knows what the most common securities are, such as stocks and bonds. But courts have found that all manner of investment schemes, including some relating to earthworms, chinchillas, and warehouse receipts for Scotch whisky, also involve a security. The student of securities law learns very quickly that the issue of whether a transaction involves a security is based on concepts completely foreign to the uninitiated.

Statutory Definition

The substantive provisions of the Securities Act begin with this definition:

Section 2(a). Definitions.—When used in this title, unless the context otherwise requires—

(1) the term "security" means any note, stock, treasury stock, bond, debenture, security future, security-based swap, evidence of indebtedness, certificate of interest or participation in any profit-sharing agreement, collateral-trust certificate, preorganization certificate or subscription, transferable share, investment contract, voting-trust certificate, certificate of deposit for a security, fractional undivided interest in oil, gas, or other mineral rights, any put, call, straddle, option, or privilege on any security, certificate of deposit, or group or index of securities (including any interest therein or based on the value thereof), or any put, call, straddle, option, or privilege entered into on a national securities exchange relating to foreign currency, or, in general, any interest or instrument commonly known as a "security," or any certificate of interest or participation in, temporary or interim certificate for, receipt for, guarantee of, or warrant or right to subscribe to or purchase, any of the foregoing.

The bulk of section 2(a)(1) is clear, and most questions concerning whether a security exists for purposes of the Securities Act can be answered by reference to that section. Further, since the Securities Act definition is virtually identical to the definition found in Exchange Act section 3(a)(10), most such questions under the Exchange Act may also be answered by reference to this same language. One item in the section 2(a)(1) list of securities has caused the majority of the trouble. That item is the "investment contract," and it will be focused on as a paradigm of the Securities Act's inclusiveness. At the other end of the spectrum is the phrase "unless the context otherwise requires," which is found at the beginning of each Act's definitions. That language offers the greatest exclusiveness in terms of defining a security. It will be taken up later in this chapter.

The term "security-based swap" was added to section 2(a)(1) in 2010. In general, "swaps" are contracts providing that the parties will exchange obligations to make payments on specified financial instruments, and jurisdiction over other than security-based swaps has been allocated to the Commodity Futures Trading Commission. A "security-based swap" is a swap on a single security or loan or narrow-based security index (generally one with fewer than nine component securities). A regulatory regime for security-based swaps was established by the SEC in 2012 but is beyond the scope of this book. That said, it is worth mentioning that section 2A of the Securities Act provides that "security-based swap *agreements*" (which basically are agreements individually negotiated by a limited group of eligible persons) are not securities at all.

Investment Contract

There long has been confusion about just what constitutes an investment contract. The main reason is that the term has no meaning in a commercial context but is simply a construct of legislators and judges. To understand the federal courts' interpretation of an investment contract, an understanding of *SEC v. W.J. Howey Co.*[1] is necessary. In the 1940s, the W.J. Howey Co. offered sections of an orange grove for sale. At the same time, a sister company offered prospective purchasers ten-year service contracts. Under those contracts, the company offered to take the plots under lease and manage every aspect of growing, harvesting, and selling oranges. The produce harvested by the service company was to be pooled, and any profit allocated to the various owners.

The Commission sought an injunction on the grounds that the Howey companies were offering and selling investment contracts that had not been registered under the Securities Act. The district and circuit courts rejected the Commission's request, but the Supreme Court reversed. As stated by the Court, "The test is whether the scheme involves an investment of money in a common enterprise with profits to come solely from the efforts of others." Applying the test, the Court found that the Howey companies were indeed offering investment contracts:

---

[1]   328 U.S. 293 (1946).

They are offering an opportunity to contribute money and to share in the profits of a large citrus fruit enterprise managed and partly owned by respondents. . . . [The offered] tracts gain utility as citrus groves only when cultivated and developed as component parts of a larger area. A common enterprise managed by respondents or third parties with adequate personnel and equipment is therefore essential if the investors are to achieve their paramount aim of a return on their investments.

In the years since *Howey*, litigation has focused on the precise meaning of the *Howey* test. For purposes of discussion, it is helpful to break the test down into four elements:

1. Investment of money

2. Common enterprise

3. Expectation of profits

4. Solely from the efforts of others

The following element-by-element discussion provides a flavor of the interpretive problems inherent in the *Howey* test.

Investment of Money

The meaning of "money" can be disposed of easily. The Securities Act covers all offers and sales of securities, regardless of the form of consideration to be exchanged in the bargain. The consideration does not actually have to be money. Perhaps the Court used "money" as a shorthand for something like "cash or checks (which would cover the *Howey* facts and those of virtually all other cases) and anything else that would constitute consideration."

For an "investment" to exist, one must put out consideration with the hope of a financial return. Perhaps the most important case discussing the meaning of "investment" is *International Brotherhood of Teamsters v. Daniel*.[2] In that case, the Supreme Court had to determine whether an investment contract existed where employers, under a collective bargaining agreement, made contributions to an employees' retirement plan to which the employees themselves did not contribute. The Court found that the employees made no investment, saying that "it seems clear that an employee is selling his labor primarily to obtain a livelihood, not making an investment."

---

[2] 439 U.S. 551 (1979).

Common Enterprise

Two clear and disparate formulations of a "common enterprise" have emerged in the courts of appeals. One is vertical commonality, which focuses on the community of interest of an individual investor and the manager of the enterprise, and the other is horizontal commonality, which concentrates on the interrelated interests of the various investors in a particular scheme.

One formulation of vertical commonality has been nicely stated in *SEC v. Koscot Interplanetary, Inc.*[3] and *SEC v. Glenn W. Turner Enterprises, Inc.*,[4] each of which involved pyramid schemes run by affiliated companies. "A common enterprise is one in which the fortunes of the investor are interwoven with and dependent upon the efforts and success of those seeking the investment or of third parties." Note that, under this formulation, there may be a common enterprise involving only one promoter and one offeree.

In *Milnarik v. M–S Commodities, Inc.*,[5] the Seventh Circuit reached a different conclusion in deciding that a discretionary commodity trading account with a broker did not involve a common enterprise. The court found horizontal commonality to be required in the Seventh Circuit and focused on the fact that the profitability of the plaintiffs' account was not influenced by the success or failure of other accounts managed by the same broker. What existed, the court found, was simply an agency for hire, with the broker's customers being represented by a common agent. In a later case involving a discretionary trading account, *Hirk v. Agri–Research Council, Inc.*,[6] the Seventh Circuit sharpened its horizontal commonality by stating clearly that both multiple investors and a sharing or pooling of funds is required for the common enterprise element to be present.

In thinking about the "common enterprise" element of the *Howey* test, it may be helpful to note that some courts have identified different versions of vertical commonality. One version, called strict vertical commonality, requires that the fortunes of the investor be linked to the *fortunes* of some other party. The other version, called broad vertical commonality, requires only that the fortunes of the investor be linked to the *efforts* of another party. (Note that courts that accept vertical commonality can be expected also to accept horizontal commonality if it happens to exist.)

---

[3] 497 F.2d 473 (5th Cir.1974).

[4] 474 F.2d 476 (9th Cir.1973).

[5] 457 F.2d 274 (7th Cir.1972).

[6] 561 F.2d 96 (7th Cir.1977).

Expectation of Profits

One of the most important cases on the *Howey* "expectation of profit" element is *International Brotherhood of Teamsters v. Daniel*. As indicated above, *Daniel* involved contributions by employers into a noncontributory pension plan maintained for their employees. As with all such plans, the managers invested the contributed funds to earn profits, which ultimately were to flow through to the employees as benefits. The Supreme Court found the "expectation of profit" element missing, however, and focused on what it viewed as the relatively small percentage of the plan's assets derived from earnings rather than from employer contributions. Logically the Court should not have cared about actual performance, since the proper focus was the reasonable profit expectations of the plan's beneficiaries. Stated simply, many investment schemes go wrong, but they do not any the less involve the sale of securities for that reason.

United Housing Foundation, Inc. v. Forman[7] is more helpful. In that case, the purchasers of interests in a cooperative housing project could receive some financial benefit from their ownership. Although no profit on a resale of interests was possible (the interests could be resold at the original purchase price only), the project leased commercial space to third parties, with any income derived to be used to reduce the rent on the housing units. That, the Court said, was "far too speculative and insubstantial to bring the entire transaction within the Securities Acts."

Neither *Daniel* nor *Forman* should be interpreted, however, as giving promoters leeway in structuring investment transactions so that they do not involve securities. In *Daniel* the Court was influenced by the fact that Congress had just subjected pensions to extensive regulation by ERISA, and in *Forman* by the obvious motivation of the purchasers to obtain a decent place to live at an attractive price. The tenor of each opinion clearly shows a desire not to find a security. Had the Court wanted to do so, it easily could have found the other way in each case.

SEC v. Edwards[8] is a case in which the Supreme Court clearly did wish to find the presence of a security. The scheme involved the sale of pay phones packaged with a five-year leaseback and management agreement, as well as a buyback agreement. The Court rejected its own dicta from an earlier case,[9] holding that the fact that a money-making scheme offers a contractual entitlement

---

[7]　421 U.S. 837 (1975).

[8]　540 U.S. 389 (2004).

[9]　*Reves v. Ernst & Young*, 494 U.S. 56 (1990).

to a fixed, rather than a variable, return, did not prevent it from being a security.

Solely from the Efforts of Others

The "solely from the efforts of others" element of the *Howey* test is perhaps the most interesting. One question, of course, has been whether to apply the test literally. The Ninth and Fifth Circuits dealt with this question in *Glenn W. Turner* and *Koscot*. Both of those cases involved pyramid schemes in which the investors were not passive. Once brought into the scheme themselves, it was their job to find new prospects and bring them to sales meetings run by the promoting companies. Those sales meetings were, the court said in *Glenn W. Turner*, "like an old-time revival meeting, but directed toward the joys of making easy money rather than salvation." It is clear that the courts were impressed with the skills of the people running the meetings, and rightly so. They undoubtedly were consummate persuaders. But the contributions of the investors also were substantial, for unless they brought prospects to the meetings, there would have been no one in which to instill the joys of making easy money.

Each court chose not to read "solely" literally, pointing out that "it would be easy to evade the test by adding a requirement that the buyer contribute a modicum of effort." The test those courts adopted, however, went far beyond that required to avoid the modicum-of-effort problem and entailed an inquiry into "whether the efforts made by those other than the investor are the undeniably significant ones, those essential managerial efforts which affect the failure or success of the enterprise." (The focus on managerial efforts as the undeniably significant ones is interesting, since the skills that seemed most important to the courts were technical rather than managerial—the ability to stir up an audience.)

The post-*Koscot* history of the "solely" element is confused. In *Forman*, the Supreme Court reaffirmed the *Howey* test and also said that its "touchstone is the presence of an investment in a common venture premised on a reasonable expectation of profits to be derived from the entrepreneurial or managerial efforts of others." But in a curious footnote on the same page, the Court indicated that it "expressed no view" on the holding of *Glenn W. Turner* that "solely" should be read flexibly rather than literally. Perhaps all the Court meant here was that its *Forman* holding did not reach that question, but it is impossible to be sure. What is known is that three years later, in *Daniel*, the Court repeated the "touchstone" formulation from *Forman* and then proceeded briefly to discuss the managerial efforts of the pension fund's trustees. But, as in *Forman*, the "solely" element was not in question in *Daniel* because all the purported investors clearly were passive. Thus, the Supreme Court has never confronted the issue presented in *Glenn W. Turner* and *Koscot*. Perhaps that, more than anything else, accounts for the confusion in its opinions.

Unless the Context Otherwise Requires

The definitional sections of both the Securities Act and the Exchange Act begin with the same words: "When used in this title, unless the context otherwise requires. . . ." Those clauses seem to have been forgotten for most of the years since those Acts were passed, at least as a stated basis for a court's analysis of whether something fell within or outside of a particular definition. Since the 1982 Supreme Court decision in *Marine Bank v. Weaver*,[10] however, those words are much in the minds of lawyers wrestling with the question of what constitutes a security.

Marine Bank involved the question of whether a certificate of deposit issued by a national bank was a security. The Court quoted the "unless the context otherwise requires" language and explained why in that instance the context "otherwise required": in large measure because a national bank is subject to comprehensive regulation designed to protect depositors, and, perhaps more important, their certificates of deposit are federally insured. Even though *Marine Bank* is apparently the first case in which the Supreme Court explicitly used the securities statutes' contextual exception as a basis for a decision, the exception arguably has underpinned earlier opinions. For example, the much-quoted statement in *Tcherepnin v. Knight*[11] that "in searching for the meaning and scope of the word 'security' in the Acts, form should be disregarded for substance, and the emphasis should be on economic reality," seems clearly to call for a contextual analysis.

The analysis of economic reality has led to two lines of cases fitting the "unless the context otherwise requires" mold. One line involved the question of whether the sale of a business, which is consummated by the sale of stock in the corporation that conducts the business, involves the sale of a security. The other deals with the issue of whether promissory notes are securities.

Under the sale-of-business doctrine, when a corporate business is sold by means of a sale of the corporation's stock, the stock is not a "security," as the term is used in the securities acts. The idea that common stock, the archetypical security, could fall outside the statutory definitions of "security" is baffling. Perhaps more baffling,

---

[10] 455 U.S. 551 (1982).
[11] 389 U.S. 332 (1967).

however, is the effect of the opposite conclusion. When a corporation's common stock is a security in that context, a strange anomaly results. An owner of a business who sells, in an arm's-length and face-to-face transaction, 100 percent of a corporation's stock to someone who wants to own and manage the corporation is subject to all of the registration and antifraud provisions of the securities acts, while another who sells his or her business by selling all of its assets is subject only to the common-law fraud rules. The illogic of that result is greater than it may at first appear, because the means by which the sale of a business is accomplished is usually a technical question, the resolution of which depends largely upon lawyers' and accountants' advice. From a business standpoint, a stock sale and an assets sale look very much the same.

Perhaps by choosing one form of bafflement over the other, courts of appeals went both ways on the sale-of-business doctrine. After viewing the struggle among the circuits, the Supreme Court decided the issue in *Landreth Timber Co. v. Landreth*.[12] That case involved the private sale of a family-owned lumber company that was accomplished by selling all of the stock of the corporation that conducted the business. Within the first few words of the Court's recitation of the facts, it was apparent that the sale-of-business doctrine was dead: "The Landreth family offered their stock for sale. . . ." By choosing to focus on the formalities of the transaction rather than the business realities, the Court foreordained its conclusion that the stock involved in the case was a security.

The sellers of the business in *Landreth* argued that prior cases, *Forman* particularly, required an analysis of the economic substance of the transaction. Relying on that analysis, the sellers stressed that the buyer "sought not to earn profits from the efforts of others, but to buy a company that it could manage and control" and pointed out that the buyer "was not a passive investor of the kind Congress intended the Acts to protect, but an active entrepreneur, who sought to [use] the business purchased just as the purchasers in *Forman* sought to use the apartments they acquired." The Court's response was simple. The prior cases, it said, "involved unusual instruments not easily characterized as 'securities.'" An inquiry was required, therefore, into the economic realities. But, in the situation at hand, what was involved was "traditional stock, plainly within the statutory definition." Therefore, there was no need "to look beyond the characteristics of the instrument to determine whether the Acts apply."

---

[12] 471 U.S. 681 (1985).

Promissory notes are interesting devices for securities lawyers. The term "note" is the first item mentioned in the definition of "security" in both the Securities Act and the Exchange Act. Complicating the matter somewhat, each Act then excludes certain notes, basically those having an original maturity not exceeding nine months, at least from certain provisions of the Act. Regardless of the language of those provisions, however, courts have used an economic reality analysis to determine whether a particular note is a security for purposes of the Securities Act or the Exchange Act. In *Reves v. Ernst & Young*[13] the Supreme Court had to decide whether promissory notes issued by the Farmer's Cooperative of Arkansas and Oklahoma were securities. The notes were payable on demand, were uncollateralized and uninsured, and paid a variable interest rate. At the outset of its decision, the Court took pains to indicate that in *Landreth* it had not rejected in general the economic reality approach it had used in *Marine Bank* and preceding cases. "While common stock [as was involved in *Landreth*] is," the Court said, "the quintessence of a security . . . , the same simply cannot be said of notes, which are used in a variety of settings, not all of which involve investments."

In analyzing the economic reality underlying the notes in the case before it, the Supreme Court in *Reves* adopted the Second Circuit's "family resemblance" test for determining whether a note is a security. Here is the test:

> [A] note is presumed to be a "security," and that presumption may be rebutted only by a showing that a note bears a strong resemblance (in terms of . . . four factors . . .) to one of the . . . categories of instrument [listed by the Second Circuit]. If an instrument is not sufficiently similar to an item on the list, the decision whether another category should be added is to be made by examining the same factors.

The categories of instrument, listed by the Second Circuit as being notes that are not securities, are the following:

> [T]he note delivered in consumer financing, the note secured by a mortgage on a home, the short-term note secured by a lien on a small business or some of its assets, the note evidencing a "character" loan to a bank customer, short-term notes secured by an assignment of accounts receivable, or a note which simply formalizes an open-account debt incurred in the ordinary course of business (particularly if, as in the case of the customer of a broker, it is collateralized).

---

[13] 494 U.S. 56 (1990).

Finally, here are the four factors to be used in considering family resemblance:

First, we examine the transaction to access the motivations that would prompt a reasonable seller and buyer to enter into it. [E.g., is the seller's purpose the raising of money and is the buyer primarily interested in making a profit on the note or, on the other hand, is the note being used to facilitate the purchase and sale of a minor asset or consumer good?]

Second, we examine the "plan of distribution" of the instrument . . . to determine whether it is an instrument in which there is "common trading for speculation or investment." [The Court noting that "common trading" does not require actual trading in the financial markets.]

Third, we examine the reasonable expectations of the investing public: The Court will consider instruments to be "securities" on the basis of such public expectations, even where an economic analysis . . . might suggest that the instruments are not "securities" as used in that transaction. [E.g., advertising notes as securities helps to make them securities.]

Finally, we examine whether some factor such as the existence of another regulatory scheme significantly reduces the risk of the instrument, thereby rendering application of the Securities Acts unnecessary.

After applying the four-factor test to the Farmer's Cooperative notes, the Court found that the notes were securities since they did not bear a sufficient family resemblance to the notes the Court had previously determined not to be securities.

As the years go by, courts all around the country add to their own disparate lists of what kinds of notes are not securities. With this in mind, one wonders how well the family resemblance test will work in the long run, especially considering the national and international nature of many transactions.

Chapter 2

WORLD OF SECURITIES LAW

The world of securities law is new to most students, and parts of it are especially new to those who have not taken a course in administrative law. In this chapter we will explain how the securities laws came about, briefly introduce each of the New Deal securities statutes, show where to find each type of "law" and appreciate its place in the hierarchy of regulation, and discuss the special position of securities lawyers with respect to professional responsibility. We also will say a brief word about state securities regulation.

New Deal Securities Statutes

The Securities Act is quintessential New Deal legislation. It grew out of the 1929 stock market crash and Franklin Roosevelt's 1932 campaign, securities law reform being one of the planks of the Democratic platform. Within weeks of his inauguration, Roosevelt moved to begin the reform. A former Federal Trade Commissioner named Huston Thompson was given the task of drafting the Securities Act. His bill went to Congress in March of 1933, accompanied by a message from the President stating his desires about the legislation. It quickly became apparent that the Thompson bill was not consistent with those desires. The President agreed with Louis Brandeis that "sunshine is said to be the best of disinfectants; electric light the most efficient policeman," and he wanted regulation through disclosure requirements. However, the Thompson bill went in another direction. It mandated what has become known as "merit regulation." This scheme, much used in state securities law, gives a governmental body the power to pass upon the merits of securities offerings and to prevent certain offerings.

In early April, a new drafting team was formed. The members' identities, their intellect, and the constraints on them as they worked are important parts of the tale. The group, which was assembled by Felix Frankfurter, consisted of James M. Landis, a Harvard Law School professor; Thomas G. Corcoran, a government lawyer recently out of a securities law practice; and Benjamin V. Cohen, a practicing lawyer. Each was brilliant, and from the statute they created it is apparent that they delighted in mental challenges involving interwoven complexities and neatly hidden traps.

The team set to work on a Friday. By late Saturday they had a draft that, more than sixty years later, still constitutes the main body of the Securities Act. The Act is a masterpiece, an intellectual tour de force. It is fun to work with once you know how. For now, realize that when one works with the Securities Act, one plays a complex mental game devised by three exceptional minds, over a weekend, more than half a century ago. (Part of the probably apocryphal lore of securities law is that the Act was drafted not only over a weekend, but over a case of Scotch.)

The Securities Exchange Act of 1934, the other statute discussed in this book in some detail, is the second part of the securities regulatory scheme that was contemplated as early as the 1932 Democratic campaign. It is substantially longer than the Securities Act, and its coverage is much more diverse. It also is more straightforward, making it easier to work with than the Securities Act. But it lacks the idiosyncratic sparkle that makes the Securities Act at once more interesting and difficult.

Since the early 1980s, the Commission has done much to integrate disclosure under the Securities Act and the Exchange Act. This has simplified practical compliance for many companies but has complicated the job of the securities lawyer.

The Securities Act and the Exchange Act constitute virtually the entire body of general federal securities regulation. Most securities lawyers deal primarily with these two Acts. There are, however, a number of other federal securities statutes, each of which deals with a specialized area. The most important of these statutes are: (1) the Trust Indenture Act of 1939, (2) the Investment Company Act of 1940, and (3) the Investment Advisers Act of 1940.

As the title of the Trust Indenture Act of 1939 suggests, it relates to trust indentures, which are contracts between the issuer of debt securities and a trustee. Included in the Act are provisions establishing requirements for trust indentures and relating to what must be in an indenture and to who may serve as a trustee, along with provisions governing the conduct of trustees. The Act applies to most indentures relating to securities that are required to be registered under the Securities Act.

The Investment Company Act of 1940, which regulates mutual funds, and the Investment Advisers Act of 1940, which regulates investment advisers, are aggressive statutes aimed at specific groups within the securities industry. Like the Trust Indenture Act, each of these statutes is the main preserve of a small percentage of securities lawyers. These three specialized acts share one important attribute—each is best approached by someone who understands the Securities Act and the Exchange Act.

Each of the statutes discussed above essentially creates a comprehensive regulatory scheme. Over the years, acts of Congress have amended and supplemented these schemes many times. Of particular note are three Acts passed in the present century: The Sarbanes–Oxley Act of 2002, the Dodd-Frank Wall Street Reform and Consumer Protection Act of 2010, and the Jumpstart Our Business Startups Act of 2012 ("JOBS").

Hierarchy of Regulation

The various federal securities statutes are, of course, the primary source of federal securities law. Congress, however, has given the Securities and Exchange Commission, which it created in section 4 of the Exchange Act, the power to supplement the securities statutes by rules. This grant is both general and specific. For example, section 19(a) of the Securities Act provides a general grant of rule-making power: "The Commission shall have authority from time to time to make . . . such rules and regulations as may be necessary to carry out the provisions of this title. . . ." Section 2(a)(15) provides an example of a specific grant:

The term "accredited investor" shall mean—

(i) [a person meeting criteria specified]; or

(ii) any person who, on the basis of such factors as financial sophistication, net worth, knowledge, and experience in financial matters, or amount of assets under management qualifies as an accredited investor under rules and regulations which the Commission shall prescribe.

Notice that, with respect to the definition of an accredited investor, Congress in section 2(a)(15) both makes its own law, in subsection (i), and gives the Commission guidance for rule-making, in subsection (ii). In other situations, Congress has chosen simply to turn everything over to the Commission. Section 14(a) of the Exchange Act provides a good example: "It shall be unlawful for any person . . . , in contravention of such rules and regulations as the Commission may prescribe . . . , to solicit . . . any proxy . . . in respect of any security . . . registered pursuant to section 12 of this title."

Congress has given the Commission's rules under Exchange Act section 14(a) the force of law, by use of the phrase, "It shall be unlawful. . . ." That is the basic way of giving rules the force of law in the Exchange Act, since section 32(a), as amended by the Sarbanes–Oxley Act of 2002, provides:

Any person who willfully violates any provision of this title, . . . or any rule or regulation thereunder *the violation of which is*

> *made unlawful or the observance of which is required under the terms of this title*, . . . shall upon conviction be fined not more than $5,000,000, or imprisoned not more than 20 years, or both, except that when such person is a person other than a natural person, a fine not exceeding $25,000,000 may be imposed. . . . (Emphasis added.)

Rules are also given the force of law in section 24 of the Securities Act:

> Any person who willfully violates any of the provisions of this title, or the rules and regulations promulgated by the Commission under authority thereof . . . , shall upon conviction be fined not more than $10,000 or imprisoned not more than five years, or both.

In administering the securities statutes, the Commission issues a large number of rules, along with many pronouncements that are not rules, at least in the usual sense of the term. Some of these pronouncements have the force of law. For example, Securities Act registration statement forms are given the force of law by Securities Act rules 130 and 401(a), the latter of which says "a registration statement . . . shall conform to the applicable . . . forms" and the former of which provides that the term "rules and regulations," as used in certain sections of the Securities Act, includes the registration statement forms.

The bulk of the Commission's pronouncements, which usually take the form of a release, do not have the force of law. The Commission has issued a large number of releases under the Securities Act and the Exchange Act. In many of these releases, the Commission promulgated a rule or made an announcement with respect to a rule, a registration statement form, or some other such matter. In others, however, the Commission, or a division of the Commission, announced a policy or an interpretation of a statute or rule. Although these policies and interpretations do not have the force of law, as a practical matter they are often given almost that effect by a securities lawyer. A litigator can expect a court to pay substantial deference to the Commission's interpretations and policies, and so he or she must consider them not far below the rules in the real-world hierarchy of securities regulation. The lawyer working as a planner, which describes securities lawyers most of the time, typically moves Commission policies and interpretations even closer to rules in the lawyer's own hierarchy. First, the planner wishes to take no avoidable chance of running afoul of the law. Second, congruence with the Commission's policies and interpretations is typically the best way efficiently to accomplish a client's transaction.

Also of substantial importance to the securities lawyer are the interpretive letters and so-called no-action letters that are issued, upon request, by the staff of a division of the Commission. In certain instances, the Commission's staff interprets a provision of law for an interested person. In other cases, the no-action letter procedure is used. The process of issuing a no-action letter begins when an interested person (or more usually his or her lawyer) writes a letter outlining a proposed transaction. If the staff is amenable, it responds by indicating that if the transaction is entered into, the staff will not recommend enforcement action to the Commission. In some areas of the law, the Division of Corporation Finance has issued staff legal bulletins, which the director of the division described as "super no-action letters."

Lawyers sometimes call the Chief Counsel's office the Division of Corporate Finance, or a staff member in the division, for an informal interpretation of some aspect of securities law. Helpfully, the Commission has published a manual of telephone responses given by the Division of Corporation Finance, and this manual may answer a lawyer's question. The manual is available online, but not updated frequently and may, with respect to some matters, be out-of-date.

Beginning in 2005, the Commission has made the staff's subsequently issued comment letters with respect to filed documents, as well as the responses to those letters by issuer's counsel, available on the Commission's website. The letters provide helpful information about the current issues being focused on by the staff.

Court decisions, of course, are as important in interpreting securities statutes and rules as they are in other areas. Coverage by case law is, however, far from uniform among the various securities statutes. Some provisions have come under continual judicial scrutiny, while others have received virtually no attention from the courts. In addition to giving the Commission the power to make rules, Congress has also given the Commission the power to sit in a quasijudicial capacity and adjudicate with respect to the statutes it administers. The adjudication process starts with a hearing before an administrative law judge, whose decision is appealable to the five Commissioners. The Commissioners' decisions look very much like those of courts and serve the same interpretive—and, in a real-world sense, law-making—function. Decisions of the Commission may be appealed to a United States Court of Appeals.

Adding the Constitution at the top, and remembering the interpretive function of courts and the Commission in its quasijudicial capacity, one finds then the following general hierarchy:

- Constitution
- Securities statutes
- Rules and other pronouncements given the force of law
- Policy and interpretive releases
- Staff legal bulletins
- Interpretive and no-action letters
- Manual of telephone interpretations
- Telephone interpretations
- Staff comments on filed documents

There is one other item that must be considered—what securities lawyers sometimes call "lore." Much of the knowledge it takes to deal with the Commission, and otherwise practice in the field, is not the subject of an official pronouncement. If, for example, a lawyer were to prepare and file a Securities Act registration statement following only the statute, rules, and registration statement form, the Commission would likely reject it as being so far afield that the staff will not deal with it. This book will try to help with lore.

Where to Find the Law

Where does one find the various statutes, rules, forms, releases, staff legal bulletins, and no-action and interpretive letters? There are at least two ways to break down the publications containing these materials: (1) official and unofficial, and (2) government and private. One should refer to the official publications when needed, but unofficial publications, and especially private ones, are generally more useful.

The most authoritative official text of federal statutes is found in the bills that contain the original statutes and amendments as passed by Congress. But, obviously, checking the text of original bills is impractical except in highly unusual circumstances.

The next most authoritative sources of federal statutes are *Statutes at Large*, which are "legal evidence" of laws, and slip laws, which are "competent evidence" of laws.[1] (There is no apparent difference between "legal" and "competent" evidence.) These sources are, however, usually too cumbersome to use in the case of the securities laws.

---

[1] 1 U.S.C. § 113.

The securities statutes are codified in title 15 of *United States Code*, making this version prima facie evidence of the law.[2] Courts have made it clear, however, that if such a section of the Code conflicts with *Statutes at Large*, the latter governs. And, whether language conflicts or not, the text of the original Act sometimes must be consulted in construing statutory language. The Supreme Court has held that a provision in the Code must be read in the context of the entire Act in which it originates,[3] and on occasion one can be misled by reading only the Code. Some text is changed systematically to enable statutes to fit into the Code. For example, the Securities Act begins, "This act may be cited . . . ," but the Code reads, "This subchapter may be cited. . . ." The greatest difference is in the area of numbering. The Securities Act, for instance, appears as title 15, sections 77a and following, with section 77a corresponding to section 1 of the Act, section 77b with section 2, and so on. The *United States Code* is updated only annually, making it of little use for research.

The best practically available government sources of Commission rules are the *Federal Register*, published daily, and the annually published codification known as the *Code of Federal Regulations*. Publication of a rule in the *Federal Register* or in *CFR* creates prima facie evidence of the text of the rule.[4] The *Code of Federal Regulations* is divided into numbered titles, parts, and sections. The rules under the securities statutes are found in title 17, beginning at part 200. In *CFR*, rules are not referred to as rules, but as sections of the Code. For example, Securities Act rule 144 appears as 17 C.F.R. section 230.144. When discussing rules, however, securities lawyers and the Commission's staff invariably use rule numbers, specifying the governing statute when there is any question. Regrettably, using *CFR* and the *Federal Register* for research is not very practical.

The Securities and Exchange Acts themselves, as well as important regulations under the securities laws, along with forms, are available at the Commission's website (www.sec.gov). They are a bit hard to find, as they are in a section called "About the SEC." The website also gives constantly expanding access to interpretative and no-action letters, Staff Legal Bulletins, and Commission releases (including administrative law decisions and rule proposals and adoptions). It is not, however, a particularly user-friendly research destination and generally is not as complete as many private commercial sources.

---

[2] 1 U.S.C. § 204(a).

[3] *United States v. Welden*, 377 U.S. 95, 98–99 n. 4 (1964).

[4] 44 U.S.C. § 1510(e).

State Securities Regulation

By the time Congress passed the Securities Act, most states had been in the business of securities regulation for many years. The New Deal securities statutes preserved the ability of the states to engage in securities regulation, and they continued vigorous activity in this area. The result was fairly comprehensive, albeit widely divergent, state regulatory schemes. In 1996, however, Congress amended federal law to reduce state jurisdiction substantially. Preemption is particularly important, as a practical matter, when considering exempt sales of securities under the Securities Act, since the use of certain federal exemptions preempts state regulation of an offering. Nonetheless, it still is not unusual for a state to exercise jurisdiction in many of the major areas covered by the Securities Act and the Exchange Act, as well as to regulate small investment advisers. Thus, like the Securities Act (but subject to its preemption for a number of issuers and transactions), the typical state statute requires that securities be registered before sale, unless an exemption is available. It also regulates brokers and dealers to some extent, overlapping here with the Exchange Act. The typical state statute also prohibits various kinds of fraud, which is proscribed by both the Securities Act and the Exchange Act. Recent assertions of anti-fraud enforcement authority by state regulators have achieved both notoriety and high-stakes settlements.

Like the more specialized of the federal statutes, state securities laws are more easily understood when they are approached by someone who knows the federal scheme. Partially for that reason, this book will touch on state securities regulation only to a very limited extent. It is important to remember, however, that state law may be involved in any particular aspect of the securities business and in any kind of securities transaction. In addition, one should realize that state securities administrators may have substantially more discretion than their federal counterparts.

Special Position of Securities Lawyers

The environment in which securities lawyers practice is quite different from that of most other lawyers. That difference is probably the result of two distinguishing characteristics of securities law practice. First, it is usually a securities lawyer who decides whether a particular transaction can proceed or, because of legal problems, must be canceled. As a matter of common practice, for example, it is often true that unless a lawyer attests to the legality of a transaction by the delivery of an opinion, the parties to the transaction will not agree to proceed. Second, a securities lawyer typically does not merely advise clients on how to accomplish a transaction but usually is an active participant in the transaction.

The first of those characteristics, coupled with the knowledge of the Commission that its own enforcement resources are wholly insufficient to police a significant fraction of securities transactions, has caused the Commission to advocate that a lawyer has a special responsibility to protect the public when working in the securities area. For example, the Commission in the past has argued that when a securities lawyer has reason to believe that a client's actions will violate the securities laws, the lawyer should have a duty to inform the Commission. Proponents of expanded responsibility for securities lawyers sometimes liken the position of the securities lawyer to that of the certified public accountant, who long ago was held to have an overriding responsibility to the public, rather than merely to his or her clients.

The second of these characteristics—active involvement by lawyers in securities transactions—sometimes insures that when the legality of a completed transaction is questioned, one or more securities lawyers will find themselves in the middle of the controversy, rather than somewhat comfortably on the sidelines.

There are two cases that point up especially well the distinguishing characteristics of securities law practice and the results that can flow from these characteristics. The first is *SEC v. National Student Marketing Corp.*[5] National Student Marketing Corp. and Interstate National Corp. had agreed to merge. At the closing of the transaction, officers of the corporations and their lawyers discussed information, provided by NSMC's accountants, concerning problems with some of the financial statements of NSMC that Interstate had provided its shareholders in connection with their vote to approve the merger. As a condition to the closing, the law firm representing each party was to deliver an opinion covering various points, including "that all steps taken to consummate the merger had been validly taken and that [its client] had incurred no violation of any federal or state statute or regulation to the knowledge of counsel." The law firms involved were two of the largest and most respected in the country: White & Case of New York for NSMC and Lord, Bissell & Brook of Chicago for Interstate.

If lawyers for either side had refused to deliver their opinion, Interstate almost certainly would not have proceeded with the closing. A theoretical solution to any legal question arising because of the financial statements was to give new statements to the Interstate shareholders and have them vote again on the merger.

---

[5]   457 F.Supp. 682 (D.D.C.1978).

There was a problem with that alternative, however. The merger agreement contained an upset date by which if the merger was not consummated, NSMC ceased to be bound, and it was impossible for the Interstate shareholders to vote before that date. Interstate's management was afraid that if it missed the upset date, NSMC would refuse to merge or might force a renegotiation of the merger's terms. That fear was well placed because the price of NSMC's stock, which NSMC was to give Interstate's shareholders, had risen substantially since the parties had finalized the merger agreement.

The law firms delivered their opinions, and the merger closed in October 1969. The price of NSMC's stock continued to rise for a time, reaching its high in mid-December. Then, in the words of the court, "in early 1970, after several newspaper and magazine articles appeared questioning NSMC's financial health, the value of the stock decreased drastically. Several private lawsuits were filed, and the SEC initiated a wide-ranging investigation. . . ."

That investigation culminated in a complaint by the Commission, filed in federal district court, that alleged securities fraud against multiple parties, including NSMC, Interstate, White & Case and one of its partners, and Lord, Bissell & Brook and two of its partners. The heart of the Commission's complaint against the law firms and the individual partners was this provision:

> As part of the fraudulent scheme [the law firms and their named lawyers] failed to refuse to issue their opinions . . . and failed to insist that the financial statements be revised and shareholders be resolicited, and failing that, to cease representing their respective clients and, under the circumstances, notify the plaintiff Commission concerning the misleading nature of the nine month financial statements.

Protracted litigation followed, with the law firms arguing vociferously that they and their clients had acted properly, considering the facts known to them at the closing.

Five years later, White & Case and its partner reached a settlement with the Commission. Without admitting or denying the allegations in the complaint, the partner consented to minor sanctions and the law firm agreed to make some changes in its internal procedures. By the time the *National Student Marketing* case was tried, only four defendants were left: the former president of Interstate; Lord, Bissell & Brook; and two of the law firm's partners, one of whom had been also a director of Interstate. The district judge found that the former president of Interstate and the lawyer-director, when acting as a director of Interstate, had violated antifraud provisions of the federal securities laws. He also found that Lord, Bissell & Brook and its two partners had aided and abetted those violations.

The other case that points up especially well the distinguishing characteristics of securities law practice, and the results flowing from them, is *In re Carter*,[6] which was a proceeding before the Commission sitting in its quasijudicial capacity. The Commission brought the action under then rule 2(e) (now rule 102) of its Rules of Practice to determine whether two partners of Brown, Wood, Ivey, Mitchell & Petty, a well-known and respected New York law firm, should be suspended or barred from practicing before the Commission because of alleged unethical or improper professional conduct.

An administrative law judge found that the lawyers had willfully aided and abetted a client's violations of various provisions of the federal securities laws. The judge also concluded that both of the partners should temporarily be suspended from practicing before the Commission. In its decision on appeal, the Commission reversed the administrative law judge, finding that the lawyers "did not intend to assist the violations by their inaction or silence," but rather, "seemed to be at a loss for how to deal with a difficult client."

Nevertheless, the Commission believed that the lawyers' conduct raised questions concerning the obligations of securities lawyers, and therefore it announced the interpretation of unethical or improper professional conduct it would apply in the future:

> The Commission is of the view that a lawyer engages in "unethical or improper professional conduct" under the following circumstances: When a lawyer with significant responsibilities in the effectuation of a company's compliance with the disclosure requirements of the federal securities laws becomes aware that his client is engaged in a substantial and continuing failure to satisfy those disclosure requirements, his continued participation violates professional standards unless he takes prompt steps to end the client's noncompliance.

Although the required prompt action could be resignation, that was not the action the Commission favored. In its view, "[p]remature resignation serves neither the end of an effective lawyer–client relationship nor, in most cases, the effective administration of the securities laws. The lawyer's continued interaction with his client will ordinarily hold the greatest promise of corrective action." Securities lawyers generally agree, however, that unless a client agrees to mend its ways immediately,

---

[6]   Exchange Act Release No. 17,597 (Feb. 28, 1981).

resignation is the only safe course. With this in mind, good securities lawyers attempt either to draft their clients' Commissions filings and other public disclosures, or to review the clients' drafts of these documents well in advance of their release. In this way, if problems arise, the lawyer has time to discuss them with management, at whatever level necessary, before having to make the decision to resign. Typically, a client can be convinced that compliance with the securities laws is in its best interest, if a lawyer has time to do it.

In both *National Student Marketing* and *In re Carter*, lawyers were accused of aiding and abetting violations of Exchange Act section 10(b). In *Central Bank of Denver, N.A. v. First Interstate Bank of Denver, N.A.*,[7] the Supreme Court determined that a private plaintiff cannot maintain an aiding-and-abetting action under that section. Exchange Act section 20 and Securities Act section 15, however, have been amended specifically to provide that the Commission has authority to bring actions for aiding and abetting the violation of any section of the Acts or of any of the Commission's rules or regulations. (A general statute[8] has long created aiding-and-abetting liability for all federal criminal offenses, and a violation of the securities laws can be a criminal offense.) In private actions, one should expect professionals, such as lawyers and accountants, to be named as primary violators of section 10(b), rather than as aiders and abettors, whenever the facts arguably would support such a claim. In *Janus Capital Group, Inc. v. First Derivative Traders*,[9] however, the Supreme Court made it clear that, in the context of a private lawsuit, section 10(b) liability for a misleading statement will attach only to those with "ultimate control" over the statement. The Court indicated that in the ordinary case attribution will be critical in determining ultimate control.

Section 602 of the Sarbanes–Oxley Act of 2002, passed as a result of the Enron and other corporate scandals involving securities fraud, codifies (with minor changes) the main part of rule 102(e) as section 4C of the Exchange Act. This section relates to improper or unethical professional conduct, and other related problems, in the context of all federal securities laws. More importantly, section 307 of Sarbanes–Oxley mandates the Commission to pass rules that set minimum standards of professional conduct for securities lawyers representing issuers. These rules appear in a compendium entitled "Standards of Professional Conduct for Attorneys Appearing and Practicing

---

[7] 511 U.S. 164 (1994).

[8] 18 U.S.C. § 2.

[9] 131 S.Ct. 2296 (2011).

Before the Commission in the Representation of an Issuer."[10] Basically, they lay reporting obligations on both in-house and outside counsel in the case of material violations of the securities laws or fiduciary duties, or similar violations. The reporting that is called for is internal to the issuer; the specific requirements and options faced by the lawyer are quite detailed.

---

[10] *See* Exchange Act Release No. 34–47276 (Jan. 29, 2003).

Chapter 3

BUSINESS CONTEXT OF SECURITIES LAW

The registration of securities is at the core of the Securities Act, and most of the Act's provisions are built around the registration framework. Before examining the registration provisions, however, it will be helpful to focus briefly on their business context because some modest understanding of that context is essential.

Reasons Companies Register Securities

There are only a few usual reasons why companies register securities for sale in a public offering. In making the decision whether to register, the expected benefits of registration must, of course, be considered along with the disadvantages. Some of the typical benefits, and the countervailing disadvantages, are discussed below. It will be apparent that the advantage/disadvantage equation changes dramatically once a company has initially registered securities. Registration marks the passage of a company from privately held to publicly held. As is typical with rites of passage, the first time through the rite has the greatest and longest-lasting consequences.

Advantages of Registration or Being Publicly Held

Cashing In

Perhaps the best reason the owners of a privately held company take it public is to "cash in" by selling some of their stock. Not uncommonly, entrepreneurs who start and build successful companies leave most of the company's profits in the company so as to help it grow—or better yet, spend the company's cash on expansion of the company before the cash can become taxable income. During this period the entrepreneur may be living on little income, even though the company is worth a great deal of money. By selling some of his or her stock to the public, such an entrepreneur can raise a large amount of cash while still retaining enough stock to control the company. Going public can be the time to trade in the ten-year-old Chevrolet on a new Mercedes.

Economy

A registered public offering may be the most economical way to raise money. Bank borrowings may or may not be possible in a given situation, and, in any case, the cost may be exorbitant. In addition, the longest term available for borrowing from a bank has usually been five years (although this appears to be changing). Many times a company has the alternative of raising the money it needs by selling securities under one of the registration exemptions. Although an exempt offering is likely to be much cheaper than a registered offering, that is not always so. Selling in an exempt offering often means dealing with venture capitalists, who are professional investors who will drive a hard bargain in negotiations. The company might save a great deal of money by avoiding those negotiations.

A company that has previously registered securities will find the registration decision easier to make on economic grounds than will the privately held company. One reason is that the company is already taking part in the disclosure system set up by the Commission, so a new registration will require relatively little work in preparing disclosure documents. In addition, the Commission allows certain public companies to file extremely simple registration statements, as discussed in Chapter 5.

Control

Companies may choose to sell securities publicly to avoid giving up some degree of control. For example, when a privately owned company sells common stock to venture capitalists, the purchasers likely will require much say in future decisions. In a public offering, that can be avoided. Also, when a publicly held company sells securities to the public rather than, say, to a group of insurance companies in an exempt offering, it avoids the restrictions on its activities that the buyers may demand in negotiations.

Creation of Liquidity

A privately owned company may register and sell newly issued stock to create a public market for its outstanding shares, which will provide its owners with liquidity. Once sold, it will immediately begin to trade in the public markets. The old shareholders will then be able to sell their shares in the trading market, as long as certain conditions, which will be discussed in Chapter 7, are met.

Often a company wishes to raise new capital by selling stock itself (which is called a primary offering), and one or more major shareholders want to generate cash by selling shares themselves (called a secondary offering). It is common, in fact, for both types of offerings to be made simultaneously (called a double-barreled offering).

Prestige

In decision making, emotional factors often pull at least as strongly as practical ones. Such an emotional pull may occur when owners of a private company consider taking it public. The prestige of becoming a major shareholder, director, and officer of a publicly held company holds a special allure for some. A basis exists for such prestige because only a company that has been successful, and whose future seems bright, has any real chance of selling securities in a public offering.

Estate Planning

The liquidity of stock in a publicly held company is helpful when the time comes to pay estate taxes. In a privately owned company, the heirs of a sole or major shareholder sometimes find themselves in a bad bargaining position when they need to find a buyer quickly. Valuation of stock in such a company is also problematical, but it is relatively straightforward in one that is publicly held. Those advantages are often overrated, however. The estate tax problem sometimes can be better handled through life insurance or through contractual arrangements. For example, a sale of stock by the estate to the company or the remaining shareholders could be arranged, either at a specified price or under a pricing formula agreed to in advance. Also, a stock's valuation for tax purposes is likely to be higher in a publicly held company.

Executive Recruiting and Retention

In certain situations, being a publicly held company can aid in executive recruiting and retention, because the company can provide relatively liquid stock as compensation. Also, the decision to "give" stock to executives in a publicly held company is a much easier decision to make than to "give" them stock in a privately held company. Taking on a few more public shareholders is of no real consequence to the company or its managers. However, taking on minority shareholders in a privately held company is a much more serious matter, as is covered in most courses in corporation law. One reason for this is that, in doing so, the managers take on a whole new set of fiduciary obligations.

Acquisitions

A publicly held company is in a much better situation than a privately owned one in terms of acquisitions. When its stock is desirable, a publicly held company can acquire other companies by using newly issued, liquid (or at least relatively liquid) stock rather than cash as consideration. Obviously, that use of stock is possible also in a private company, but it raises the issues discussed in the preceding paragraph.

Disadvantages of Registration or Being Publicly Held

Expense

A major disadvantage of registration is the direct and indirect expense involved. Of the direct expenses, the highest is the compensation to the securities firms that sell the securities. For an offering of common stock of a few million dollars, the compensation typically is approximately 10 percent of the public offering price, or about $1,000,000 for a $10 million offering. For larger offerings, especially for those involving debt rather than equity, the percentage compensation is lower, finally diminishing to less than one percent for the largest offerings of bonds. The next highest costs are legal, accounting, and printing expenses. For an initial public offering, those items easily can total $500,000; they can be much higher when complications are encountered. Filing fees, usually totaling a few thousand dollars, must be paid to the Commission, to the Financial Industry Regulatory Authority, and to most states in which the securities are to be sold. Miscellaneous expenses, including fees for a transfer agent and registrar of the securities, total another few thousand dollars.

A prospective issuer must also consider that direct expenses are just the starting point in a registered offering. Indirect expenses are substantial, especially so because they continue indefinitely. Once a company registers securities under the Securities Act, it becomes subject to the reporting requirements of the Exchange Act.[1] Annual and other reports, containing specially prepared financial statements and detailed information about a wide range of subjects, must be prepared and filed. Except in rare cases, after a Securities Act registration, the company also meets the requirements for registration of its securities under the Exchange Act.[2] That registration subjects it to additional continuing expenses, primarily for complying with the Commission's proxy rules at least annually. In total, Exchange Act compliance costs a company at least a few tens of thousands of dollars annually in legal, accounting, and printing costs. Beyond those expenses, a publicly held company has the annual fees of a transfer agent and registrar and the costs involved with continued dealings with securities analysts and shareholders.

The Sarbanes–Oxley Act of 2002 imposed costly certification and other requirements on companies reporting under the

---

[1] Exchange Act § 15(d).

[2] Exchange Act § 12(g) and rule 12g–1.

Exchange Act. The JOBS Act of 2012, however, ameliorates some requirements for many issuers during the first five years after their initial registration under the Securities Act. These issuers are known as "emerging growth companies" and are further described in Chapter 4.

Disclosure of Information

The Commission requires that a great deal of information about a company be made public in a Securities Act registration statement. Periodic updating of that information, and disclosure of new information, is then required by the Exchange Act. Although much of that disclosure of updated and new information is due to the Exchange Act's reporting and proxy requirements, some disclosure is required by the antifraud provisions of both Acts. Much of the information that must be disclosed concerns topics the company would rather keep private. As one entrepreneur who took his company public has said, "Much of what goes on in the bedroom is visible to those who sit in the parlor."[3]

Freedom of Action

Former owner-managers often find unpalatable the new limits on their freedom of action that taking a company public brings. The owners are often used to making decisions as they please, and formalities of decision making are often minimal. The decision-making process must change after stock is sold to the public. The greatest change stems from the legal imposition upon major owners, directors, and officers of companies of fiduciary obligations to the shareholders. Those obligations, the proxy rules, and the floodlight of disclosure encourage greater formality and less flexibility in decision making.

Income Expectations

One objective in a private company is usually to minimize current income so as also to minimize the company's income tax. That goal is accomplished by spending cash, before it can be realized as income at the end of the year, in ways that are designed to help the company grow and prosper in the future. The managers of a company that has recently gone public must execute an immediate about-face in terms of income strategy. Even though a prosperous future and a minimization of taxes are in all the shareholders' long-term interest, public shareholders have an insatiable appetite for current earnings. The reason for that attitude, of course, is that the average shareholder has no

---

[3] Salomon, *Second Thoughts on Going Public*, HARV. BUS. REV. 126, 128 (Sept./Oct. 1977).

particular long-term interest in the company. Shareholders want a steep, quick rise in the stock's price that allows them to sell and take their profits. This puts heavy pressure on the managers of a publicly held company to use every means to boost current earnings, and to do so on a quarterly basis. One simple way to increase current earnings is to cut development expenses for future products or services. Often managers see the long-term dangers of doing that, but the pressures are hard to resist. And resisted or not, those pressures constitute one of the greatest disadvantages of being publicly held.

Functions of Securities Firms

Securities firms perform a number of different functions, both in connection with registered offerings and otherwise. When they perform those functions, the firms are referred to by various descriptions that relate to the function that is performed. The major aspects of those functions are outlined below.

Underwriting

Underwriting generally refers to the function of helping a company, or one or more of its major shareholders, sell securities to the public through an offering registered under the Securities Act. That function is accomplished in one of three ways:

1. *Firm Commitment Underwriting.* In the typical firm commitment underwriting, a syndicate of underwriters purchase securities from a company, or one or more major shareholders, at an agreed price. The underwriters then attempt to resell those securities to the public at a profit. The syndicate acts through a managing underwriter or underwriters, which make all the arrangements with the issuer and puts together the syndicate. The managing underwriter receives a fee for its efforts, paid out of the proceeds of sale.

2. *Best Efforts Underwriting.* In the best efforts underwriting, an underwriter or group of underwriters agrees to use its best efforts to sell an agreed amount of securities to the public. The underwriters may simply agree to sell whatever portion of the total they can. On the other hand, their agreement may be on an all-or-none, or an agreed-minimum-percentage basis.

3. *Standby Underwriting.* The standby form of underwriting is typically used in so-called rights offerings. In such an offering, a company directly offers its existing security holders the right to purchase additional securities, at a given price, and underwriters agree to purchase from the company any securities that are offered to the security holders but not purchased by them.

For business reasons, basically relating to the volatility of securities prices, underwriters in a firm-commitment underwriting wish to dispose of an entire issue almost immediately. (When securities remain unsold after about two days, the deal is considered "sticky," and the underwriters become very concerned.) To accomplish that quick sale, the underwriters often sell a portion of the securities—at a discount from the public offering price—to other securities firms, which in turn attempt to resell them to the public. As discussed below, those other firms function as dealers, since they take title to the securities. Underwriters with a large sales force and an ability to sell securities quickly may sell all or most of the securities they are underwriting. Others may sell few or even none themselves.

The financial arrangements in an underwriting of stock might work like this for each share sold:

Public offering price	$10.00
Price to underwriter	9.00
Gross profit to underwriter	$ 1.00
Fee to managing underwriter	.20
Profit to underwriter if it sells the share to the public	$ .80
Discount to dealer	.50
Profit to underwriter if it sells the share to a dealer	$ .30

Acting as Dealer, Broker, and Market Maker

In industry parlance, the term "dealer" refers to a firm when it buys and sells securities for its own account (except the term is not used when the firm does that as an underwriter). Some firms that operate as dealers never function as underwriters in any registered offering, but others may be an underwriter in some offerings and a dealer in others. In addition to operating as dealers in registered offerings, securities firms also function as dealers in the trading markets. The term "broker" refers to a firm when it buys or sells as an intermediary for a customer, rather than taking or giving title itself. Some confusion is created by the Securities Act, which in section 2(a)(12) includes brokers within the definition of "dealer." Industry practice, however, is to use those terms with specificity. Further confusion is created by the use of the term "market maker" to describe a dealer that functions in the trading market by maintaining an inventory of a particular company's securities and holding itself open, on a continuing basis, as willing to buy and sell those securities.

Investment Banking

The term "investment banking" can be used to encompass any of the above functions, and any person in a firm performing any of those functions could be called an investment banker. By convention, however, those terms usually are used less broadly. In large securities firms, for example, there are a number of departments. The one most visible to the public handles trades for individuals. The technical term for the persons working with customers in that department is "registered representative," but those persons are often called brokers or stockbrokers. Insiders would not call them investment bankers. A department almost invisible to the public handles underwritings and performs a wide range of services primarily for client companies. Among those are: (1) assisting companies in the sale of securities, almost always in large amounts, to such private purchasers as insurance companies; (2) finding acquisition partners for companies that wish to acquire or be acquired by others; and (3) giving financial advice of various sorts to client companies. That department is likely to be called the investment banking department. In any case, its functions are at the heart of the insiders' conception of investment banking. When referring generally to firms that perform investment banking functions, the term "investment banking firm" or, less commonly, "investment bank" is used.

Effects of Financial Unrest

Certainly, as IPOs dwindled in 2008, it stood to reason, and seemed to be the case, that underwriters would be forced into increased competition. In some instances, this has led to the involvement of multiple firms to perform the underwriting functions described above (without any concomitant increase in the fee to the issuer). More significant, however, has been the exit from the field of a number of "investment banks"—many of which had incurred huge debts to acquire highly risky mortgage-backed securities. Even such established entities as Bear Stearns and Lehman Brothers went bankrupt. Another, Merrill Lynch, was acquired by the Bank of America, and two others (Goldman Sachs and Morgan Stanley) converted themselves to bank holding companies. In this form, they have access to customer deposits as well as to credit facilities made available by the federal reserve. The price was to subject themselves to an additional layer of regulation (by bank authorities).

This does not mean that the functions of securities firms described above have ceased to exist. A more dire threat (from the standpoint of those performing those functions) may be posed by the Internet. Brokerage and underwriting services presently are offered online, but the nature of the services themselves may change as savvy investors and issuers find ways of doing for themselves the things they used to rely on well-connected financial intermediaries to do.

Steps in a Registered Offering

In approaching the material that follows in the next chapter, it is helpful to have as background a conception of the broad sweep of events in a registered public offering. Here are the steps in a typical initial public offering:

1. A company wishing to sell securities gets together with a firm that wishes to serve as its managing underwriter. The initial contact can be by either party, and often it is by an investment banking firm seeking underwriting business. At that point, the parties do not enter into a binding agreement, but they may sign a letter of intent.

2. Counsel for the company begins drafting the registration statement. The managing underwriter engages a law firm to represent it and the underwriting syndicate that is to be formed. That counsel begins drafting the underwriting agreements. Typically, there are three types of agreements relating to the underwriting. First, there is an agreement among the underwriters in which the underwriters agree to act together in the underwriting and agree on which firm is to be the managing underwriter. Second, there is an agreement between the company and the underwriters in which the company agrees to sell and the underwriters agree to buy a specified amount of securities at an agreed price. Third, there are a series of agreements between the underwriters and the dealers relating to the sale of securities to the dealers at a discount from the public offering price. Those agreements may informally be agreed to early on, but they are not executed until much later.

3. Company counsel does any "housekeeping work" that is needed. This often involves clean-up work. For example, company counsel may find that the board of directors has not authorized certain actions of corporate officers that were beyond the officers' authority. In that case, the directors may need to ratify past actions. Also, in the usual first public offering, the issuer's capital structure has to be changed. For example, a small private company that wishes to offer 500,000 shares, representing a 25 percent interest in the company, must have authorized in its charter at least 2,000,000 shares, and 1,500,000 of those must be outstanding in the hands of the current owners. It is highly unlikely that that situation will exist by chance. Counsel can, as covered in a corporations class, accomplish the required change in capital

structure by a charter amendment that provides for an increase in authorized capital and a stock split.

4. The managing underwriter begins putting together the underwriting syndicate. That effort usually involves telephone calls and meetings with investment bankers in other firms. Any agreements reached are informal and nonbinding.

5. When the company and its counsel, and the managing underwriter and the underwriters' counsel, are satisfied with the draft of the registration statement, the company files it with the Commission. Historically, the staff has attempted to provide comment within 30 days. Now, pursuant to the JOBS Act of 2012, emerging growth companies (as defined in Chapter 4) can submit their registration statements for comment before publicly filing them. The effect on the timing of staff comment remains to be seen.

6. The managing underwriter continues to work on forming the underwriting syndicate and begins tentatively to form a prospective dealer group.

7. The prospective underwriters and dealers begin sending copies of a preliminary prospectus (an offering document that makes up the bulk of the registration statement) to customers and begin telephoning customers in an attempt to create interest in the offering.

8. The company files one or more amendments to the registration statement in preparation for its effectiveness. A company may file an amendment because material events have occurred since the filing of the registration statement. Often it files one because the Commission's staff finds problems in the registration statement as originally filed. At other times, a company files an amendment to fill in blanks that originally appeared in the registration statement.

9. When the registration statement is ready to become effective, the company and the managing underwriter make a final decision as to whether to proceed with the offering, and under what terms. Typically, they complete final negotiations after the close of the securities markets on the day before expected effectiveness. That day is one agreed to by all parties and the Commission's staff, and so it does not come as a surprise. On the morning of effectiveness, the underwriters sign the agreement among underwriters and the company and the underwriters enter into the underwriting agreement.

10. On the morning of effectiveness, the company may file a so-called price amendment to the registration statement, making final corrections and changes and adding previously unknown

information such as the price to the underwriters, the price to the public, the discount to dealers, and the names of all the underwriters. Securities Act rule 430A allows issuers in most cases to forego the filing of a price amendment when the only changes to be made relate to certain limited information, such as specified information about the volume of securities offered, pricing, and underwriting arrangements. Such information may be simply included in the so-called final prospectus, which under rule 424 must be filed within some days after effectiveness.

11. The registration statement becomes effective.

12. The underwriters and the dealers, after signing a dealer agreement, begin making sales to the public.

13. The closing, at which securities and money change hands, occurs, usually three business days after effectiveness.

14. The managing underwriter closes the books on the offering and either distributes profits to the underwriters or calls on them to pay their share of the loss.

Chapter 4

WHAT CAN BE DONE DURING SECURITIES ACT REGISTRATION

Types of Issuers

In 2005, the Commission adopted a number of new rules designed to ease compliance with the regulatory framework of Securities Act registration. Without a doubt, it succeeded both in easing practical compliance and in complicating legal analysis. Both of these effects were amplified in 2012 when the JOBS Act was signed into law. Many of these changes related to the creation of different categories of issuers. As one approaches the succeeding materials, it is helpful to know in advance that different types of issuers are subject to different requirements. The basic types of issuer are described below.

Non-Reporting Issuers. These are issuers that are not required to file reports under the Exchange Act, nor voluntarily doing so. Most commonly, they are first time registrants under the Securities Act. "Non-reporting issuer" is not actually a term defined in the Commission's rules, although it is a discernible and useful concept.

Unseasoned Issuers. These are issuers that are required to file reports under the Exchange Act, or are voluntarily doing so, but that do not qualify as seasoned issuers (described immediately below). As covered in more detail in Chapter 9, issuers are required to report under the Exchange Act if they (a) have a class of security traded on a national exchange, (b) have in excess of $10,000,000 in assets and a class of equity security in the hands of a specified number of holders (with the number varying according to the type of holders), (c) have registered securities under the Securities Act within the last year, or (d) have registered securities under the Securities Act that are in the hands of at least 300 holders. Once again, "unseasoned issuer" is not actually a term defined in the Commission's rules.

Seasoned Issuers. In general terms, these are issuers that have filed reports under the Exchange Act for at least twelve months and either (a) have at least $75 million of common equity held by non-affiliates, or (b) meet certain other tests and are offering non-convertible debt. This group is identified, although not defined, in Rule 433(b) by reference to the issuer's qualification to use Securities Act Form S–3 to register securities.

Well-Known Seasoned Issuers. In general terms, these are seasoned issuers that have either (a) $700 million of common equity held by non-affiliates or (b) (if the issuer is registering non-convertible securities other than common equity) issued for cash more than $1 billion of registered non-convertible securities other than common equity in the last three years. The technical definition of this class of issuer is contained in Securities Act Rule 405, which incorporates by reference portions of the Instructions to Securities Act Form S–3.

Emerging Growth Companies. An emerging growth company is an issuer, other than a well-known seasoned issuer, whose initial public offering was or will be completed after December 8, 2011 and had annual gross revenue of less than $1 billion during its most recent fiscal year. Qualifying for this category, which is defined in new Section 2(a)(19), permits certain types of solicitational activity that otherwise would be prohibited. The status continues for five years after the company's initial public offering.

As far as the first four categories are concerned, the more information that is publicly available about an issuer, and the more likelihood that the available information is being actively considered by the market, the more relaxed compliance becomes. The clarity of the compliance picture was, however, fuzzied a bit by the invention of the emerging growth company in 2012. The differences are addressed in more detail below and are summarized at the end of the chapter.

Securities Act Section 5

Once the types of issuers are understood, consideration of the regulatory framework of registration logically begins with the Securities Act, and because of the way the Act is structured, it is essential to begin by considering section 5. In doing so, it is most helpful to examine the various subsections of section 5, not in the order in which they appear, but rather as they relate to the three time periods in an offering: (1) the period before a registration statement is filed (the prefiling period), (2) the period after filing but before the registration statement becomes effective (the waiting period), and (3) the period after effectiveness (the posteffective period). The following table shows the basic applicability of the various subsections:

PREFILING	WAITING	POSTEFFECTIVE
§ 5(a), (c)	§ 5(a), (b)(1)	§ 5(b)

The following sections of this chapter examine the regulatory framework of each of those periods, beginning in each case with the most basically relevant provisions of section 5. Whenever statutory sections are discussed in this and later chapters, it will be helpful to refer to the sections themselves.

Prefiling Period

Scheme of the Statute

The provisions of section 5 applicable to the prefiling period are sections 5(a) and (c). They provide:

Prohibitions Relating to Interstate Commerce and the Mails

Section 5. (a) Unless a registration statement is in effect as to a security, it shall be unlawful for any person, directly or indirectly—

(1) to make use of any means or instruments of transportation or communication in interstate commerce or of the mails to sell such security through the use or medium of any prospectus or otherwise; or

(2) to carry or cause to be carried through the mails or in interstate commerce, by any means or instruments of transportation, any such security for the purpose of sale or for delivery after sale.

. . .

(c) It shall be unlawful for any person, directly or indirectly, to make use of any means or instruments of transportation or communication in interstate commerce or of the mails to offer to sell or offer to buy through the use or medium of any prospectus or otherwise any security, unless a registration statement has been filed as to such security, or while the registration statement is the subject of a refusal order or stop order or (prior to the effective date of the registration statement) any public proceeding or examination under section 8.

It is best to begin an analysis with section 5(c), since it relates to offers and is applicable in its entirety to the prefiling period (except for provisions on registration statements that are the subject of a refusal order, stop order, public proceeding, or examination, which are rare occurrences that are discussed in Chapter 5). Section 5(a), on the other hand, deals with sales (which chronologically follow offers) and is applicable to the waiting period as well as the prefiling period.

The most helpful first step in understanding section 5(c) is the culling of language that does not aid comprehension. For example, "directly or indirectly" adds little to understanding, and "through the use or medium of any prospectus or otherwise" adds nothing. The clause relating to "means or instruments of transportation or communication in interstate commerce or of the mails" is a bit trickier. It is a practical impossibility to complete the usual securities offering without using one of the named "jurisdictional means." Of course, it is possible that a particular act, such as the making of a specific offer, might be done without use of those means. The concept of jurisdictional means, however, is broad. Any use of the telephone by the offeror almost certainly satisfies the requirement, and it can be met in much more abstruse ways. For example, when the president of an issuer by chance encounters a friend at the country club and offers to sell the friend securities, the president probably has not used any jurisdictional means. But if the friend telephones for more information, a court probably would find that jurisdictional means had been used to "offer" the securities, because the offeror reasonably could have foreseen the use of the telephone by the offeree. Lawyers litigating securities cases may sometimes find "no jurisdictional" means arguments helpful. Others will find such arguments too dangerous to rely on, and they can virtually ignore the jurisdictional means language of section 5. That is what generally will be done in this book. After culling the above language and setting aside language relating to refusal orders, stop orders, public proceedings, and examinations, one is left in section 5(c) with this: "It shall be unlawful for any person . . . to offer to sell or offer to buy . . . any security . . . unless a registration statement has been filed as to such security. . . ."

All that remains, then, for understanding section 5(c) is an understanding of what its various words and phrases mean. That is not as simple as it may seem. An examination of the definitions, contained in section 2, shows that some of those words and phrases have special meanings. After a reading of definitions, one is ready to consider rules, releases, cases, and so on in an attempt more fully to understand those terms.

After considering offers under section 5(c), one should turn to section 5(a). Taken to its essentials, section 5(a)(1) prohibits the sale of securities unless a registration statement has become effective (that is, at the end of the waiting period). The major problem in that area is determining what constitutes a sale. A look at section 2(a)(3) shows that the word has special meanings, which are discussed below. Section 5(a)(2) contains a rather straightforward prohibition against transmitting unregistered securities through the mail, or by means of interstate commerce, for purposes of sale or delivery after sale. That provision is an important enforcement tool of the

Commission, but one that relates to problems a securities lawyer rarely encounters while working as a planner.

Reading the basic portions of sections 5(c) and 5(a)(1) together, the rule for the prefiling period is: no offers, no sales. Whether an activity constitutes a sale may be an issue in the prefiling period, but that issue is typically of more concern in the waiting period. For that reason, the discussion of sales appears in the context of the waiting period. Offers present the main problem of the prefiling period, and they are discussed here.

What Is an Offer

Statutory Definition

The starting point for understanding the concept of an offer under the Securities Act is the definition contained in section 2(a)(3), which in its basic part provides: "The term 'offer to sell,' 'offer for sale,' or 'offer' shall include every attempt or offer to dispose of, or solicitation of an offer to buy, a security or interest in a security, for value." The provision does not purport to be a complete definition, because it speaks only in terms of what an offer "shall include." Presumably the drafters intended to take the common-law definition of offer as a beginning and modify it. The modification immediately apparent is that the solicitation of an offer to buy is considered an offer to sell. As a result, it is not possible to avoid the "no offer to sell" prohibition of section 5(c) by phrasing an offer in terms of a solicitation of an offer to buy.

The language of section 2(a)(3) may have been meant to modify the common law definition of "offer" in a more significant way. It can be argued that the intent of the phraseology "shall include *every* attempt or offer to dispose of" (emphasis added) was to push the perimeters of the ordinary definition outward, so as to encompass activities that otherwise would not constitute offers. The full intent of the drafters is not clear, but a desire for expansiveness is not unlikely. In any case, the Commission has read the definition broadly, particularly in terms of prefiling activities that, while falling far short of common-law offers, condition the market for the securities to be sold.

Conditioning the Market

The concept of conditioning the market was first articulated by the Commission in Securities Act Release No. 3,844 (October 8, 1957). After referring to the definition of "offer" in section 2(a)(3), the Commission stated without analysis that, in the prefiling period, it is not legally possible to begin a public offering *or* "initiate a public sales campaign." The use of the connector "or" causes confusion. A public sales campaign is only unlawful when it involves an offer as defined in the Act. When it does, the campaign should be encompassed in the term "public offering." Presumably, the Commission used that latter term in the more restrictive sense of a formal offering, but it is difficult to be sure. What is clear in the release, and in later pronouncements on the subject, is that the Commission has not been precise or analytical in fitting its ideas into the statutory scheme.

As detailed below, there are now a number of activities that are specifically permitted by statute or rule notwithstanding the fact that they otherwise might constitute market conditioning (or outright offers under any definition). The concept of market conditioning still is of concern, however, particularly for first-time registrants. Moreover, attempted reliance on a specific statutory provision or rule does not preclude reliance on the argument that a communication is not an offer under earlier interpretive guidelines. The Commission's pronouncements on the subject of what constitutes conditioning the market thus continue to be important.

In Release No. 3,844, the Commission emphasized that:

[T]he publication of information and statements, and publicity efforts, generally, made in advance of a proposed financing, although not couched in terms of an express offer, may in fact contribute to conditioning the public mind or arousing public interest in the issuer or in the securities of an issuer in a manner which raises a serious question whether the publicity is not in fact part of the selling effort.

The Commission chose to explain itself through the use of examples. One example concerns promoters and prospective underwriters of a mining company in the development stage who "arranged for a series of press releases describing the activities of the company, its proposed program of development activities, estimates of ore reserves and plans for a processing plant." Those activities were determined to have violated section 5. A more subtle example, also involving a mining venture, concerned the distribution by a prospective underwriter of a brochure that described "in glowing generalities the future possibilities for use of the mineral to be explored for and the profit potential to investors" in the industry. Neither the venture nor any security was mentioned, but the brochure did bear the underwriter's name. The Commission said that that clearly was the first step in a sales campaign and that it violated section 5.

A year after Release No. 3,844, events occurred that gave the Commission the chance to put greater force behind its expansive concept of what constitutes an offer. It did so in *In re Carl M. Loeb,*

Rhoades & Co.,[1] a disciplinary proceeding against two securities firms registered under the Exchange Act. The problems began when the co-managing underwriters put out press releases concerning the issuer, a real estate development company, before a registration statement was filed. The releases described the property involved, related the company's development plans in general terms, outlined the proposed securities offering, and mentioned the names of the two managing underwriters. Although the releases did not directly offer to sell any securities, the Commission concluded that publicity of that type and in that situation "must be presumed to set in motion or to be a part of the distribution process and therefore involve an offer to sell or a solicitation of an offer to buy . . . securities." Focusing on the more extensive of the releases and the resultant publicity, the Commission found that "such release and publicity was of a character calculated, by arousing and stimulating investor and dealer interest in the securities . . . , to set in motion the process of distribution."

After *Loeb, Rhoades*, securities lawyers have counseled caution in the release of any publicity about the issuer or its industry that might fall under Release No. 3,844 or *Loeb, Rhoades*. However, since issuers usually depend on publicity to sell their products and services, it is impractical to suggest that all publicity be stopped. The Commission has long recognized, in fact, that publicly held companies should keep their security holders informed about company affairs, and in the years since *Loeb, Rhoades* there has been an increasing recognition of the obligation of such companies to do so. Those conflicting duties have led to the fear that publicity may get a company in trouble under the Securities Act, and the lack of it may result in violations of the Exchange Act.

In response to that tension, the Commission issued Securities Act Release No. 5,180 (August 16, 1971). There are two basic themes in that release. The first theme, which deals with publicity, is that while a publicly held company may not legally initiate publicity that is for the purpose of facilitating the sale of securities, a "business as usual" general publicity effort probably does not run afoul of section 5(c). The second theme relates to the kinds of information publicly held companies may provide when inquiries are directed to them by shareholders, securities analysts, the press, and others. Here the Commission emphasized that although factual information should be provided, responses involving predictions, forecasts, projections, and opinions concerning value are not acceptable. Although the Commission refrained from giving a list of what can and cannot be done by a publicly held company during the prefiling and later periods of an offering, it declared that a company should:

---

[1]   38 S.E.C. 843 (1959).

1. Continue to advertise products and services.

2. Continue to send out customary quarterly, annual, and other periodic reports to stockholders.

3. Continue to publish proxy statements and send out dividend notices.

4. Continue to make announcements to the press with respect to factual business and financial developments; i.e., receipt of a contract, settlement of a strike, opening of a plant, or similar events of interest to the community in which the business operates.

5. Answer unsolicited telephone inquiries from shareholders, financial analysts, the press, and others concerning factual information.

6. Observe an "open door" policy in responding to unsolicited inquiries concerning factual matters from securities analysts, financial analysts, security holders, and participants in the communications field who have a legitimate interest in the corporation's affairs.

7. Continue to hold shareholder meetings as scheduled and to answer shareholders' inquiries at shareholder meetings relating to factual matters.

Although the release helps the publicly held company to a fair extent, it does little to aid the first-time issuer. The first item on the list provides some help, since the continued advertising of products and services seems equally applicable to public and private companies. But even there, the issues may be complex. For example, a new advertising campaign might raise questions, especially when it is presented in media that seem calculated to reach investors rather than merely customers.

The releases just discussed were written before the advent of the Internet. Now, the Commission's staff scrutinizes an issuer's website carefully to see if it conditions the market for an upcoming offering. In doing this, the staff takes a common sense view of the question, based on the experience of viewing many websites. A particularly difficult problem arises when a company has not had a website in the past, but wants to initiate one when an offering is likely. Such a website will come under heightened scrutiny, and even more judgment is involved. In reviewing websites, hyperlinks must be considered carefully. The Commission has indicated, in what probably should be taken as understatement, that hyperlinking information that meets the broad definition of "offer," "raises a strong inference that the hyperlinked information is attributable to the issuer for the purposes of a section 5 analysis."[2] On the other hand, rule 433, added in 2005, provides that historical issuer information identified as such and located in a separate section of the issuer's website is not considered an offer unless it is used or identified in connection with an offering.

The need for large measures of judgment is unavoidable when making decisions on questions relating to publicity. In exercising that judgment, a lawyer needs to focus on the real reason for a particular action. If the action is designed to help sell securities, the inquiry is ended—the act cannot be done. But the opposite is not true, because an inquiry cannot end with a determination that the real reason for an advertising campaign is product sales or another acceptable goal. The securities lawyer must remember that questions of that nature are often examined, long after the fact, in the context of a lawsuit. In the typical case, the transaction involved in the suit is a failure in financial terms, and a court may not perceive the equities to be on the side of the issuer. In dealing with questions concerning the real reason for publicity, the most important issue may be what an advocate can make reality appear to be to a fact finder already negatively disposed.

General Exceptions

There are now several generally applicable exceptions to the definition of "offer." The first is found in section 2(a)(3) itself:

> The terms defined in this paragraph and the term "offer to buy" as used in subsection (c) of section 5 shall not include preliminary negotiations or agreements between an issuer (or any person directly or indirectly controlling or controlled by an issuer, or under direct or indirect common control with an issuer) and any underwriter or among underwriters who are or are to be in privity of contract with an issuer (or any person directly or indirectly controlling or controlled by an issuer, or under direct or indirect common control with an issuer).

It is important to note that, so far as securities firms go, the exception is limited to underwriters, and therefore does not cover dealers. During the prefiling period, then, the company can find a managing underwriter, or a prospective managing underwriter can find a company interested in doing a public offering, and the managing underwriter can work with other securities firms to gauge their interest in joining the underwriting syndicate. However, the managing underwriter cannot begin to assemble the dealer group, even tentatively.

---

[2] Securities Act Release No. 7,856 (Apr. 28, 2000).

The second generally applicable exception is contained in Securities Act rule 135, which begins:

> For the purpose only of section 5 of the Act, a notice given by an issuer that it proposes to make a public offering of securities to be registered under the Act shall not be deemed to offer any securities for sale if such notice states that the offering will be made only by means of a prospectus and contains no more than the following additional information. . . .

The information that may be included is very basic and does not go much beyond the type and amount of securities to be offered, the anticipated timing of the offering, and a brief statement of the purpose of the offering. Underwriters may not be named.

There is a third exception applicable to all issuers that are not disqualified. (Basically, the most common categories of disqualified issuers are blank check companies, shell companies, and penny stock issuers, all of which are generally not permitted to take advantage of any recent reforms.) It is expressed in rule 163A, which provides that any communication made by or on behalf of an issuer more than 30 days prior to the filing of a registration statement will not be deemed to be an offer if that communication does not refer to the offering of securities. The issuer must, however, take reasonable steps to control further distribution or publication of the communication within 30 days before such a filing.

Several years ago, the Commission also added safe harbors that, though intended for use by different classes of issuers, have broad effects. One of these, contained in rule 169, permits non-reporting issuers to continue to communicate factual business information regularly released to persons other than in their capacity as investors or potential investors. Another, set out in rule 168, permits companies reporting under the Exchange Act (as well as certain others) to continue to communicate regularly released factual business and forward-looking information, notwithstanding the type of recipient. Finally, rule 163 permits a great deal of flexibility to well-known seasoned issuers. These issuers may make oral or written offers at any time. Written offers, however, must bear certain legends, be retained for three years and be filed with the Commission. Written offers meeting these conditions are referred to as "free writing prospectuses."

The Commission's reforms partially were geared toward easing Securities Act compliance for larger issuers. In 2012, the pendulum swung and Congress attempted to help out the "little guy"—that is, the emerging capital growth company. Perhaps not everyone would agree with the chosen line of demarcation; nonetheless, as set out at the beginning of this chapter, any issuer that is not a well-known seasoned issuer and that has less than $ 1 billion in annual revenue generally may (for five years) qualify for various exemptions from otherwise applicable Securities and Exchange Act requirements. For the purpose of defining what is and what is not an offer, there are two exemptions available to emerging growth companies. One of these is fairly straightforward: Section 5(d) provides that the issuer or someone (including an underwriter) acting on its behalf may "test the water" for market interest by communicating with institutions meeting certain size or deemed sophistication tests. In addition, Section 2(a)(3) now excludes from the definition of "offer" any research report on an emerging growth company by a broker or dealer (whether or not such a broker or dealer is participating in the offering).

Special Situations

Section 2(a)(3) contains two provisions relating to special situations. The first provision serves as an example of the drafters' skill at anticipating possible loopholes:

> Any security given or delivered with, or as a bonus on account of, any purchase of securities or any other thing, shall be conclusively presumed to constitute a part of the subject of such purchase and to have been offered and sold for value.

Actually, that exception is unnecessary because neither the Commission nor a court was likely to accept any other interpretation.

The other exception provides:

> The issue or transfer of a right or privilege, when originally issued or transferred with a security, giving the holder of such security the right to convert such security into another security of the same issuer or of another person, or giving a right to subscribe to another security of the same issuer or of another person, which right cannot be exercised until some future date, shall not be deemed to be an offer or sale of such other security; but the issue or transfer of such other security upon the exercise of such right of conversion or subscription shall be deemed a sale of such other security.

This exception usually applies to a convertible security or an option (often called a warrant). Examples are preferred stock convertible into common stock, and a warrant to purchase additional common stock that is sold along with common stock. Under the provision, the underlying security does not have to be registered originally when the conversion or exercise cannot occur at this time, but rather can only take place at some point in the future. Although section 2(a)(3) does not specifically address the issue, at the time the conversion or exercise can occur, an offer exists, and the filing of a registration statement, or the availability of a registration exemption, is required. Logic leads to that conclusion because the no offer exception speaks only to the time of original issue or transfer, and the requirement of later registration is dealt with in the legislative history.

A number of Securities Act rules contain exceptions to the definition of "offer" that relate to special situations. Those include situations involving general advertising concerning investment companies (rule 135a), the use of certain materials concerning options trading (rule 135b), and publication by securities firms of research reports in the ordinary course of business (rules 138 and 139).

Waiting Period

Scheme of the Statute

During the waiting period, section 5(a) continues to apply, prohibiting all sales and all transportation, by the mails or in interstate commerce, of securities for sale or delivery after sale, and section 5(b)(1) becomes applicable also as a practical matter (though it technically applied during the prefiling period). It provides:

(b) It shall be unlawful for any person, directly or indirectly—

(1) to make use of any means or instruments of transportation or communication in interstate commerce or of the mails to carry or transmit any prospectus relating to any security with respect to which a registration statement has been filed under this title, unless such prospectus meets the requirements of section 10. . . .

When the language concerning interstate commerce and the mails is ignored, the section provides that it is unlawful to use any prospectus unless it satisfies the requirements of section 10. The definition of "prospectus" is found in section 2(a)(10), which reads:

The term "prospectus" means any prospectus, notice, circular, advertisement, letter, or communication, written or by radio or television, which offers any security for sale or confirms the sale of any security; except. . . .

Stripped of its detail, section 2(a)(10) defines a prospectus as a written offer or a confirmation of sale (setting aside the exceptions and the concepts of radio or television offers). Exception (a) in section 2(a)(10) relates to the posteffective period and is not considered here. Exception (b) is a typical administrative law provision. It sets out the law regarding which communications are not deemed a prospectus, and then gives the Commission power to supplement it:

(b) a notice, circular, advertisement, letter, or communication in respect of a security shall not be deemed to be a prospectus if it states from whom a written prospectus meeting the requirements of section 10 may be obtained and, in addition, does no more than identify the security, state the price thereof, state by whom orders will be executed, and contain such other information as the Commission, by rules or regulations deemed necessary or appropriate in the public interest and for the protection of investors, and subject to such terms and conditions as may be prescribed therein, may permit.

To supplement that provision, the Commission adopted rule 134, which is discussed below.

In their essentials, then, sections 2(a)(10) and 5(b)(1) provide that, during the waiting period, no offer, in writing or by radio or television, may be made except by a section 10 prospectus or a communication meeting the requirements of exception (b) to section 2(a)(10). Additionally, those sections prohibit confirmations of sale. During the waiting period, the prohibition on oral offers, included in section 5(c)'s general prefiling period prohibition of offers, is lifted. As discussed above, section 5(a) continues to apply during the waiting period, prohibiting all sales and all transportation, by the mails or in interstate commerce, of securities for the purpose of sale or delivery after sale.

Section 10 is entitled "Information Required in Prospectus." Section 10(a) provides that a prospectus "shall contain the information contained in the registration statement," with some exceptions. That requirement may lead to two misconceptions. First, it may seem that a registration statement is filed and a prospectus subsequently is drafted based on the filed document. Actually, a prospectus is drafted for inclusion in a registration statement. Practicality dictates this, and this is what is contemplated by the Commission's registration statement forms and rules. The Commission requires the prospectus to contain most of the registration statement disclosure. The nonprospectus disclosures make up a small percentage of the total registration statement. Second, the statute's language may make it appear that any prospectus included as part of a registration statement necessarily must satisfy the requirements of section 10(a), whether or not the registration statement actually contains the information it is supposed to contain. That is not the case. Although the exact requirements of the section are somewhat unclear, as discussed below, at least it can be said that a prospectus does not comply with section 10(a) when it contains blanks where required information is to be added by amendment.

It may be possible for the prospectus as originally filed to comply with the requirements of section 10(a). Usually, however, certain required information is unknown at the time of filing. For example, the underwriting syndicate is seldom established at that time, and the names of the underwriters must usually be added by an amendment just before the registration statement becomes effective. The price of the securities to be offered is also typically left blank originally, along with miscellaneous other information. In the usual case, then, a section 10(a) prospectus is not available in the waiting period. A prospectus that meets the requirements of section 10(b) is available. That section gives the Commission authority to permit the use of a prospectus, for the purpose of section 5(b)(1), that omits or summarizes information required by section 10(a). The Commission has exercised that authority in rules 430 and 431. The first of those rules allows the use, during the waiting period, of what is called variously a "preliminary prospectus" or a "prospectus subject to completion." This prospectus may contain omissions, and any of its contents may later be changed. The second covers "summary prospectuses" and allows their use in certain circumstances.

The Commission also has exercised its section 10(b) authority to adopt rule 433, which (together with rule 164) permits the use, after a registration statement is filed, of something called a "free writing prospectus." Free writing prospectuses generally must bear a prescribed form of legend and, in many cases, must be filed with the Commission. (Those that are not filed must be retained for three years.) Though filed, they do not become part of the registration statement. If a free writing prospectus is prepared by or on behalf of an issuer, or by or on behalf of a participant in an offering by an issuer, it must be accompanied or preceded by a section 10 prospectus other than a summary prospectus or another free writing prospectus —in other words, during the waiting period, it is supposed to be accompanied or preceded by the preliminary prospectus authorized under rule 430. If the free writing prospectus is electronic and contains a hyperlink to the preliminary prospectus, the preliminary prospectus is deemed to accompany it.

Even more lenient treatment applies, however, to some classes of issuers. Seasoned (including well known seasoned) issuers are permitted by Rule 433 to use free writing prospectuses without regard to whether they are accompanied or preceded by any other prospectus.

What Is a Sale

The definition of "sale" contained in section 2(a)(3) does not purport to be complete. Its basic provision is: "The term 'sale' or 'sell' shall include every contract of sale or disposition of a security or interest in a security, for value." Similar to its treatment of offers, the Securities Act takes the common law meaning of the term "sale" as its base and then expands it. The most striking thing about section 2(a)(3) is its inclusion of contracts of sale within the ambit of "sale." That inclusion is a drafters' technique that allows provisions such as section 5(a) to be written a little more cleanly, but at a price, for by that technique the drafters laid a little trap. In the waiting period, certain offers may be made. The trick is that when an offer is accepted and a contract is created, section 5(a)(1) has been violated because a sale has occurred. As a practical matter, then, ordinary offers should not be made in the waiting period, but rather offerors should condition their offers in such a way that they cannot be accepted until the registration statement is effective. Partly for that reason, during the waiting period, securities firms make conditional offers and collect responses called "indications of interest," with the hope of turning those indications of interest into sales shortly after effectiveness.

As with offers, the Commission reads the section 2(a)(3) definition of "sale" liberally, leading to an expansive application of an already expanded concept. By including in the definition not only contracts of sale, but *"every* . . . disposition of a security . . . for value" (emphasis added), the drafters of section 2(a)(3) provided the Commission a reasonable basis for that reading. An example of the Commission's expansive reading is found in *In re Franklin, Meyer & Barnett*.[3] In that case, during the waiting period, salesmen in a securities firm performed two acts that might be considered to be consummating sales. First, they accepted checks sent by customers in payment for offered shares. Except for one instance, there was no indication that those checks were sent at the behest of, or even with the prior agreement of, the salesmen. The checks were deposited in the customers' accounts with the firm, and there was no finding that funds were taken out of those accounts prior to effectiveness. Second, the salesmen sold other securities for customers and held the proceeds for application against the purchase price of the offered shares. In most cases, those sales of other securities were at the suggestion of the salesmen. In each instance, the Commission found that the salesmen had made sales during the waiting period. It gave no helpful analysis, other than to say that the salesmen "accepted orders" prior to the effective date.

In contrast to that expansiveness is the exception in section 2(a)(3), introduced in connection with the prefiling period, that relates to "preliminary negotiations or agreements" between an issuer and underwriters, or among underwriters. That exception

---

[3] 37 S.E.C. 47 (1956).

provides that all the terms in section 2(a)(3), including "sale," do not include those negotiations or agreements. On its face, the exception is ambiguous because it cannot be determined from the words themselves whether "preliminary" modifies only "negotiations" or whether it also modifies "agreements." If the latter were the case, neither the agreement among underwriters nor the underwriting agreement could be entered into during the waiting period, since those are not "preliminary" agreements. Everyone—including the Commission—wants the underwriting arrangements finalized prior to effectiveness. Perhaps because of that, a problem has never existed with interpretation: "preliminary" modifies "negotiations" only. It is then unclear how negotiations are so limited. It seems that there is no limitation, because the parties must finalize negotiations before they can sign agreements. It may be argued that by adding the word "preliminary," the drafters attempted to make clearer the distinction between negotiations and agreements: negotiations are preliminary to agreements, and agreements are not part of negotiations.

Special Situations

This and the following subsections will cover some special situations involving the sale of securities in transactions other than the straight sale of stock to the public. The non-securities law issues involved are covered in a corporations or commercial law class.

Acquisitions

There never has been any question regarding the existence of a sale in the context of an acquisition by means of a stock-for-stock tender offer. When the acquiring company asks the target company's shareholders to tender their shares and promises its own stock in return, that is an offering of securities. And a sale inarguably occurs when the parties become bound by contract to consummate the transaction as planned, since under Securities Act section 2(a)(3), entering into a contract of sale constitutes a "sale." In that situation, the analysis is made easy because the acquiring company deals directly with the target's shareholders, each of whom makes an individual investment decision.

When dealing with mergers and stock-for-assets acquisitions, the issues are more complex. In those transactions, the target's shareholders often receive securities issued by the acquiring company, either because the plan of merger provides for that or because after the target company has sold its assets in exchange for stock of the acquiring company, it dissolves and distributes the stock to its shareholders as part of the liquidation process. Unlike the tender offer, however, the decisions behind the stock's finding its way into the hands of the target's shareholders are not, on the surface at least, the shareholders' individual decisions. Rather, those decisions can be viewed simply as decisions of the target corporation.

For a number of years, the Commission followed that reasoning and maintained that the transactions described above involve no sale of the acquiring company's securities to the target's shareholders. As a result, no registration of the securities was necessary, and the antifraud provisions of the securities laws did not apply. In 1972, the Commission reversed field, saying that "formalism should no longer deprive investors of the disclosure to which they are entitled."[4] It accomplished that change of position in rule 145, which fits the described transactions, and some similar ones, into the ordinary framework of a Securities Act offering.

Under rule 145, an offering of securities is made to the target's shareholders when certain acquisition plans are presented to them for approval, and a sale occurs when the requisite contract is entered into. The acquiring company is the issuer. It has no direct dealings with the target's shareholders, but rather those dealings are handled within the target company in the context of a shareholders' meeting. In other words, the target company acts as a middleman, and the Securities Act provides that in certain circumstances such a middleman is considered to be an underwriter. Rule 145 now applies the "deemed underwriter" doctrine to the target company, and any affiliate (which is a person in a control relationship with the company), publicly offering or selling securities received by the target in an acquisition covered by the rule, but only if one of the parties to the covered transaction is a shell company (basically, one with neither significant business operations nor significant assets other than cash or cash equivalents). For the target company deemed to be an underwriter, the primary result is that it is subject to underwriter's liability, most directly under section 11 of the Securities Act, for disclosure problems in connection with the offering. What may be of more immediate concern to affiliates of the target is the notion that underwriter status brings restrictions on their ability to resell any securities they receive in a rule 145 transaction. Resale limitations on affiliates are discussed in Chapter 7. For now, it is perhaps best just to note that the rule creates those limitations and that it then provides a mechanism for resales by affiliates on certain conditions.

When securities are offered and sold in connection with certain business combinations, such as mergers and tender offers, the Commission's rules permit somewhat more and different communications with security holders and the securities markets than are discussed in this chapter.

---

[4] Securities Act Release No. 5,316 (Oct. 6, 1972).

Spin-Offs and "Free" Stock Offerings

The question of whether and under what circumstances the corporate spin-off involves a sale is both interesting and slippery in terms of analysis. In a spin-off, a corporation takes stock that it owns in another corporation and distributes that stock to its shareholders as a dividend. When the corporation engaging in the spin-off is publicly held, the corporation spun off becomes publicly held also. Some shareholders will immediately want to sell their newly acquired shares, and a trading market will develop to facilitate that.

There are many permutations of that scenario. One such permutation involves a publicly held corporation's acquiring, for minimal consideration, partial ownership of a private company and then, without registration under the Securities Act, spinning off most, but not all, of the acquired shares. A business purpose for the acquisition of the shares by the publicly held corporation, other than benefits from the subsequent spin-off, is lacking. Those benefits may be substantial and will be spread fairly broadly. First, the owners of the private company benefit because they can take the company public with little cash outlay, while retaining a substantial percentage ownership. Second, since the publicly held corporation keeps some of the shares it acquires, it later can sell those shares for a profit. Third, the publicly held corporation's shareholders may come close to getting something for nothing, because although their company has paid little for the shares it has distributed to them, and they have paid nothing for those shares, the shares have value in the market.

The losers in such a transaction are those who buy the shares in the trading market without the benefit of disclosure. Because of that, the Commission has worked to conclude that such a spin-off cannot be done without registration. There is more than one theory involved, but the best one is that the spin-off involves a sale. Reaching that conclusion requires a little work. Dividends of a company's own stock have never been considered to involve a sale because a stock dividend is not a disposition of a security "for value." Taking that as a given, it might be difficult to understand how the opposite conclusion can be reached in the case of the spin-off described above. The big difference is that in such a spin-off, the company performing the spin-off stands to benefit from the creation of a public market for the shares it has retained for itself. Since the spin-off, and the trading market that inevitably develops, provide value to the company engaging in the spin-off, the spin-off can be considered a disposition of a security "for value" and therefore a sale under Securities Act section 2(a)(3). Courts have agreed with this analysis.[5]

More garden variety spin-offs may or may not involve sales, depending on the details of the transaction. The Commission's staff has issued a large number of no-action letters involving spin-offs, and in 1997 it issued a staff legal bulletin on the subject. Among other requirements, the staff has shown a properly serious concern that adequate public information be available about the spun-off securities and their issuer and that there be a legitimate business purpose for the spin-off.

On a related front, the Commission has attempted to prohibit unregistered offerings of "free" stock over the Internet.[6] The typical "free" stock offering required the "investor" to sign up with the issuers' website and disclose personal information in order to obtain shares. In some cases, additional shares were given for soliciting additional investors, for linking the investor's own website to the issuer's website, or for purchasing additional services. According to the Commission, "[t]hrough these techniques, issuers received value by spawning a fledgling public market for their shares, increasing their business, creating publicity, increasing traffic to their websites, and, in two cases, generating possible interest in projected public offerings."

Pledges

In common law terms, and under the Uniform Commercial Code, a pledge obviously is not a sale, and most students who have not had a class in securities law almost certainly would never consider that a pledge may be a sale under the Securities Act. Over the years, a number of courts have considered the issue. The most important case is *Rubin v. United States*,[7] which involved the question of whether a pledge of stock to a bank as collateral for a loan involves the sale of a security under section 17(a) of the Securities Act, which deals with fraud. The Supreme Court began its analysis with the definition of sale contained in Securities Act section 2(a)(3), noting that that definition includes the concept of "disposition of an interest in a security, for value." The Court held that a pledge of stock as collateral for a loan "unmistakably involves" such a disposition because, although less than a transfer of absolute title is involved, an "interest in a security" is transferred nonetheless.

---

[5] The leading cases are *SEC v. Datronics Engineers, Inc.*, 490 F.2d 250 (4th Cir.1973), and *SEC v. Harwyn Industries Corp.*, 326 F.Supp. 943 (S.D.N.Y.1971).

[6] *See* Securities Act Release No. 7,879 (Aug. 8, 2000).

[7] 449 U.S. 424 (1981).

What Is a Prospectus

Under the language of section 2(a)(10), without the exceptions, any written offer, offer by radio or television, or confirmation of sale is a prospectus. (In this book, radio or television offers are considered special varieties of written offers and so are not always specifically mentioned.) An understanding of the concept of "offer" provides a foundation for understanding what makes up a prospectus, because a determination of what constitutes an offer is much more complex than a determination of whether something is written or transmitted by radio or television. One difficult part of the task, therefore, has been accomplished in the discussion of the prefiling period. It is worth pausing, however, to review this discussion, and especially to note that some regularly released factual and (in the case of companies registered under the Exchange Act) forward-looking information will not be regarded as an offer, whether or not it is in writing. Moreover, with respect to emerging growth companies, neither brokers' or dealers' research reports nor communications with certain institutions will be regarded as offers.

What remains is to discuss the "written or by radio or television" aspects of prospectuses, to cover the exceptions to the definition of the term prospectus, and to discuss the possible application of a 1995 Supreme Court case.

In connection with the waiting period issue of what constitutes a prospectus, *Gustafson v. Alloyd Co.*,[8] which is discussed in Chapter 8, needs to be considered. This case deals with litigation under Securities Act section 12(a)(2), which provides a civil remedy in the case of offers or sales "by means of a prospectus or oral communication" that contains a materially false or misleading statement. In reaching its decision, the Court discussed the meaning of the term "prospectus." For example, the Court indicated that the definition of the term in section 2(a)(10) "refers to documents of wide dissemination." The Court also indicated that it could not "accept the conclusion that [the term 'prospectus'] means one thing in one section of the Act and something quite different in another." These statements, however, along with other broad language in the opinion, are merely dicta with respect to matters outside the holding of the case, and it remains to be seen how wide the effect of this opinion will be. Partly because, as discussed in Chapter 8, the decision was based on an exceedingly flawed understanding of the Securities Act, one might expect that ultimately it will be overturned or that, in any case, it will not be applied to the conception of what constitutes a prospectus in a registered offering. Otherwise, some of the discussion in this chapter of what constitutes a prospectus may change in ways

---

[8]   513 U.S. 561 (1995).

that are difficult fully to predict. Until more is known about this, a lawyer operating as a planner would be wise not to change his or her advice to clients about what can and cannot be done during the course of a Securities Act registration, based on the assumption that *Gustafson* provides added flexibility.

Indirect Offers

Garden variety written offers are spotted easily enough. It is indirect offers that cause a problem. Written publicity concerning the issuer or its industry that conditions the market for a security is the most common example of an indirect offer. The discussion of publicity in connection with the prefiling period is equally applicable here. For instance, the examples discussed above from Release No. 3,844, and the facts of *Loeb, Rhoades*, involved press releases and a brochure. Those publicity items were in writing and, therefore, constituted prospectuses because they made offers. Release No. 3,844 directly speaks to that point in connection with a discussion of the waiting period and gives a waiting period example involving the distribution of a report concerning an issuer prepared by a third party.

The "written or by radio or television" aspects of publicity can be more subtle than the examples discussed above. Take, for instance, an oral announcement by the president of an issuer at a press conference that, if in writing, would constitute a prospectus under the section 2(a)(10) definition. There is little doubt that, when a reporter incorporates the announcement in an article, the president has made an offer that is "written." Analytically, it can be said that the president caused the writing, and that that is enough to make the offer one that is by means of a prospectus. Clearly, the statute does not speak in terms of who the scrivener is. Harder questions are presented by responses to press inquiries. Upon analysis, however, it becomes clear that the hardest questions relate to whether a particular statement involves an offer, rather than to whether the offer was "written or by radio or television." But that is not to say, for example, that a newspaper article including a puffing answer to a reporter's unsolicited question about a company's product would be as likely to constitute a section 5 problem as would prepared statements at a called press conference. The newspaper article would be less dangerous, but primarily because a court would not be as likely to decide that the answer involved an offer, written or otherwise.

Written publicity is not, of course, the only way indirect written offers can be made. *In re Franklin, Meyer & Barnett*, discussed above, offers an interesting example. During the waiting period, a securities salesman sent a customer a preliminary prospectus that satisfied the requirements of section 10(b). That prospectus was allowed under section 5(b)(1). The salesman also enclosed his business card, on which he wrote, "Phone me as soon as possible as my allotment is almost complete on this issue." The Commission found that the business card solicited an offer to buy and was therefore a prospectus. That conclusion seems clear enough. A different situation would be presented if the salesman had called the customer and, finding him not in, had left the above message, which was reduced to writing. One way to approach that situation is to begin with the above analysis relating to press inquiries. Would the idea of "causing" a writing be extended to encompass the salesman's acts? It is hard to say. Considering the flexibility inherent in the concepts discussed above, it might depend on how badly the Commission or a court wanted to expand the concept.

Factual permutations would make an affirmative answer to the question more or less likely. For example, it would be important to know if the salesman specifically asked that the message be put in writing or that it not be. Agency concepts should help the salesman in an argument along these lines: (1) that in the one situation the press is the agent of the issuer, whereas in the other whoever answered the customer's telephone is the customer's agent, not the salesman's; (2) that the oral statement to the agent was the equivalent of an oral statement to the customer directly; and (3) that the note-taking by the agent was therefore analytically indistinguishable from note-taking by the customer.

Technology has presented new challenges for those seeking to define "writing." For instance, practitioners grappled for several years with whether e-mail is more like a substitute for a telephone conversation or (given its ability to be forwarded, downloaded, etc.) more like a mailed document. In 2005, in an amendment to rule 405, the Commission specified that "written communication" includes any "graphic communication." "Graphic communications" include Internet communications, e-mails, electronic postings on websites, and broadly disseminated or "blast" voice mail messages. Specifically excluded, however, are live communications carried in real time to a live audience, unless they are radio or television broadcasts. Special treatment for electronic road shows is set out in the revised rule.

Exceptions

Exception (b) to section 2(a)(10), which is discussed above, allows certain written offers in the waiting period by deeming them not to be prospectuses. In supplementation of that provision, and as an exercise of the power given it in section 19(a) to make rules relating to definitions, the Commission has adopted rule 134. That rule offers a great deal more leeway than the statute. The rule is complex, following this form: (a) can be done if (b) is done, but (b) does not have to be done if either (c)(i) or (c)(ii) is done, and if its terms are followed, (d) can be done. Any type of communication that is written or by radio or television can meet the requirements of rule 134. Press releases and letters are typical examples. Also common, although used more in the posteffective than in the waiting period, is the so-called tombstone advertisement, which gets its name from its stylized format. Those are found most often in the financial section of newspapers, with the *Wall Street Journal* often including a number of them.

In addition to rule 134, the Commission has adopted rule 134a, which is a highly specialized rule providing that certain written material relating to standardized options, as defined in Exchange Act rule 9b–1, is not deemed a prospectus. Unlike rule 134, which takes exception (b) to section 2(a)(10) as its starting point, rule 134a's real foundation is the Commission's general rule-making power found in section 19(a).

The applicability of rule 135, discussed in connection with the prefiling period, is uncertain in the waiting period. Rule 135 provides that certain notices "by an issuer that it proposes to make a public offering of securities to be registered under the Act shall not be deemed to offer any securities for sale." Its thrust clearly is toward the prefiling period. Everything supports that conclusion, including the rule's focus on offers, rather than on prospectuses as in rules 134 and 134a, and statements by the Commission in the adopting release. None of that means, however, that rule 135 could not apply during the waiting period. The important phrases in the rule to consider are "proposes to make a public offering" and "to be registered." In the usual situation, securities firms begin a public offering immediately after a registration statement is filed. In that situation, rule 135 clearly could not continue to be used, because the issuer no longer merely "proposes to make" an offering. However, an offering sometimes is delayed until later, for example, until the registration statement becomes effective. (Note, however, that there is a theory that the offering begins either on the filing of the registration statement or on its being made public by the commission, which occurs almost immediately.) The phrase "to be registered" is more problematical. In a technical sense, securities are still "to be registered" during the waiting period, since they are not "registered" until the registration statement is effective. But the term may be used in a somewhat looser sense, similar to the phrase "to be the subject of a registration statement." Usually, of course, it does not matter whether rule 135 applies during the waiting period, because of the availability of rule 134. But the question may be important to the occasional issuer that has published a notice meeting the information requirements of rule 135 but not those of rule 134. (This typically would happen when someone marked up a notice from a prior transaction without realizing that the notice was a rule 135 notice.)

Preliminary Prospectus Delivery Requirements

The Commission has perceived a shortcoming in section 5 of the Securities Act, which allows, but does not require, that preliminary prospectuses be distributed during the waiting period. It views that as a shortcoming because securities firms direct much of their sales effort at customers during that period. Since the Commission cannot rewrite section 5, it has corrected that shortcoming by two roundabout means. First, the Commission has indicated in rules 460 and 461, read together with Securities Act Release No. 4,968 (April 24, 1969), that it will not "accelerate" the effective date of a registration statement unless certain distributions of preliminary prospectuses have been made. Acceleration is discussed more fully in the next chapter, but for present purposes it is necessary to appreciate the importance of acceleration in many offerings. Section 8 of the Securities Act provides that a registration statement becomes effective twenty days after filing, or after the filing of any amendment. It also provides that a registration statement may become effective on "such earlier date as the Commission may determine" or, in securities parlance, that its effective date may be "accelerated." The problem for issuers is that a registration statement rarely can be complete at the time it is filed. Certain information, such as the name of each underwriter in the syndicate, usually cannot be supplied until just prior to effectiveness. Thus, acceleration typically is required as a practical matter.

The second means by which the Commission forces the distribution of preliminary prospectuses is even more roundabout than the first. Exchange Act section 15(c)(2) prohibits securities firms from engaging "in any fraudulent, deceptive, or manipulative act or practice" and gives the Commission power to determine what acts and practices fit within that prohibition. In Exchange Act rule 15c2–8, the Commission requires underwriters and dealers to take reasonable steps to furnish copies of the preliminary prospectus to any person who makes a written request for a copy. It also requires underwriters and dealers to furnish copies of the preliminary prospectus to their sales personnel, and the managing underwriter to provide the underwriters and dealers with sufficient quantities of the prospectus to meet their delivery requirements. Further, in the case of offerings by non-reporting issuers (which includes many first-time registrants), the rule requires underwriters and dealers to "deliver a copy of the preliminary prospectus to any person who is expected to receive a confirmation of sale at least 48 hours prior to the sending of such confirmation." The teeth behind those requirements is the Commission's determination, in rule 15c2–8, that a failure to make those deliveries constitutes a deceptive act or practice under Exchange Act section 15(c)(2).

In response to the evolving use of the Internet in business communications, the Commission issued a number of releases addressing electronic delivery of prospectuses. One of these is Securities Act Release No. 7,856 (April 28, 2000), which provides that electronic delivery is permissible if the recipient gives informed consent, and that such consent can be given telephonically if a record is kept of the call. This release also gives guidance as to what other electronic material will be considered part of the prospectus, what material will be considered delivered concurrently, and what the issuer's responsibility is for the content of its website and hyperlinked materials. In addition, the release sets out basic principles to be observed in conducting an offering entirely online. The Commission's releases have been augmented by the adoption of rule 433, which provides that an electronic preliminary prospectus that is hyperlinked to a free writing prospectus is deemed to accompany or precede it.

Posteffective Period

Scheme of the Statute

Section 5(b)(1), discussed in connection with the waiting period, continues to apply during the posteffective period. That section proscribes the use of any prospectus, unless it satisfies the requirements of section 10. During the waiting period, rules adopted pursuant to the Commission's section 10(b) authority permit use of preliminary prospectuses (rule 430), summary prospectuses (rule 431), and free writing prospectuses (rule 433). Summary prospectuses may be used after effectiveness, in certain circumstances. Free writing prospectuses also may be used, although, in the case of issuers that are not seasoned or well-known seasoned issuers, the free writing must be accompanied (including by hyperlink) or preceded by the "final prospectus" called for by section 10(a). For reasons that soon will become apparent, a writing that is accompanied or preceded by the final prospectus is not technically a prospectus at all.

Once the registration statement becomes effective, a few additional rules come into play under section 10(b). These are rules 430A, 430B and 430C (the last two of which were adopted in 2005). These rules permit, in the case of certain types of offerings and/or certain types of issuers, the use of prospectuses lacking specific items of information.

Usually, the only prospectus that complies with the requirements of that section is the prospectus that is included in the registration statement just before it becomes effective (the registration statement having in most cases been amended shortly before effectiveness to make final changes and to include information, such as the names of all the underwriters, that was left blank in the preliminary prospectus). Also, during that period a new exception is applicable to the definition of "prospectus." That is exception (a) in section 2(a)(10), which provides that a communication is not deemed a prospectus when it is accompanied or preceded by a prospectus that meets the requirements of section 10(a). The term traditionally used to describe communications allowed by that exception is "free writing." Because, in the post-effective period, many of the free writing prospectuses now allowed must be accompanied or preceded by a section 10(a) prospectus, they technically cease to be free writing "prospectuses" and become merely free writing.

After effectiveness, section 5(b)(2) comes into play. It provides:

(b) It shall be unlawful for any person, directly or indirectly—

(2) to carry or cause to be carried through the mails or in interstate commerce any such security for the purpose of sale or for delivery after sale, unless accompanied or preceded by a prospectus that meets the requirements of subsection (a) of section 10.

As a practical matter, this section provides that a security may not be delivered to a buyer unless the buyer simultaneously receives, or has received, a copy of the final prospectus. Rule 172(b), however, now provides that for purposes of this section the final prospectus is deemed, in most instances, to be delivered when the registration statement becomes effective. Notwithstanding this largesse (known as the "access equals delivery" model), rule 173 requires (though not as a condition of reliance on rule 172) that issuers, underwriters and dealers provide their purchasers either final prospectuses or a prescribed form of notice within two business days of completing the sale. Non-participating dealers may be exempt from this requirement as described at the end of this chapter.

The final piece to the post-effective statutory puzzle lies in understanding the treatment of confirmations of sale, which generally are not sent until the post-effective period, the first time at which the sale itself lawfully may occur. Under section 2(a)(10), confirmations of sale are included in the definition of "prospectus." Section 2(a)(10) then provides, in exception (a), that a communication sent during the post-effective period and accompanied or preceded by a final prospectus will not be considered a prospectus after all. Because business practice essentially requires that confirmations be delivered, and rule 10b–10 under the Exchange Act explicitly requires such delivery, the statute would demand delivery of a final prospectus as well. Under rule 172(a), adopted in 2005, however, most confirmations limited to the information necessary to comply with rule 10b–10 (and notices of allocations) are exempt from the provisions of section 5(b)(1).

During the post-effective period, then, oral offers may be made, since section 5(c) does not apply during this period (except in the case of a registration statement that is the subject of a stop order or of a public proceeding instituted before the effective date). Written offers may be made by means of the final prospectus, as contemplated by section 5(b)(1) and, in some cases, by summary, rule 430A, 430B or 430C prospectuses. They may also be made by free writing, when accompanied or preceded by a final prospectus, as provided in section 2(a)(10). Seasoned (including well-known seasoned) issuers may continue to use free writing prospectuses that are not accompanied or preceded by any other prospectus. Offers may continue to be made under exception (b) to section 2(a)(10) and under rules 134 and 134a. Sales may be made, since the prohibition on sales contained in section 5(a)(1) no longer applies. Section 5(a)(2)'s prohibition of pre-effective deliveries ceases to pertain, and section 5(b)(2)'s requirement that security delivery must be accompanied or preceded by a final prospectuses generally will be deemed satisfied, thanks to rule 172(b). Nonetheless, issuers, underwriters and some dealers must deliver either the final prospectuses or the notice prescribed by rule 173.

Section 5(b) and Defective Prospectuses

As indicated above, during the posteffective period, section 5(b)(1) allows the use of a prospectus that meets the requirements of section 10, and section 5(b)(2) requires that a section 10(a) prospectus accompany or precede the delivery of a security. But what if a final prospectus is defective because it is materially false or misleading? Does such a defect prevent the prospectus from meeting the requirements of section 10(a)?

The place to start to answer that question is section 10(a) itself, which provides that "a prospectus . . . shall contain the information contained in the registration statement. . . . "On its face, that language seems to require only that the prospectus track the registration statement, defective or otherwise, although as the prior discussion of section 10(a) has indicated, to comply with that section the prospectus must at least be complete. The language of the section itself, then, provides no help in answering questions concerning materially false or misleading prospectuses.

The Commission and the Second Circuit have provided their answer in *SEC v. Manor Nursing Centers, Inc.*[9] In that case, developments subsequent to the effective date of a registration statement and final prospectus made the information in the prospectus materially false and misleading. The Commission alleged that the continued use of the prospectus constituted a section 5(b)(2) violation, and the Second Circuit agreed:

> We hold that implicit in the statutory provision that the prospectus contain certain information is the requirement that such information be true and correct. A prospectus does not meet the requirements of § 10(a), therefore, if information required to be disclosed is materially false or misleading.

Although the First Circuit has followed *Manor Nursing*,[10] it has done so without analysis. And the Fifth Circuit has criticized the case strongly. In *SEC v. Southwest Coal & Energy Co.*,[11] the court was faced with a situation in which *Manor Nursing* was relevant by analogy. In rejecting the Second Circuit's thesis, the Fifth Circuit focused its analysis not on section 10(a), but on the violence *Manor Nursing* does to other sections of the Securities Act. False or misleading statements in a prospectus are the subject of specific antifraud provisions, and in those provisions Congress provided for defenses available in certain circumstances. By finding that a false or misleading prospectus violates section 5(b)(2), the Second Circuit pushed aside the tailor-made antifraud provisions, rendering them, in the words of the Fifth Circuit, "essentially superfluous as remedial mechanisms" and obliterating the defenses they provide.

When events occur after the effectiveness of a registration statement that make the final prospectus materially false or misleading, or when prior defects are discovered after effectiveness, the prospectus must be corrected (because of the antifraud provisions of the securities laws, if for no other reason). That correction can be performed in one of two ways. First, an issuer may file a posteffective amendment to the registration statement containing the correction, which may be contained in either an amended final prospectus or a supplement to the final prospectus. (In industry usage, an amended prospectus is one that has been rewritten to reflect changes, while a supplemented prospectus is one to which a sticker incorporating changes has been added to the cover page.) Second, an issuer usually may amend or supplement the final prospectus without filing a posteffective amendment, as long as, under rule 424(b), the new form of prospectus is filed with the Commission within a specified number

---

[9] 458 F.2d 1082 (2d Cir.1972).

[10] *A. J. White & Co. v. SEC*, 556 F.2d 619, 622 (1st Cir.1977).

[11] 624 F.2d 1312, 1318 (5th Cir.1980).

of days. Traditionally, issuers handle relatively discrete corrections by the rule 424(b) mechanism and more extensive corrections through the filing of a posteffective amendment.

Final Prospectus Delivery Requirements

As indicated in the discussion relating to the waiting period, section 5 does not require that preliminary prospectuses be delivered. Section 5(b)(2), however, does require that a final prospectus be delivered along with the security purchased, unless the security has been preceded by a copy of that prospectus (assuming the use of jurisdictional means).

As described above, section 5(b)(2) stipulates that securities cannot be delivered unless accompanied or preceded by a final prospectus. This presents interesting theoretical questions about what constitutes delivery in, *e.g.*, the case of uncertificated shares, and whether delivery to a "street name" holder constitutes delivery to the beneficial owner. These questions largely are moot owing to rule 172(b)'s "access equals delivery" approach (providing that section 5(b)(2) generally is satisfied when the registration statement becomes effective) and the requirement in rule 173 that issuers, underwriters and some dealers deliver either a final prospectus or a prescribed form of notice within two days of completing a sale.

Section 5(b)(2) aside, there is an additional reason why final prospectuses must be delivered to purchasers as part of the initial distribution of shares. Exchange Act rule 15c2–8, which was discussed in connection with the waiting period, establishes much the same requirements for limited distributions of final prospectuses that it establishes for preliminary prospectuses. Basically, they are to be furnished to sales personnel, and to other persons on written request. Remember, however, that the commission has approved the delivery of prospectuses through electronic means, provided specified conditions are met.

If no written offers (or offers by radio or television) ever were made in the post-effective period other than by section 10 prospectus, the provisions discussed thus far (section 5(b)(2), Securities Act rules 172 and 173, and Exchange Act rule 15c2–8) would tell the whole story about final prospectus delivery requirements. Inevitably, however, such offers will be made, giving rise to additional obligations by way of section 5(b)(1), discussed in connection with the waiting period. As mentioned above, rule 172 usually takes care of the problem that otherwise would be presented by the confirmations of sale mandated by Exchange Act rule 10b–10. Other writings and broadcasts must be separately analyzed as described earlier in this chapter.

In the case of dealers who are not participants in the distribution that is the subject of registration, however, there is now an easy answer. Under rule 174 (adopted pursuant to authority granted the Commission in Section 4(a)(3)), prospectus delivery requirements are deemed satisfied once the registration statement has become effective.

Summary

The following chart provides, in general terms, a summary of the communications that are specifically permitted (or, in some cases, required) by the regulatory framework discussed in this chapter.

Type of Issuer	Prefiling Period	Waiting Period	Posteffective Period
Non-reporting	**Permitted:**	**Permitted:**	**Permitted:**
	• Preliminary negotiations and agreements with underwriters (Section 2(a)(3))	• Oral offers	• Oral offers
		• Preliminary negotiations and agreements with underwriters (Section 2(a)(3)	• Sales
	• Communications pursuant to Rule 135		• Communications pursuant to Rule 134
		• Communications pursuant to Rule 134 (or Section 2(a)(10)(b))	
	• Communications more than 30 days in advance that do not reference the offering (Rule 163A)		• Section 10 prospectuses (no longer including the preliminary prospectus)
		• Section 10 prospectuses:	
	• Regularly released factual information (Rule 169)	○ Preliminary (Section 10(b) and Rule 430)	• Free writing (Section 2(a)(10)(a; must be accompanied or preceded by a final prospectus)
		○ Summary ((Section 10(b) and Rule 431)	
		○ Free writing (Section 10(b) and Rules 164 and 433; must be accompanied or preceded by preliminary prospectus)	
	If also an emerging growth company:	**If also an emerging growth company:**	**If also an emerging growth company:**
	• Communications with certain institutional investors (Section 5(d))	• Communications with certain institutional investors (Section 5(d))	• Communications with certain institutional investors (Section 5(d))
	• Brokers' and dealers' research reports (Section 2(a)(3))	• Brokers' and dealers' research reports (Section 2(a)(3))	• Brokers' and dealers' research reports (Section 2(a)(3))

Type of Issuer	Prefiling Period	Waiting Period	Posteffective Period
Non-reporting		**Required:**	**Required:**
		• Distribution of preliminary prospectus per Exchange Act Rule 15c2–8	• Written confirmation (Exchange Act Rule 10b–10)
			• Delivery of final prospectus or Rule 173 notice unless exempt under Section 4(4) or Rule 174
			• Delivery of final prospectus to accompany or precede delivery of securities (deemed under Rule 172(b) to occur at effectiveness)
			• Distribution of final prospectus per Exchange Act Rule 15c2–8
Unseasoned	**Same as Nonreporting,** *plus*:	**Same as Nonreporting,** *except*:	**Same as Nonreporting,** *except*:
	• Regularly released forward-looking information is permitted (Rule 168)	• Exchange Act Rule 15c2–8 compliance is less demanding	• Only participating dealers are non-exempt under Section 4(3) and Rule 174
			• Exchange Act Rule 15c2–8 compliance is less demanding
Seasoned	**Same as Unseasoned**	**Same as Nonreporting and Unseasoned,** *except*:	**Same as Unseasoned,** *plus*:
		• Free writing prospectuses need not be accompanied or preceded by preliminary prospectus (Rule 433)	• Free writing prospectus permitted that is not accompanied or preceded by final prospectus (Rule 433) (Note that this is in addition to free writing under Section 2(a)(10)(a))

Type of Issuer	Prefiling Period	Waiting Period	Posteffective Period
Well-Known Seasoned	**Same as Unseasoned and Seasoned, *plus*:** • Oral offers at any time (Rule 163) • Free writing prospectuses at any time; need not be accompanied or preceded by any other prospectus (Rule 163)	**Not applicable**	**Same as Seasoned**

Chapter 5

HOW SECURITIES ARE REGISTERED UNDER THE SECURITIES ACT

Scheme of the Statute

Sections 6, 7, and 8 of the Securities Act contain the statutory scheme for the registration process. Section 6:

1. Provides that securities may be registered by filing a registration statement with the Commission;

2. Specifies who must sign the registration statement; and

3. Sets the formula for the registration fee. The fee, which for fiscal year 2014 will be $128.80 for each million dollars of the maximum proposed public offering price, is to be adjusted to produce target amounts set by Congress for each year thereafter. Congress still must pass revenue measures each year with respect to the fee, however, and in the past it often has delayed passing a measure on time. This causes the preexisting fee to stay in effect until the revenue measure is passed and signed by the President.

The registration statement must be signed by the issuer, the principal executive officer, the principal financial officer, the comptroller or principal accounting officer, and a majority of the directors or persons performing similar functions. (As will be seen in Chapter 8, everyone who signs the registration statement is subject to liability under section 11 for any material misstatement or omission in the registration statement.)

New section 6(e), added by the JOBS Act of 2012, provides that emerging growth companies (described in Chapter 4) contemplating their initial public offerings may submit a confidential draft registration statement to the Commission for feedback. Public filing must occur at least 21 days before the date on which the issuer conducts a road show.

Section 7 deals primarily with what a registration statement must contain and sets forth schedule A to the Securities Act as the technical starting point for most issuers. That schedule is a thirty-two-item list presenting a few pages of disclosure requirements. Congress did not intend to tie the Commission's hands with that schedule, however, and until 2010 section 7 gave the Commission full authority to add or subtract information requirements. The Commission did so to such a degree that schedule A is now essentially irrelevant. The registration statement forms promulgated by the Commission have become the practical starting point for determining disclosure requirements. In 2010, however, the Dodd-Frank Act amended Section 7 to direct the Commission to require certain disclosures from the issuers of asset-backed securities (which were deemed to have contributed to the financial turmoil beginning in 2008). In 2012, the JOBS Act limited financial information that could be required from an emerging growth company.

Section 8 covers the effectiveness of registration statements. That section provides that a registration statement automatically becomes effective twenty days after filing, or after the filing of any amendment. That provision is in section 8(a), which also gives the Commission the power to accelerate the effective date. The rest of section 8 gives the Commission the means to prevent materially defective registration statements from becoming effective or to suspend the effectiveness of such statements. Those means are refusal-order proceedings under section 8(b) and stop-order proceedings under section 8(d). Section 8(e) covers examinations that the Commission may make to determine whether a stop order should be issued. As is discussed below, practice deviates substantially from what might be expected after reading section 8.

As will be seen below, the Commission has done much tinkering with the statutory scheme. Two of its changes have been particularly significant. First, the Commission has devised a method to delay effectiveness in order to permit time for review and comment. Second, it has provided that the registration statements of well-known seasoned issuers (as discussed in Chapter 4, those issuers that have been Exchange Act reporting companies for at least twelve months and that meet certain size requirements) become effective immediately.

Drafting a Registration Statement

Registration Statement Forms

As indicated above, the registration statement forms promulgated by the Commission provide the real starting point for determining what must be included in a registration statement. Securities Act rules 130 and 401 give those forms the force of law, which makes their requirements mandatory. There are a number of different forms, each for use in a specific situation. The forms are generally short because the bulk of the disclosure requirements are not usually contained in the forms themselves, but in a central repository called regulation S–K. (There is also a repository called regulation S–X for information required in financial statements).

Generally, the forms simply contain lists of regulation S–K items with which an issuer must comply. The forms break the disclosure requirements into two parts: information required, and not required, in the prospectus. The former is information to be provided to investors, while the latter is basically for the Commission's review.

Form S–1 is the general, catch-all form that is used when no other form is authorized or prescribed. For the typical issuer and the garden variety security, it contains the Commission's most extensive disclosure requirements. A Form S–1 registration statement may be several dozen pages in length. Some issuers, however, may take advantage of a Commission initiative called "integration." For most of the history of the Securities Act and the Exchange Act, the disclosure requirements of the two acts operated independently. When a company wished to register securities under the Securities Act, it filed a registration statement containing full disclosure about itself and its business. Although this requirement made sense for a first time issuer, it ignored the fact that for others essentially the same information had been disclosed, and continuously updated, in reports filed under the Exchange Act and that this information had almost certainly found its way into the market place through the work of securities analysts and others in the securities industry.

In recognition of these factors, and the fact that Exchange Act reports now easily may be accessed via the Internet, the Commission now permits issuers that are reporting companies under the Exchange Act to incorporate into their Form S–1 registration statements a significant amount of information by reference to their already-filed Exchange Act reports. In order to take advantage of incorporation by reference, an issuer must have filed an annual report under the Exchange Act for its most recent fiscal year and meet certain other tests. When a company meets the tests, its registration statement for most transactions may be a combination of spelled-out disclosures and the incorporation by reference of information from Exchange Act sources (which must be made accessible on the issuer's website). The prospectus used by such an issuer must state where the information incorporated by reference may be found and state that the issuer will deliver that information upon request.

Form S–3 is available for specified transactions to companies that meet certain additional tests. Most notably, companies that have filed Exchange Act reports for twelve months and satisfy one of four requirements relating either to past issuance of non-convertible securities registered under the Securities Act or to specified relationship with a well-known seasoned issuer may register non-convertible debt on Form S–3. Companies that have filed Exchange Act reports for twelve months and are issuing common stock for cash may use Form S–3 if the company's outstanding voting and non-voting common equity held by non-affiliates[1] has a market value of at least $75 million. (These two groups also comprise the class of seasoned issuers referred to in Chapter 4; the seasoned issuer concept, in fact, is defined by reference to eligibility to use Form S–3 for primary offerings.) In addition, issuers that have a class of common equity listed and registered on a national exchange and have not been a "shell" company within the last twelve months may use Form S–3 for primary offerings of common equity not exceeding, in a twelve-month period, one-third of their public float. (These issuers, however, are not "seasoned.") In a Form S–3 registration statement, the issuer basically gives information particular to the transaction at hand and then incorporates by reference from Exchange Act documents—both those that have been filed and those that will be filed before the offering is complete. This registration statement usually runs only to several pages.

The Commission has long realized that the burdens of registration were greater than could be borne by many small companies and that this burden created an impediment to capital formation. It has now built into Regulation S–K special, less demanding requirements with which qualifying small issuers may elect to comply on an "*a la carte*," or item-by-item, basis. These qualifying small issuers, known as "smaller reporting companies" (although the designation is not dependent on reporting status under the Exchange Act), must have either less than $75 million of public float, or, if they have no public float, less than $50 million in annual revenue. Congress also has exhibited concern for what it considers smaller companies and, as indicated above, decreed in the JOBS Act that the financial information required from emerging growth companies was to be limited. It also directed the Commission to study Regulation S–K for ways to streamline the registration process for emerging growth companies.

Other registration statement forms relate to particular kinds of issuers (for example, forms F–1 and F–3 for certain private foreign issuers, S–6 for unit investment trusts, and S–11 for certain real estate companies) and special types of transactions (for example, S–4 for mergers and other acquisitions). In some instances, one of

---

[1] Under Securities Act Rule 405, an "affiliate" is someone in a control relationship with someone else either controlling, controlled by, or under common control. "Control" is a tricky concept that will be discussed in Chapter 7. Generally, directors, at least some officers, and substantial shareholders are affiliates of an issuer.

those specialized forms must be used, but in others an issuer can use the specialized form or one of the general forms.

Rules, Regulations, and Industry Guides

Regulation S–K serves as the Commission's general repository of disclosure requirements. Regulation C under the Securities Act contains rules in the 400 series and relates to various aspects of the registration process. Basically, it is a catch-all of rules relating mostly to formal and procedural matters. As examples, the requirements of regulation C address such matters as dating of prospectuses (rule 423) and procedures for abandoning registration statements (rule 479).

A detailed discussion of regulation C would not be helpful here, but one rule merits special attention. This is rule 408, which provides:

> In addition to the information expressly required to be included in a registration statement, there shall be added such further material information, if any, as may be necessary to make the required statements, in the light of the circumstances under which they are made, not misleading.

This rule, as a practical (though not technical) matter, reduces to a requirement that anything material must be disclosed. The concept of "materiality" is significant across all areas of securities law. A good starting point for an understanding of the concept is rule 405, which provides: "The term 'material,' when used to qualify a requirement for the furnishing of information as to any subject, limits the information required to those matters to which there is a substantial likelihood that a reasonable investor would attach importance in determining whether to purchase the security registered." In real-world securities practice, rule 408 is the centerpiece of disclosure. Good securities lawyers make certain they cover all the specific disclosure requirements, but that is somewhat mechanical. For the securities lawyer worrying about disclosure, digging to find nonspecified information and then determining whether it is material takes the most skill and judgment.

The forms and rules discussed above are promulgated by the Commission itself and have the force of law. In a different category are the Industry Guides, which are expressions of the policies and practices of the Commission's Division of Corporation Finance. Although the guides lack the legal status of forms and rules, in practical terms they are not of much less real importance. There are six Securities Act Industry Guides:

1. [Reserved]

2. Disclosure of oil and gas operations.

3. Statistical disclosure by bank holding companies.

4. Prospectuses relating to interests in oil and gas programs.

5. Preparation of registration statements relating to interests in real estate limited partnerships.

6. Disclosures concerning unpaid claims and claim adjustment expenses of property-casualty insurance underwriters.

7. Description of property by issuers engaged or to be engaged in significant mining operations.

The guides generally have the look of regulation S–K disclosure requirements, except for guide 5, which goes much further and is essentially a blueprint for drafting the prospectus.

Getting the Job Done

Although the registration statement form is the starting point for determining disclosure requirements, it does not provide a model for drafting. Assuming a first public offering, the issuer's counsel invariably uses recent prospectuses from other issues for this purpose. The managing underwriter typically is the best source for hard copies of those prospectuses, and they will be available by computer as a result of the Commission's Electronic Data Gathering, Analysis and Retrieval System, which everyone refers to as EDGAR.[2] The registration statement drafter may be lucky and find one or more recent prospectuses that tell the same basic story the drafter has to tell. The more recent the models the better, because if they are final prospectuses they may give a good idea of disclosures favored by the current Commission staff.

There are other ways to find out what currently favored disclosures are. Sometimes the Commission issues a release on particular disclosure points. Letters of comments from other registrations also provide insights into the staff's thinking—and the more recent the letter the better.

After studying other prospectuses, and keeping in mind the various other sources of information concerning disclosure, the drafter is ready to begin work. The first thing to do is to amass information about the issuer. That task is easy in the case of an Exchange Act reporting company because most of the work has already been done. For nonreporting companies, such research can be difficult, and it requires good investigative skills. Many

---

[2] Information on how to access documents filed under EDGAR is available at the Commission's website, www.sec.gov.

discussions with company officers are required, along with much digging in the company's files and examining its operations. Many companies have prepared, often in connection with loan applications, a report that describes the company and its business. Those reports can be helpful. If a company has sold securities in an exempt offering, an offering memorandum probably was prepared. Depending largely on the type of exemption involved, and the ability of the lawyers who drafted it, the memorandum may be good enough to use as a rough prospectus draft.

Once enough information concerning the issuer is at hand, a lawyer can begin drafting the registration statement. Drafting the prospectus portion is the challenge, since the rest of the registration statement is straightforward. Since a prospectus is the main document that offers a security, one might expect it to be upbeat.

As discussed in Chapter 8, however, heavy liabilities may result from a misstatement or omission in a prospectus. Largely because of that, lawyers and investment bankers do not much think of a prospectus as a selling document, but rather as one to protect against liability. In a well-drafted prospectus a reader is hard pressed to find the slightest puffing. In fact, simple positive statements tend to be made only when they can be backed by unimpeachable authority. And even then, the drafter often includes some negative statement as an offset. For example, a drafter might write: "The company is the country's largest producer of dog collars," and then add: "but there can be no assurance that the company can maintain that position, or even if it can, that competitive or other factors will not make the manufacture and sale of that product unprofitable."

Under rule 421(d), issuers must prepare the front and back cover pages of the prospectuses, as well as the summary and risk factors sections, in what the Commission refers to as "plain English." The thrust of the rule is that these parts of prospectuses must comply with six basic plain English principles such as the use of short sentences and of the active voice.

Drafts of the registration statement are circulated to the managing underwriter, its counsel, officers, and perhaps directors of the issuer. Each of those persons may give comments, and typically one or two all-day meetings are held to discuss the registration statement before it is put in final form. In connection with their review of registration statement drafts, the managing underwriter and its counsel do a so-called due diligence examination designed to ensure as best they can that the registration statement is completely accurate and contains no material omission (these are done partly to make sure the document is correct and partly to protect against section 11 liability if something material is missed but the due diligence effort nonetheless satisfies the requirements of that section). A due diligence examination includes discussions with the issuer's officers, examining documents in the issuer's files, and visiting the issuer's facilities.

At some point in the drafting process, a registration statement usually is sent to a financial printer to be set in type. Financial printers are high-quality, quick-turnaround businesses found only in a few financial centers. When necessary, they can produce a registration statement overnight. When everyone is satisfied with the document, the printer makes the final agreed changes, often in a late-night session attended by junior members of the various teams, and the issuer files the registration statement with the Commission. The filing must be done electronically under the EDGAR system. Wise securities lawyers typically call the Commission to learn who the examiner will be and send the examiner, by overnight delivery, a paper copy of the registration statement done in regular type rather than in the more difficult to read EDGAR format.

Procedures of the Commission

Review and Comment Procedure

Under the Commission's review and comment procedure, registration statements of first-time issuers are given a thorough review by the staff of the Commission's Division of Corporation Finance, and statements filed by second and later issuers are reviewed selectively. A number of staff members work on a registration statement. An examiner takes responsibility for reviewing the bulk of the document. The financial disclosures are reviewed by an accountant. The examining team reports to an assistant director, who makes the final decision concerning comments to be made to the issuer.

The goal of securities lawyers is compliance with staff comments, and any suggested change in the registration statement that can be made with a reasonable expenditure of time and effort is typically made with little question. Sometimes, however, the cost of compliance would be too great or the time required would be too long. Occasionally, a requested change would cause the registration statement to be materially false or misleading. In one of those instances, the issuer's counsel calls the examiner and tries to reach an agreement on changes. If they cannot come to terms, issuer's counsel sometimes then appeals informally, by telephone, to the assistant director and, if necessary, to those higher up in the Division of Corporation Finance.

Changes in the registration statement may be handled in a couple of ways. When the changes are at all extensive, an amendment is filed. A number of amendments may be required before the staff gives its clearance. Sometimes, when the changes to be made are relatively minor, draft language is given to the examiner for informal clearance without the filing of an amendment. In that case, agreed-to changes are included in the so-called price amendment, which often is filed just before effectiveness to make final corrections and changes and to add previously unknown information to the registration statement.

If substantial final corrections and changes are not necessary, rule 430A may allow the issuer to forego the filing of a price amendment and simply add to the final prospectus information about pricing and the underwriting arrangements. (For issuers utilizing "shelf" registration, discussed below, rule 430B permits even more flexibility in omitting information from the prospectus contained in the registration statement when it becomes effective and adding the information when it becomes known.) Under rule 424, the final prospectus must be filed shortly after it is used. The information that is added is deemed to be a part of the registration statement. Under Rule 430C, this is also true of prospectuses filed to reflect substantive changes in prior information.

In terms of timing, the first staff review of a registration statement for an initial public offering typically takes a month or a little more, but that can vary depending on the staff's work load. After the assistant director issues comments, the staff responds quickly to inquiries from the issuer's counsel and to amendments. Depending on the time it takes to comply with staff comments and the number of amendments, it may take anywhere from another few days to a few months before the registration statement is ready to go effective. In light of that, one might wonder what has happened to the twenty-day waiting period written into section 8(a).

Delaying and Accelerating Effectiveness in a Traditional Registration

Remember that section 8(a) provides for the automatic effectiveness of registration statements twenty days after filing, or twenty days after the filing of an amendment. The statutory automatic effectiveness was virtually a dead letter from the beginning. It could not work in most offerings because a registration statement rarely can be complete when filed. In the typical offering, the registration statement needs to have added to it information (such as pricing and the names of the underwriters) that cannot be determined twenty days in advance. The resulting problem is that, under section 8(a), if an issuer files an amendment adding this information, the twenty-day waiting period begins again. Circumventing both the automatic twenty-day effectiveness and the twenty-day waiting period after filing an amendment has been, therefore, a practical necessity from the beginning.

The only way to avoid automatic effectiveness is to amend the registration statement before the twenty-day period has run. By means of a creative mechanism provided in rule 473, an issuer may include a paragraph on the cover of a registration statement that effects its continuing amendment. The paragraph reads:

> The registrant hereby amends this registration statement on such date or dates as may be necessary to delay its effective date until the registrant shall file a further amendment which specifically states that this registration statement shall thereafter become effective in accordance with section 8(a) of the Securities Act of 1933 or until the registration statement shall become effective on such date as the Commission, acting pursuant to said section 8(a), may determine.

The idea of that paragraph's serving as a continuing amendment may seem a little strange, but it is clever and it works.

Avoiding the twenty-day wait after filing an amendment is handled by the Commission using its power under section 8(a) to accelerate the twenty-day period. The mechanisms of that procedure are simple. After the Commission's staff is satisfied that a registration statement is ready to become effective, the issuer and the managing underwriter decide the timing of effectiveness and agree on final business terms. Then, as provided in rule 461, each requests acceleration, specifying the day and time they desire the registration statement to become effective. In the usual case, acceleration is granted pro forma, with the staff working to meet any reasonable time schedule.

The Commission extracts a price for that cooperation, however, in that it uses the implied threat of acceleration denial to force actions not required by the statute. That power was examined in the last chapter in the discussion of distribution of preliminary prospectuses. Although the Securities Act does not require use of preliminary prospectuses, the Commission will deny acceleration unless they are distributed during the waiting period, assuming a sales effort went on during that period. Rule 461 contains a list of other factors the Commission considers in connection with acceleration requests, including whether "the Commission is currently making an investigation of the issuer, a person controlling the issuer, or one of the underwriters ... pursuant to any of the Acts administered by the Commission."

Technically, of course, an issuer does not have to use a delaying amendment. If it refused to do so, however, its registration statement would be turned over to the enforcement division for their examination. The enforcement staff could then be expected to begin an examination, under powers given the Commission under section 8(e), into whether a stop order should be issued. The registration statement would become effective in the statutory twenty days, but that would be of no help to the issuer, because under section 5(c) no offers may be made while an examination instituted before the effective date is in progress, and such an examination likely would take several months to complete. What it comes down to is this: If an issuer wants to cooperate with the Commission staff, the staff will cooperate with it. But, if someone forces a confrontation, the staff can handle that too.

Shelf Registration Under Rule 415

The last sentence of section 6(a) provides that "[a] registration statement shall be deemed effective only as to the securities specified therein proposed to be offered." The Commission traditionally has interpreted this language to mean that securities generally can not be registered unless there is an intention to offer them in the "proximate future." Major exceptions to this approach have been embodied in rule 415, which has taken on great significance. This rule allows the registration, in certain circumstances, of securities that are to be offered on a continuous or delayed basis. In popular terminology, it provides for "shelf registration."

The traditional offering focused on so far, which is designed to be completed promptly after effectiveness, does not satisfy the needs of all issuers. Sometimes the transaction an issuer contemplates requires that securities be offered and sold over a long period, on a continuous basis. A good example is common stock offered under an employee stock purchase plan, when the plan gives employees the right to purchase shares anytime they wish during the life of the plan. In other cases, issuers may wish to register securities and put them "on the shelf" so the securities will be immediately available for sale when needed. A traditional example of this is an issuer which is engaged in a program of acquiring other companies and wishes to have registered securities available to use as consideration for the purchase of these companies. The Commission long ago established exceptions for these (and similar) transactions; these exemptions now are included in rule 415.

Rule 415 also is available for, among other things, offerings by issuers eligible to use Form S–3 or F–3. Another important, permitted use is as for sales of asset-backed, investment grade debt by other companies. Once the registration is accomplished, issuers relying on rule 415 can watch the advances and declines in market prices and wait for an advantageous market window through which to slip their securities. This ability to time an offering precisely can greatly minimize the qualifying issuer's cost of capital. Further savings to issuers can be made through registering the securities without naming underwriters and then shopping for the best underwriting deal, or choosing underwriters by competitive bid at the last minute. Empirical studies of issuance costs have found rule 415 costs to have been lower than in traditional offerings.

Described in broad strokes, rule 415 permits a registration statement to become effective even though the prospectus it contains omits information that is not yet known (such as the names of the underwriters) but which otherwise would be required. The information then is added, either through post-effective amendment or (more usually) by use of the rule 424 process, when the information becomes available. (Rule 430B deals with the interim use of prospectuses omitting the otherwise required information.)

Of particular note, rule 415 permits the shelf registrations of well-known seasoned issuers (as described in Chapter 4, companies meeting more stringent requirements than merely seasoned companies) to become effective automatically upon filing. The registration statement may cover unspecified amounts of specified classes of securities, and easily may be amended to add to or change the classes that are covered. Filing fees may be paid in advance or on a "pay-as-you-go" basis at the time of an actual offering. Shelf registrations of this type (as well as certain others) remain in effect for three years.

Refusal Orders, Stop Orders, and Withdrawal of Registration Statements

Because of the Commission's review and comment procedure, refusal and stop orders rarely are used to prevent the effectiveness of a registration statement. Refusal orders are, in fact, unlikely ever to be used, because the requirements are tougher on the Commission in refusal-order proceedings under section 8(b) than in stop-order proceedings under section 8(d), and because it long has been held that stop orders may be used in the place of refusal orders. The section 8(e) examination also has been used rarely. Only when the Commission is faced with what it considers an egregious case, or a particularly recalcitrant issuer, is an examination or stop order at all likely. When the Commission and an issuer cannot come to terms on a registration statement, voluntary withdrawal, as provided for in rule 477, is much more likely.

Chapter 6

EXEMPTIONS FROM THE REGISTRATION REQUIREMENTS

Scheme of the Statute

Exemptions from the Securities Act's registration requirements are found in sections 3 and 4, and section 28 gives the Commission broad powers to create other exemptions. Section 4 is entitled "Exempted Transactions," which provides an accurate description of its coverage. The title of section 3, "Exempted Securities," is, however, somewhat of a misnomer. It is true that most of the securities referred to in section 3(a) are, in all circumstances, exempted from the registration requirements of section 5. Examples are government securities (section 3(a)(2)) and securities issued by religious, educational, charitable, and other such organizations (section 3(a)(4)). Those securities never have to be registered under the Securities Act.

The misnomer mainly exists in three other situations: securities exchanged with existing security holders (section 3(a)(9)), securities issued under a plan of exchange approved by a court or other governmental authority (section 3(a)(10)), and securities issued in an intrastate transaction (section 3(a)(11)). Those subsections do not deal with exempted securities, but rather with exempted transactions, and logically they should be in section 4.

Section 3(b)(1) authorizes the Commission to add other securities to those exempted by section 3 when it finds that registration is not necessary "by reason of the small amount involved or the limited character of the public offering." That subsection, however, places a dollar limit on the aggregate offering price of an issue of securities that may come within its coverage, and the limit currently is $5 million. Pursuant to section 3(b)(1), the Commission has adopted various exempting rules. The most important of them will be discussed below. It is important to realize that, like certain exemptions provided in section 3(a), those exemptions established by the Commission under the authority of section 3(b)(b) are transaction exemptions only.

Two developments complicate the study of section 3(b)(1). First, in 1996, section 28 was enacted. This section gives the Commission authority to "exempt any person, security, or transaction, or any class or classes of persons, securities, or transactions, from any provision" of the Securities Act, so long as the "exemption is necessary or appropriate in the public interest, and is consistent with the protection of investors." (Note that under section 2(b), added along with section 28, the Commission must, when considering what is in the public interest, also consider whether a rulemaking action "will promote efficiency, competition, and capital formation.") One important aspect of section 28 is the ability it gives the Commission to raise the dollar limit of exemptive rules it previously adopted under section 3(b)(1).

The second complicating development was the enactment in 2012 of section 3(b)(2) (which required the provision previously number 3(b) to be renumbered as 3(b)(1)). Section 3(b)(2) requires the Commission to adopt an exemption for offerings not exceeding $50,000,000.

Section 4 contains only transaction exemptions. Of those, the private placement exemption provided in section 4(a)(2), the accredited investors exemption found in section 4(a)(5), and the new crowdfunding exemption contained in Section 4(a)(6), will be discussed in this chapter. Section 4(a)(3) was examined briefly in Chapter 4, and sections 4(a)(1) and 4(a)(4) will be discussed in the next chapter.

When considering sections 3 and 4, it is important to understand the limits of the exemptions those sections provide. Section 4 states that the registration requirements of section 5 do not apply to the transactions covered in section 4. All the other sections of the Securities Act, of which the liability provisions are the most important, do apply. Section 3 provides that the provisions of the Securities Act do not apply to the securities enumerated in section 3 "except as . . . expressly provided." One of the major liability sections of the Act, section 12(a)(2), provides that offers or sales of all securities, except government securities and certain security futures products, exempted from the registration provisions by section 3 are nevertheless subject to section 12(a)(2). The antifraud provision, section 17, is expressly applicable to all securities, including those exempt from registration under section 3. Liability issues will be discussed in Chapter 8.

Private Placements

Section 4(a)(2) provides that the registration requirements of section 5 do not apply to "transactions by an issuer not involving any public offering." These transactions are called private placements, private offerings, or non-public offerings. Since the definition of "issuer" in the Act is straightforward, the only thing necessary to understand the legal requirements for a private placement is knowing what constitutes a "public offering." Regrettably, that term is not defined in the statute. The basic contours of a public offering, however, are well established in case law and in pronouncements by the Commission.

The most important Commission action on section 4(a)(2) has been the adoption of rule 506. That rule is part of regulation D, which is a collection of rules that governs the limited offer and sale of securities without Securities Act registration. Rule 506 is a safe-harbor rule under section 4(a)(2) that an issuer is free to use as it pleases. The private placement exemption under that section and the limited offering exemption under rule 506 tend as a practical matter to be regarded as separate exemptions. For that reason, the statutory exemption is discussed here, and rule 506 is examined later in the chapter along with the rest of regulation D.

The private placement traditionally has been the most important registration exemption available to issuers. It retains major importance even with the safe harbor of rule 506. There are a number of reasons for that. First, the importance of having a fallback exemption, available for use when a rule 506 limited offering or some other exemption is tried but fails, should not be underestimated. Second, in some types of transactions there is no doubt about the private nature of the transaction, and no safe-harbor rule is needed to help secure the section 4(a)(2) exemption. Third, the requirements of section 4(a)(2) can more easily be satisfied by chance than most other exemptions, some of which contain filing or other requirements that require advance planning. In cases when a lawyer is called in after the fact, the private placement exemption may be the only exemption available to save a client from civil and criminal liability.

The leading case concerning the requirements for a private placement is *SEC v. Ralston Purina Co.*,[1] in which the issuer sold unregistered stock to a wide variety of nonmanagement employees. The Commission brought suit for violation of the registration requirements of section 5. The district court dismissed on a finding that the company met the requirements of section 4(a)(2), and the court of appeals affirmed. In its opinion reversing the lower courts, the Supreme Court laid down its guidelines for determining the difference between a public and a private offering.

Focusing on the legislative history of section 4(a)(2), the Court found that the exemption was included in the Securities Act because it was thought to describe transactions "where there is no practical need for [the Act's] application." Thus, the Court said, the applicability of the exemption "should turn on whether the particular class of persons affected needs the protection of the Act." In defining that class, the Court set forth a general criterion of

---

[1] 346 U.S. 119 (1953).

"those who are shown to be able to fend for themselves" and then discussed the satisfaction of that requirement in terms of access to information on the part of the offerees. The exemption was not available to Ralston Purina, the Court determined, because the employees "were not shown to have access to the kind of information which registration would disclose."

Three aspects of the Supreme Court's handling of the issue of access to information have particular continuing interest. First, the Court spoke of the requirement that offerees "be shown" to meet the test. It is critical to realize that the burden of proof is on the person who wants the protection of an exemption. Second, the general requirement that an offeree be able to fend for himself has given the Commission and lower courts substantial leeway in establishing specific criteria for meeting the general requirement. Third, the requirement that offerees have access to "the kind of information which registration would disclose" is somewhat flexible. The Court did not require that an offeree have access to "the" information that would be available in a registered offering, but only that he or she have access to the "kind" of information that would be available.

Next to rule 506, the most important Commission pronouncement on section 4(a)(2) has been Securities Act Release No. 4552 (November 6, 1962). In that interpretive release, the Commission elaborated on what it considers to be the requirements for a private placement. According to the release, all the surrounding circumstances must be considered, "including such factors as the relationship between the offerees and the issuer, the nature, scope, size, type and manner of the offering." Regrettably, this statement is not of much help to lawyers.

Release No. 4552, however, discusses two other concepts that are involved in establishing the limits of a particular offering. The first is "coming to rest," and the second is "integration." "Coming to rest" deals with the issue of when a particular offering is over. The Commission considers the offering to continue until the offered securities have "come to rest" in the hands of persons who are not "merely conduits for a wider distribution."

"Integration" is also an important concept. There the question is whether what purports to be a single offering should be combined with one or more other purportedly separate offerings. When offerings are integrated in that way, the larger offering, viewed as a whole, must meet the requirements of an exemption or all the securities must be registered. In Release No. 4552 the Commission gave the following list of factors relevant to the question of integration. The Commission looks at whether:

1. The different offerings are part of a single plan of financing.

2. The offerings involve the issuance of the same class of security.

3. The offerings are made at or about the same time.

4. The same type of consideration is to be received.

5. The offerings are made for the same general purpose.

Unfortunately, the Commission has not provided much help in understanding the various factors included in this list. "Single plan of financing," "about the same time," and "same general purpose" offer obvious problems in interpretation. As to the timing issue, some help may be given by the fact that, for purposes of regulation D, the Commission uses six months as the integration cutoff. In general, however, the vagueness of the concepts involved has led to a good deal of worry, and conservative advice, on the part of securities lawyers.

Courts of appeals deciding cases following *Ralston Purina* have gone a long way in answering questions about the requirements for a valid private placement. In doing so, they have devised their own lists of factors to consider, based on *Ralston Purina* and Release No. 4552. A committee of the American Bar Association attempted to combine and distill those factors in a 1975 position paper. After looking at judicial precedent and Commission pronouncements, the ABA committee decided that there are only four factors of real significance in determining the availability of the private placement exemption: (1) offeree qualification, (2) availability of information (remember that *Ralston Purina* spoke in terms of "the kind of information which registration would disclose"), (3) manner of offering, and (4) absence of redistribution (which relates to the "coming to rest issue"). Only the first of those factors requires much discussion here, because the second and fourth factors are discussed above, and the third can be summarized briefly. In the committee's words: "All forms of general advertising and mass media circulation should be avoided."

Offeree qualification is a complex factor. Every securities lawyer would agree that offers in private placements may be made only to qualified offerees. The problem is in deciding what is required for qualification. The ABA committee indicates that an offeree may qualify on a number of independent bases, which it identifies as: (1) risk-bearing ability, (2) degrees of sophistication with respect to business and finance, (3) the offeree representative principle (the idea that the sophistication of an agent can be imputed to an offeree), (4) the manner of disclosure (the theory being that the clearer and more detailed the disclosure, the less sophistication is required of offerees), (5) nonqualified offerees (here the ABA committee argues that the exemption for the entire transaction should not necessarily be lost simply because there are one or more unqualified offerees or purchasers), and (6) economic bargaining power (a concept that essentially is a shorthand for describing institutional and some other types of professional investors).

It may cause confusion that such factors as the number of offerees and the size of the offering do not have any "real significance" in the view of the ABA committee, especially since both the Commission and a number of courts list them as relevant. The number of offerees is important, but only in a special way. Theoretically, it has no significance. The problem is that the more offerees there are in an offering, the greater is the risk that an offer will be made to someone not qualified to be an offeree. At some point that risk becomes too great to be reasonable, since one illegal offer in a private placement may well remove the exemption for the whole offering.

The ideal technique for conducting a private placement is quite simple: view the plans for the offering as if through the eyes of a plaintiff's lawyer and change anything that would provide a reasonable argument against the exemption. In the usual circumstance, that means offering only to people with sophistication in business and finance, coupled with high income or substantial assets. It also means providing, to each ordinary offeree, an offering memorandum that is much like a prospectus in a registered offering. Although institutions and some other professional investors, along with executive officers and some others having special relationships to the issuer, can be provided access to information rather than a complete memorandum, the access has to be full, and there can not be any question concerning the ability of such an offeree to fend for himself or herself. Conducting a careful offering means limiting the number of offerees and purchasers, and keeping complete records of who the offerees were. It also means taking effective steps, through contractual provisions and legends on stock certificates, to prevent any resales that might make the offering illegal because of the coming to rest problem.

Intrastate Offerings

Securities Act section 3(a)(11) exempts from the registration requirements of the Act:

Any security which is a part of an issue offered and sold only to persons resident within a single State or Territory, where the issuer of such security is a person resident and doing business within, or, if a corporation, incorporated by and doing business within, such State or Territory.

As in the case of section 4(a)(2), the Commission has adopted a safe-harbor rule, rule 147, that issuers may use to secure a section 3(a)(11) exemption.

Before examining the rule, however, it is important to understand the statutory exemption outside the rule. It is impossible to appreciate the importance of the rule without understanding the situation outside the rule. In addition, it is often wise to comply with the requirements of the statutory exemption and the rule, so that if for some reason the requirements of the rule are not satisfied, the issuer has a fallback position. Also, in some limited situations, especially when the statutory exemption is considered a remote backup for the private placement or other exemption, an issuer may not wish to comply with the rule. Finally, the rule is usually not satisfied by chance, and lawyers giving after-the-fact advice concerning the availability of an exemption typically find the rule of no help.

Statutory Exemption

The requirement for understanding section 3(a)(11), of course, is an appreciation of what its various words and phrases mean. It is easiest to discuss the troublesome ones in the order in which they appear. Since "security" has already been discussed in Chapter 1, the most difficult concept has been dealt with. The next troublesome word to appear is "issue." That term also has been explored. In the last section the concepts of integration and "coming to rest" were discussed, and those are the concepts involved in delineating a single securities "issue."

Little further discussion of integration is needed here, except to point out that the Commission has cautioned, that the "Section 3(a)(11) exemption should not be relied upon for each of a series of corporations organized in different states where there is in fact and purpose a single business entity or financial venture."[2] In other words, what may be thought of as two or more exempt intrastate offerings by different issuers may be, in fact, a single illegal interstate offering. That possibility makes an already loose and difficult concept even more troublesome to apply.

As indicated in the previous discussion of "coming to rest," that concept involves the question of when an issue of securities has been completed. In the case of an intrastate offering, the concept is a logical necessity. The drafters of the statute could hardly have

---

[2] Securities Act Release No. 4,434 (December 6, 1961).

expected the exemption to be available, for example, when a New York corporation sells securities to a group of New York securities firms, who then immediately resell to investors around the country. If that were the case, registration almost always could be circumvented.

The problem, of course, is in determining how much time must pass before an issue of securities is considered to have come to rest in the hands of state residents, so that a resale to a nonresident does not destroy the issuer's exemption. After more than sixty years there is little case law on that subject, but as early as 1935 the Commission suggested the passage of one year as a presumption of fact subject to refutation upon a showing that distribution was completed within less than one year. On the other hand, it is possible, though unlikely, that a court would find one year not to be long enough in a particular offering. Confusing the issue somewhat is *Busch v. Carpenter*,[3] in which the Tenth Circuit indicated that if an issuer makes a prima facie showing that securities initially were sold only to state residents, it can get summary judgment on the coming to rest issue, regardless of the purchasers' holding period, unless the other party produces some evidence to the contrary.

The next two troublesome terms—"offered" and "sold"—have been discussed in previous chapters. Residence is the next concept to be discussed here. Outside rule 147, the Commission has traditionally read "residence" to mean "domicile". The trouble with "domicile" is that it is a subjective concept that involves intent. It is somewhat uncertain how the Commission currently would interpret the statutory language and even more uncertain how a court would do so. Caution dictates, therefore, using both domicile and residence as standards when planning an intrastate transaction.

The last statutory term to discuss is "doing business." That term is the trickiest one, because the interpretation by courts and the Commission is so at variance with the ordinary legal conception. Most business lawyers know that it takes little business activity in a state before a foreign corporation is considered to be doing business there. That interpretation of "doing business," however, does not hold under section 3(a)(11). In its main release on the intrastate offering exemption, the Commission indicated that an issuer must conduct "substantial operational activities in the state of incorporation" to be considered to be doing business there.[4] The Commission also cautioned that the "doing business" requirement is not met in certain situations in which the proceeds of an offering are to be used primarily outside the state.

---

[3] 827 F.2d 653 (10th Cir.1987).

[4] Securities Act Release No. 4,434 (December 6, 1961).

Eight years after those Commission interpretations, the Sixth Circuit carried the requirement further, indicating that to meet it an issuer must conduct a predominant amount of its business within the state in which the securities are sold.[5] Not to be outdone, the Commission then said in a release that the principal or predominant business must be conducted in that state.[6] The Commission also took the opportunity to strengthen its stand on the permissible use of proceeds from the offering, saying that substantially all of the proceeds must be used in the local area.

Rule 147

As a consequence of the substantial uncertainties involved in the statutory intrastate offering exemption, it is only the safe harbor of rule 147 that makes section 3(a)(11) generally very useful. The rule goes through the elements of section 3(a)(11) step by step and adds a note of certainty at each point. For example, the integration problem is handled by removing from the possibility of integration most offers or sales made more than six months before, or more than six months after, any offers or sales made under the rule. For the purposes of the rule, "principal residence" satisfies the residence requirement of individuals. In addition, the rule provides objective tests for determining the residence of corporations, partnerships, and other types of business organizations. The rule also sets objective tests for the doing business requirement, basically pitched at the 80 percent level for assets located in, gross revenues derived from, and proceeds to be used in the state in which the offering is made. Under the rule, the "coming to rest" problem is solved by setting nine months from the date of the last sale by the issuer as the cut-off point for limitations on out-of-state resales.

The rule contains technical requirements for precautions against interstate offers and sales of securities that are not likely to be satisfied by chance, such as placing legends on certificates representing the securities sold, issuing stop-transfer instructions to transfer agents, obtaining written representations from purchaser as to residence, and disclosing the resale limitations in writing.

---

[5] *Chapman v. Dunn*, 414 F.2d 153, 159 (6th Cir.1969).

[6] Securities Act Release No. 5,450 (Jan. 7, 1974).

Limited Offerings: Sections 3(b)(1), 3(b)(2), 4(a)(2), 4(a)(5), 4(a)(6), and 28; Regulations A, D, CE and S; Rules 701, 801 and 802

Sections 3(b)(1), 3(b)(2) and 28

Securities Act section 3(b)(1) authorizes the Commission to exempt securities from registration when it finds that registration is not necessary because of the small dollar amount involved or the limited character of the public offering. The Commission's exempting authority is limited, however, to offerings not in excess of $5 million. The Commission has established various exemptions under section 3(b)(1), the most important of which are regulation A, rules 504 and 505 of regulation D, and rule 701.

Going much further than section 3(b)(1) is section 28, which was adopted in 1996. This section gives the Commission authority to "exempt any person, security, or transaction, or any class or classes of persons, securities, or transactions, from any provision" of the Securities Act, so long as the "exemption is necessary or appropriate in the public interest, and is consistent with the protection of investors."

In 2012, the JOBS Act threw new section 3(b)(2) into the mix. This Section was intended to liberalize regulation A, discussed below. It requires the Commission to add an exempted class of securities the aggregate offering amount of which that is "offered and sold within the prior 12-month period in reliance on the exemption" does not exceed $50 million (subject to inflation adjustment every two years).

Regulation A

Although regulation A provides an exemption from the registration requirements of the Securities Act, as a practical matter its requirements closely mimic those for registration. Regulation A transactions have, in fact, traditionally been called short-form registrations.

Regulation A offerings differ significantly from registered offerings in certain respects, however. One of the more important differences is that, in regulation A offerings, an issuer may formally "test the waters," by oral and written communications to potential buyers that are designed to gauge interest in the offering. The written document that may be used for this purpose is very limited, though, and it is to be filed with the Commission before it is used (although the failure to file will not destroy the exemption provided by regulation A).

Regulation A is available only to certain United States or Canadian companies. Among other requirements, the issuer can not be an Exchange Act reporting company or an investment company, and (unless the Commission decides otherwise) it can not have run afoul of specified laws in the past. The maximum dollar amount of securities that may be sold under regulation A is $5 million in a twelve-month period, and $1.5 million of that amount may be sold by security holders. In 2012, the JOBS Act added section 3(b)(2) targeted at increasing the applicable amount that could be raised to $50 million. (Note, however, that section 3(b)(2) does not specifically refer to regulation A). The Commission must require issuers using the "new" exemption to file audited financial statements annually and may require other periodic disclosures. It is permitted to impose such other terms, conditions, or requirements as deemed necessary in the public interest and for the protection of investors. The exemption is to be available for equity securities, debt securities (including those convertible to equity), and any guarantees of such securities.

Section 4(a)(5)

Section 4(a)(5) provides a registration exemption for offerings to accredited investors, in amounts up to the dollar limit of section 3(b)(1), as long as the issuer files the required notice with the Commission. The term "accredited investor" is defined in section 2(a)(15) to include certain institutions, such as banks and insurance companies, and "any person, who, on the basis of such factors as financial sophistication, net worth, knowledge, and experience in financial matters, or amount of assets under management qualifies as an accredited investor under rules and regulations which the Commission shall prescribe." The Commission has adopted rule 215, which sets forth requirements for qualification of accredited investors. For natural persons, the basic tests are either net worth, with one's spouse, of more than $1 million (not including primary residence or any debt associated with such a residence) or net income of more than $200,000 in each of the two most recent years (or $300,000 with one's spouse).

Regulation D

Regulation D is an interesting amalgam. Of its three exempting rules, rules 504 and 505 are rules under section 3(b)(1), and rule 506 is a rule under section 4(a)(2). Regulation D contains a number of rules that provide information and establish requirements that are applicable to the three exempting rules. Rule 501 is the definitional rule. Among other things, it establishes the requirements for classification as an accredited investor, which has substantial regulation D consequences. The requirements are the same as under rule 215, referred to above. Rule 502 provides a number of conditions for establishing a regulation D exemption, which may or may not apply to a particular exempting rule. For example, it sets forth requirements for the information to be furnished to investors. Those requirements vary with the exemption used and with the nature of both issuers and investors. It also proscribes general solicitations or advertisements in most situations and sets forth a number of requirements designed to prevent illegal resales by purchasers, such as the requirement of placing restrictive legends on certificates representing securities. The rule also provides help with the integration question by, in most cases, removing from the possibility of integration offers and sales that occur more than six months before the start of a regulation D offering or more than six months after its completion. Rule 503 provides the requirements for filing notices of sales, and the Commission has provided form D for the purpose. Form D is a simple, fill-in-the-blanks form. Interestingly, as the exempting rules are written, one can get the benefit of the regulation D exemptions without filing the form D. Rule 507 provides, however, that if an issuer or a predecessor or affiliate has been the subject of an injunction because of a failure to file the form required by rule 503, then regulation D is no longer available for use by that issuer, unless the Commission specifically determines otherwise. Finally, rule 508 provides that, in certain circumstances, an insignificant deviation from the requirements of one of regulation D's exempting rules, rule 504, 505, or 506 will not result in the loss of the registration exemption provided by the rule. Main among those circumstances is a good faith and reasonable attempt by the issuer to comply with the rule.

The following table shows the basic requirements and limitations on offerings under rules 504, 505, and 506. Note that when the dollar limit is relatively low ($1 million under rule 504), the requirements and limitations are few. The requirements and limitations rise along with the increase in the dollar limit (to $5,000,000 under 5ule 505) and then increase again (under rule 506) when the dollar limit is lifted entirely. This correlation is, however, now somewhat reversed in the case of general solicitation. Although rule 506 is a safe harbor under section 4(a)(2), it was given something of a life of its own in 2012. Section 201 of the JOBS Act required the Commission to revise the rule so as to permit general solicitation and advertising, provided that all actual purchasers are accredited investors. Issuers are to be required to make such efforts as the Commission specifies to make sure that purchasers indeed are accredited investors. Section 4 of the Securities Act simultaneously was amended, by the addition of new sub-section (b), to provide that offerings under Rule 506 will be non-public (and thus exempt under Section 4(a)(2)) notwithstanding general solicitation or advertising.

Regulation D Exemptions

	Rule 504	Rule 505	Rule 506
Aggregate Offering Price Limitation	$1 million (12 mos.)	$5 million (12 mos.)	Unlimited
Number of Investors	Unlimited	35 plus unlimited accredited	35 plus unlimited accredited
Investor Qualifications	None required	None required	Purchaser must be sophisticated (alone or with representative); accredited presumed to be qualified
Sales Commissions	Permitted	Permitted	Permitted
Limitation on Manner of Offering	Usually no general solicitation permitted*	No general solicitation	General solicitation permitted provided all purchasers are accredited investors
Limitation on Resale	Usually restricted**	Restricted**	Restricted**
Issuer Qualifications	No Exchange Act, "blank-check,"*** or investment companies	No investment companies or issuers disqualified under Regulation A (except upon Commission determination)	No issuers disqualified under Regulation A (except upon SEC determination)

	Rule 504	**Rule 505**	**Rule 506**
Notice of Sales	Form D to be filed within 15 days after first sale (but not a condition of exemption)	Same as 504	Same as 504 and 505
Information Required	None	1. If purchased solely by accredited investors, no information required. 2. If purchased by nonaccredited investors, information as specified.****	Same as 505

* This requirement, and the "restricted" nature of the securities (see following item in table), are lifted basically when (i) the securities are registered under a state law requiring public filing and delivery of a disclosure document before sale, and such a document is delivered, or (ii) the securities are offered and sold exclusively under a state law exemption that permits solicitations, so long as sales are made only to accredited investors.

** "Restricted" securities are defined in rule 144, which is discussed in the next chapter. For the purposes of this table, they can be viewed as securities that cannot be resold in a public sale until certain requirements, including in most cases a one-year holding period, are met.

*** A "blank-check" company is a development-stage company that either has no specific business plan or purpose or has indicated that its business plan is to engage in a merger or acquisition with an unidentified company or companies or other entity or person.

**** If securities are purchased by nonaccredited investors,

    a. nonreporting companies under the Exchange Act must furnish the same kind of information as in a registered offering, or in a regulation A offering if eligible, but with modified financial-statement requirements;

    b. reporting companies must furnish (i) specified Exchange Act documents or (ii) information contained in the most recent specified Exchange Act report or Securities Act registration statement on specified forms, plus, in any case, (iii) updating information and limited additional information about the offering;

c. issuers must make available prior to sale: (i) exhibits, (ii)written information given to accredited investors, (iii)opportunity to ask questions and receive answers;

d. issuers must advise purchasers of the limitations on resale.

Section 4(a)(6): "Crowdfunding"

Section 4(a)(6) was added in 2012 by a title of the JOBS Act. The exemption itself is stated in section 4(a)(6), but section 4A imposes additional requirements for issuers and financial intermediaries involved in crowdfunding and also must be considered. Although the Commission was given both fairly broad discretion to tinker with the details and a list of instructions to address such matters as "bad actor" disqualifiers, the new exemption has the following notable requirements:

1. The issuer must be a domestic company not required to file Exchange Act Reports;

2. The aggregate amount of securities sold to all investors by the issuer and its controlled or controlling entities within a 12-month period cannot exceed $1,000,000 (subject, as are all dollar amounts in section 4(a)(6), to inflation adjustments every five years);

3. The aggregate amount sold to any investor within a 12-month period cannot exceed (a) for investors with an annual income or net worth less than $100,000, the greater of $2,000 or 5 percent of annual income or net worth; and (b) for investors with an annual income or net worth of at least $100,000, 10 percent of annual income or net worth, not to exceed a maximum aggregate amount sold of $100,000;

4. The transaction must be conducted through a broker or "funding portal" complying with a panoply of requirements, including registration under the Exchange Act, ensuring investor understanding of, and ability to bear, the risk of investment, and taking steps to ensure that no investor in a 12-month period purchases under section 4(a)(6) securities that, in the aggregate from all issuers, exceed the limits described in (3) above;

5. The issuer must file with the Commission, and provide to investors and the relevant broker or funding portal, a variety of information and certifications that depend on the offering's target size;

6. The issuer must not advertise the terms of the offering, except for notices which direct investors to the relevant funding portal or broker; and

7. Securities acquired subject to the exemption cannot be transferred for one year other than to a list of specified parties including family members and accredited investors or as part of a registered offering.

Regulation CE

Regulation CE is exceedingly short. It contains only one rule, rule 1001. Basically, the rule provides a registration exemption for offers and sales of securities that satisfy the conditions of section 25102(n) of the California Corporations Code, up to a total of $5 million per offering. (Note the implications of the fact that the amount limitation is "per offering." If, for example, $3 million of an offering were under section 25102(n) and $3 million were under another exemption, the amount limitation would be exceeded.)

Rule 701

Prior to the passage of rule 701 in 1988, issuers who wished to offer securities to employees under stock purchase, stock option, or other benefit plans or contracts often found that an exemption from the Securities Act's registration requirements was not available. Perhaps recognizing the special relationship between an issuer and its employees, the Commission adopted rule 701 to make an exemption available for such offerings, along with offerings to others having specified relationships with the issuer. Rule 701 is not available to Exchange Act reporting companies or investment companies. The maximum amount of securities that can be sold in a twelve-month period is the greater of $1 million, an amount equal to 15% of the issuer's total assets, or 15% of the outstanding securities of the class. If more than $5 million of securities are sold, specified disclosures must be provided.

Rules 801 and 802

The Commission has long been interested in helping facilitate international securities transactions, for example by providing the specialized registration forms F–1 and F–3 for foreign issuers that correspond to Forms S–1 and S–3. By the late 1990s, it became clear to the Commission that registration exemptions were necessary for international transactions involving rights offerings, exchange offers, and business combinations involving foreign private issuers. Rule 801 was the Commission's response with respect to rights offerings and Rule 802 its response for exchange offers and business combinations. These rules are further discussed in Chapter 15.

Regulation S

Regulation S does not provide an exemption from the Securities Act's registration requirements. Rather, it is an interpretive regulation by which one can determine if a particular offshore transaction is subject to the Securities Act. In practice, however, lawyers often think of it, and use it, almost as if it did provide a registration exemption. It, too, is further discussed in Chapter 15.

Chapter 7

RESALES BY SECURITY HOLDERS

The Securities Act registration exemption that allows most security holders to sell securities without registration is section 4(a)(1), which covers "transactions by any person other than an issuer, underwriter, or dealer." It is easiest to determine the availability of that exemption when a preliminary question is answered first: Are the securities proposed to be sold control securities or restricted securities? (As noted in Chapter 6, securities sold under the intrastate offering exemption have their own basic resale limitations, which are discussed in that chapter.)

Control and Restricted Securities

Control securities are securities owned by a person who is an affiliate of the issuer. To understand the concept of control securities, it is helpful first to look to Securities Act rule 405, which contains definitions of terms. "Affiliate" and "control" are both defined:

> *Affiliate.* An "affiliate" of, or person "affiliated" with, a specified person, is a person that directly, or indirectly through one or more intermediaries, controls or is controlled by, or is under common control with, the person specified.

> *Control.* The term "control" (including the terms "controlling," "controlled by" and "under common control with") means the possession, direct or indirect, of the power to direct or cause the direction of the management and policies of a person, whether through the ownership of voting securities, by contract, or otherwise.

To understand the concept of "control," one must understand what the Commission means by the "power to direct or cause the direction of . . . management and policies." Familiarity with two theories concerning control aids in that understanding. One is the idea that the unexercised ability to control is control. When, for example, a shareholder owns sufficient stock in a corporation that management is likely to be responsive to the shareholder's requests or demands, the Commission says the shareholder is an affiliate of the corporation. That leads to the question of how much stock is enough to control a corporation. There is not a firm answer, but ten percent traditionally has been used as a rough rule of thumb. Securities lawyers begin worrying about control, however, when well below this percentage of stock is involved.

The other theory to understand is that of the control group. Under that theory, a person is in control if he or she is a member of a group that controls. That theory applies to shareholders who may be considered part of a control group. A family is a classic example. The theory also is used to bring corporate officers and directors under the concept of "control."

The concept of "restricted securities" is simpler in a way than that of "control securities." A definition is contained in rule 144(a)(3):

The term "restricted securities" means:

(i)   Securities acquired directly or indirectly from the issuer, or from an affiliate of the issuer, in a transaction or chain of transactions not involving any public offering;

(ii)   Securities acquired from the issuer that are subject to the resale limitations of Rule 502(d) under Regulation D or Rule 701(g);

(iii)   Securities acquired in a transaction or chain of transactions meeting the requirements of Rule 144A;

(iv)   Securities acquired from the issuer in a transaction subject to the conditions of Regulation CE;

(v)   Equity securities of domestic issuers acquired in a transaction or chain of transactions subject to the conditions of Rule 901 or 903 under Regulation S;

(vi)   Securities acquired in a transaction made under Rule 801 to the same extent and proportion that the securities held by the security holder of the class with respect to which the rights offering was made were as of the record date for the rights offering "restricted securities";

(vii)   Securities acquired in a transaction made under Rule 802 to the same extent and proportion that the securities that were tendered or exchanged in the exchange offer or business combination were "restricted securities"; and

(viii) Securities acquired from the issuer in a transaction subject to an exemption under Section 4[(a)(5)] of the Act.

That definition is convoluted, but it is readily understandable with a little explanation. The best way to accomplish that explanation is to break the definition into parts, and then discuss each part in turn. It will help to realize that there are overlaps among the parts.

The first part of the definition relates to "Securities acquired directly or indirectly from the issuer, or from an affiliate of the issuer, in a transaction or chain of transactions not involving any public offering." That part of the definition covers securities that: (1) at one point were sold by the issuer under a section 4(a)(2) nonpublic offering exemption (either in a statutory private placement or in a sale under Securities Act rule 506) or a section 4(a)(5) limited offering exemption; or (2) at one point were sold by an affiliate of the issuer in a private resale using the section 4(a)(1) exemption (which is discussed below). When there is such a chain of transactions, each intervening sale must be a private resale that uses the section 4(a)(1) exemption. Thus, the straightforward thrust of this part of the definition is that purchasers in transactions under section 4(a)(2) or 4(a)(5) buy restricted securities.

The second part of the definition of restricted securities covers "Securities acquired from the issuer that are subject to the resale limitations of Rule 502(d) under Regulation D or Rule 701(g)." That phrase includes all securities purchased directly from an issuer in any transaction under rule 701(g), or under rules 505 or 506 of regulation D, because all securities sold under those rules have resale restrictions.

The third part of the definition covers "Securities acquired in a transaction or chain of transactions meeting the requirements of rule 144A." Rule 144A is discussed at the end of this chapter. It relates to resales of securities by security holders to "qualified institutional buyers."

The fourth part of the definition covers "Securities acquired from the issuer subject to the conditions of regulation CE." Regulation CE exempts offerings and sales of securities that satisfy the conditions of section 25102(n) of the California Corporations Code, up to a total of $5 million per offering. Regulation CE provides that all securities issued under the regulation are restricted securities.

The fifth part of the definition covers "Equity securities of domestic issuers acquired in a transaction or chain of transactions subject to the conditions of Rule 901 or Rule 903 under Regulation S." Regulation S relates to the offshore offer and sale of securities.

Like the fifth part of the definition of restricted securities, the sixth and seventh parts of the definition exemplify the Commission's initiative to facilitate international securities transactions. The sixth part relates to cross-border rights offerings made in accordance with rule 801 by foreign private issuers. The seventh part covers securities subject to cross-border exchange offers and business combinations made under rule 802 by such issuers.

The eighth part was added in 2007 to clarify the treatment of securities acquired under section 4(a)(5) (which, as discussed above, already were covered in part one).

Before leaving the discussion of restricted securities, it will be helpful to introduce one further concept: fungibility. Under that concept, if a person owns both restricted and nonrestricted securities of the same class and from the same issuer, the nonrestricted securities take on the taint of restricted status. That occurs because, for some purposes, securities are considered to be fungible. In the release in which it adopted rule 144, however, the Commission indicated that the concept of fungibility will not apply for the purposes of the rule.

Public Resales Outside Rule 144

Rule 144 provides a means for selling both control and restricted securities. However, rule 144 is not exclusive, and sellers sometimes wish to sell outside the rule. Also, the rule often is of no use when lawyers are called in after the fact, since it has requirements that may demand advance planning. In addition, the rule is mechanistic rather than analytic, and it provides little help in understanding section 4(a)(1) and its place in the regulatory scheme. Without that understanding, some of the provisions of the rule are quite opaque. For these reasons, public resales of control and restricted securities outside rule 144 are discussed at this point.

Sales of Control Securities

As indicated at the beginning of this chapter, section 4(a)(1) provides the exemption that allows most security holders to sell securities without registration. To determine when that exemption is available, it is important to determine whether the proposed transaction is "by an issuer, underwriter, or dealer." Here are the section 2 definitions of "issuer" and "dealer":

The term "issuer" means every person who issues or proposes to issue any security. . . .

The term "dealer" means any person who engages either for all or part of his time, directly or indirectly, as agent, broker, or principal, in the business of offering, buying, selling, or otherwise dealing or trading in securities issued by another person.

Except in an unusual situation, then, an investor who wishes to sell securities under section 4(a)(1) is neither an issuer nor a dealer.

The consequences of holding control securities are found in the definition of "underwriter." In its most basic provision, section

2(a)(11) defines the term to mean "any person who has purchased from an issuer with a view to, or offers or sells for an issuer in connection with, the distribution of any security." For an affiliate who holds securities that are control securities and not also restricted securities, there would be little problem if the definition stopped there. It does not, however. The last sentence of section 2(a)(11) adds: "As used in this [section 2(a)(11)] the term 'issuer' shall include, in addition to an issuer, any person directly or indirectly controlling or controlled by the issuer, or any person under direct or indirect common control with the issuer." In other words, the basic definition of "underwriter" should be treated as if it read: "the term 'underwriter' means any person who has purchased from an issuer or affiliate of the issuer with a view to, or offers or sells for an issuer or an affiliate of the issuer in connection with, the distribution of any security." "Distribution" is not defined in the statute, but it is understood essentially to be synonymous with "public offering." For example, in an early case the Commission established that a distribution comprises "the entire process by which in the course of a public offering a block of securities is dispersed and ultimately comes to rest in the hands of the investing public."[1]

Because of the way in which the term "underwriter" is defined, a securities firm that handles the sale of control securities in the public markets may be considered an underwriter. If it handles the sale as a dealer (as the term is used in the securities industry, i.e., if it buys the securities itself with the idea of reselling them), it may be considered to have "purchased from an issuer with a view to . . . distribution." If it handles the transaction as a broker (i.e., if it merely sells the securities for the affiliate), it may be considered to have offered or sold "for an issuer in connection with . . . the distribution." When that is the case, section 4(a)(1) is not available, and the registration requirement of section 5 is violated.

It may appear that securities would always have to be registered before an affiliate could sell them publicly, because it may seem that such a sale always would constitute a distribution. That result is not what was contemplated by the drafters of the Securities Act, and the Commission has never taken that extreme position. Rather, the Commission has built some flexibility into the Securities Act by manipulating the concept of distribution.

As discussed above, the Commission in its early years of operation established that a distribution comprises "the entire process by which in the course of a public offering a block of securities is dispersed and ultimately comes to rest in the hands of

---

[1] *In re Oklahoma–Texas Trust,* 2 S.E.C. 764, 769 (1937).

the investing public." Notwithstanding the expansive nature of that conception, prior to the mid-1940s the Commission allowed affiliates publicly to sell unregistered control securities in limited circumstances. The Commission considered no distribution to be involved when an affiliate sold control securities, on a stock exchange, in a transaction in which the selling broker limited its activities to the usual brokerage functions—and, most important, when the broker did not solicit any orders for the securities. Under that rather generous interpretation of "distribution," affiliates had a ready market for their securities, as long as the amount of securities involved in a particular sale was small enough to be salable, at a reasonable price, without one or more securities firms' drumming up buyers.

The Commission's generosity came to an end in a 1946 case heard by the Commission sitting in its quasijudicial capacity, *In re Ira Haupt & Co.*[2] In that case, affiliates sold during a five-and-a-half-month period of 1943, publicly and through a broker, stock representing approximately 38 percent of their company's common stock. The ability of the broker to accomplish that sale seems to have been related to two factors. First, the prosperity of the World War II years had created a hot stock market; one in which sales of large blocks were possible without any unusual sales effort. Second, the company announced that it was considering an unusual and apparently economically favorable plan under which it would sell its product, whiskey, at cost to its shareholders.

By its finding that the *Haupt* facts constituted a distribution, the Commission made it clear that, although it was willing to allow control securities to trickle into the market, it would not allow a flood. That decision made the securities firm that handled the sales an underwriter, which caused the section 4(a)(1) exemption to be unavailable. In reaching that result, the Commission disregarded the contention of the securities firm that the brokers' exemption of section 4(a)(4), which exempts from the registration requirements of section 5 "brokers' transactions executed upon customers' orders . . . but not the solicitation of such orders," was available to protect its conduct. That exemption, said the Commission, is available only to brokers selling for ordinary investors and cannot be used by a firm that is an underwriter involved in a distribution.

It was not until 1954, when it adopted rule 154, that the Commission took definitive action on the questions left open in *Haupt*. That rule, which was later superseded by rule 144, used the old Commission staff interpretations as a starting point and added

---

[2] 23 S.E.C. 589 (1946).

an "amount of securities sold" test to determine the existence of a distribution. That rule alleviated a good bit of the problem generated by *Haupt*. As discussed below, its concepts were carried over into rule 144.

Sales of Restricted Securities

Outside of rule 144, there never has been a corollary to rule 154 relating to the sale of restricted securities. There are, however, administrative interpretations that allow restricted securities to be sold publicly without the sale's being treated as a distribution. Before the adoption of rule 144 in 1972, those interpretations had a great deal of vitality, and securities lawyers spent substantial amounts of time struggling with them. In Securities Act Release No. 5223 (January 11, 1972), the release in which the Commission announced rule 144, the Commission asserted that the rule is not exclusive. Subsequently, the Commission amended the rule to provide that explicitly. It must be remembered, however, that the Commission almost certainly lacked the power to adopt an exclusive resale rule, and so its failure to do so tells little about its real desires in the matter. The language the Commission used in Release No. 5223 is the best gauge of those desires, and it clearly discourages reliance on the pre-existing interpretations for sales of restricted securities, except for securities purchased before the effective date of the rule. The tone of the release accomplishes that discouragement, as do two statements in the release relating to restricted securities purchased after the effective date of the rule: (1) the change-of-circumstances doctrine (discussed below) would have no further effect and (2) the Commission's staff would no longer issue no-action letters in connection with resales. (The Commission later relented on the latter point and will give no-action letters on resale questions that are unusual.)

Still, rule 144 is not exclusive for restricted securities purchased after its effective date, and there may be an occasion for a holder of such securities purposely to sell them publicly outside the rule. That rarely would be wise, however. The interpretations pre-existing rule 144 are of much greater current importance for two other reasons: (1) they foster an understanding of the workings and effect of the rule, and (2) they may have to be relied upon in cases in which a holder of restricted securities, without proper planning, sells those securities publicly without following the requirements of the rule.

One interpretation relates to how long restricted securities are held before resale. That factor is important because it is thought that the length of the holding period is objective evidence of the holder's investment intent, or the lack thereof, at the time of original purchase. A purchaser's investment intent is important because the opposite of investment intent is "view to distribution." And, under section 2(a)(11), purchasing with a view to distribution makes the holder an underwriter.

Alternatively, a person who sells restricted securities too soon after their purchase may be considered an underwriter under the theory that the sale is, under section 11, "for an issuer in connection with [a] distribution." Reasoning to that conclusion starts with the idea that a distribution is not complete until the securities have come to rest in the hands of persons who are not what the Commission calls "merely conduits for a wider distribution." The argument may then proceed that: (1) the issuer knows or should know that some purchasers of restricted securities will want to resell fairly quickly after their purchase; (2) a purchaser is able to resell quickly only because the issuer does not take effective steps to prevent it (such as contractual provisions prohibiting the resale and legends on the certificates representing the securities); and (3) since the issuer is responsible for the resale, the resale will be considered as simply a part of a larger distribution of the securities, by the issuer, to the public through an underwriter.

The obvious question, of course, is how long a holding period is required to avoid these problems. It is clear that no holding period removes the taint of underwriter status from someone who has purchased with a distribution in mind. In the usual situation, however, a sufficiently long holding period dispels any notion that a reseller of restricted securities is an underwriter, and two years came to be viewed by securities lawyers as the minimum safe holding period of restricted securities before a public sale. *United States v. Sherwood*[3] helped in that respect by declaring that the passage of two years between the purchase and resale involved in the case was an "insuperable obstacle" to a finding that the reseller was an underwriter. Before the passage of rule 144, the Commission's staff responded to a multitude of no-action letter requests in connection with potential resales of restricted securities. The staff freely granted no-action letters when restricted securities were held for three years, but was much less likely to do so in the case of a two-year holding period.

The other interpretation pre-existing rule 144 that must be discussed is the change-in-circumstances doctrine. Since the Commission has asserted that the doctrine should no longer be relied upon in the case of securities purchased after the effective date of rule 144, a change in circumstances is of much less help to a post-rule 144 purchaser than is a sufficiently long holding period. In

---

[3]   175 F.Supp. 480 (S.D.N.Y.1959).

fact, it has always been of less importance than the holding period. The thrust of the change-in-circumstances doctrine is that the inference of underwriter status that may accompany a too-short holding period can be avoided when the holder of restricted securities proves that the desire to resell arose because of changed circumstances. The Commission made it clear in Securities Act Release No. 4552 (November 6, 1962) that factors such as an advance or decline in a stock's price or in an issuer's earnings "are normal investment risks and do not usually provide an acceptable basis for a claim of changed circumstances." An examination of pre-rule 144 no-action letter requests and responses shows little staff acceptance of change-in-circumstances arguments. Perhaps the usual effect of the doctrine in the pre-rule 144 period was to give comfort to those involved in a transaction by a security holder who barely met a minimally acceptable holding period.

Public Resales Under Rule 144

As indicated by the title of rule 144, "Persons Deemed Not to Be Engaged in a Distribution and Therefore Not Underwriters," the rule is designed to provide a mechanism for avoiding underwriter status. It is complex because it is detailed and covers a variety of circumstances, and also because it combines provisions relating to control and restricted securities. Nonetheless, for those familiar with the rudiments of the section 4(a)(1) exemption, which is what compliance with the rule secures, understanding the rule should present few problems.

Rule 144 begins with definitions, the most important of which are those of "affiliate" and "restricted securities." Both of these definitions are discussed above. The next most important definition is that of "person" when that term is used to refer to the seller of securities under the rule. Here the Commission has played a little drafting trick by including other people within the definition, such as certain relatives who share the same home. This has significant importance, including for the purpose of determining whether certain limitations in the rule are satisfied.

Rule 144(b) declares, by cross-referencing other parts of the rule, the basic terms with which persons hoping to take advantage of the rule's protection must comply. For purposes of further analysis, these persons should be divided into two groups and separately considered. These two groups are (1) non-affiliates who hold restricted securities, and (2) affiliates and those who act on their behalf.

Non-Affiliates

The Commission has vastly simplified the analysis of the position of non-affiliates holding restricted securities. (Note, however, that to qualify as a non-affiliate one must not have been an affiliate during the three months prior to the contemplated sale.) If the securities were issued by a company that has been subject to the Exchange Act's reporting requirements for at least 90 days prior to the contemplated sale, and has filed all of its required reports for the preceding twelve months (or such shorter period as it has been subject to reporting requirements), a six-month holding period must be satisfied. Otherwise—that is, if the issuer has not been an Exchange Act reporting company for an adequate period or has not complied with its reporting requirements—the non-affiliate must satisfy a twelve-month holding period.

Holding periods are calculated in accordance with rule 144(d)(3). An important special situation dealt with is when restricted securities are resold in a private transaction. In that case, the holding period of a new owner generally begins when the securities were purchased from the issuer or an affiliate of the issuer. Also of importance is the treatment of gift shares (which are deemed to have been acquired by the donee when acquired by the donor) and shares owned by an estate (which, in the case of non-affiliates, are exempt from the holding period requirement). The rule deals with a number of other situations as well.

Affiliates and Those Selling on Their Behalf

The analysis of the position of affiliates and those selling on their behalf is, of necessity, more complicated. There are three steps to understanding why this is so. (1) An affiliate (like a non-affiliate) may have purchased restricted securities from the issuer with a view to distribution, and thus be an underwriter under section 2(a)(11). Satisfaction of some holding period thus comes into play to establish that no such view was held. (2) An affiliate may be acting on behalf of an issuer in connection with a distribution and thus be an underwriter under section 2(a)(11). This is trickier to handle; basically, the Commission seeks to assure that when any securities are sold by an affiliate the effect on the market is sufficiently minimal to allay any concerns that a distribution is taking place. (3) Someone selling on behalf of an affiliate in connection with a distribution may, by reason of section 2(a)(11)'s wording, also be an underwriter. Once again, the matter is handled by assuring that no distribution is taking place.

Affiliates and Unrestricted Shares

The first situation to consider, then, is that of an affiliate (or a broker acting on behalf of an affiliate) who wishes to sell unrestricted securities. This can occur, under rule 144, only if (a) there is specified information currently available to the public about the issuer, (b) the sale occurs subject to restrictions on volume, (c) the sale occurs subject to limitations on the manner of sale, and (d) appropriate notice of reliance on the rule is given.

Under rule 144(c), it is theoretically possible for an issuer to satisfy the "publicly available information" requirement simply by making public the required information. As a practical matter, it is rarely met other than by companies who are Exchange Act reporting companies. Because of this, some companies that have not been legally required to register securities under the Exchange Act have done so to make rule 144 available for use by their affiliates. Although it may not be strictly obvious why an informational requirement is relevant to a determination of when a distribution occurs, it can be explained in two ways. First, of course, it simply goes to the Commission's assessment of the public's need for protection in various situations. Second, it is reasonable to think that securities sold into a fully informed market will have less of an impact on market price.

The generally applicable volume limitation for affiliates' sales (including those made on their behalf) is, under rule 144(e), the greater of one percent of the class of securities outstanding or of the average weekly trading volume of the class of securities during the preceding four weeks. Again, there are a number of provisions for special situations (including for debt securities).

In the usual case, rule 144(f) provides that all securities sold by an affiliate or on an affiliate's behalf must be sold in a broker's transaction (as defined in rule 144(g)) or directly to a market maker. In the case of a broker's transaction, no solicitation of buyers or extraordinary commission is allowed, and other limitations pertain. The requirements of rule 144(f) do not, however, apply to debt securities or securities sold by an estate (provided the estate itself is not an affiliate of the issuer).

Finally, rule 144(h) states the circumstances in which a notice of reliance on rule 144 must be filed with the Commission. Basically, form 144 must be filed if sales during a three-month period exceed 5,000 shares or $50,000.

Affiliates and Restricted Shares

The last task in understanding rule 144 is the treatment of an affiliate's sale (or a sale on behalf of an affiliate) of restricted shares. One might think that if the volume and manner of the sale of shares has a sufficiently negligible impact on the market for a security, it would not also be necessary to assure that the seller harbored no "view" to resale at the time the shares were acquired. This has not, however, been the view adopted by the Commission. Restricted shares held by an affiliate are subject to the requirements described immediately above and are subject to mandatory holding periods. These holding periods are the same as in the case of a non-affiliate.

Practical Compliance

Actually using rule 144 requires something in addition to an understanding of its requirements: a knowledge of the practices that have developed to effect compliance. The typical task for a lawyer representing a seller, in addition to being personally satisfied that the rule is available, is determining what is required by the issuer's lawyers and by the securities firm that is to handle the sale. Many securities firms and law firms have worked out a detailed set of requirements, sometimes even providing drafts of documents. Usual requirements include letters or certificates attesting to the facts supporting rule 144 compliance, along with an opinion of counsel that the requirements of the rule are met. Handling all the details may take some weeks, and legal fees typically run at least some hundreds of dollars. For those reasons, the rule is not so useful as it may at first seem for the sale of a relatively small amount of securities.

Rule 144A and Other Private Resales

When certain conditions are satisfied, the section 4(a)(1) exemption can be available for a private offering of control or restricted securities. Here the analysis proceeds in the same way that it does for the public resale of control and restricted securities. That analysis leads to the conclusion that, as in the case of a public sale, the troublesome question is whether an underwriter will be involved in a proposed transaction. Also as with public resales, that question is answered by answering a more basic question: Will the transaction involve a distribution? When there is no distribution, there is no underwriter, since the definition of "Underwriter" in section 2(a)(11) is tied exclusively to a distribution. When there is no underwriter involved in a sales transaction, the section 4(a)(1) exemption is available to any security holder other than the issuer or a dealer.

Since "distribution" essentially is synonymous with "public offering," the necessity for doing an exempt private resale of control or restricted securities is that the sale not involve a public offering. It is apparent that there is substantial learning available on the question of what constitutes a public offering and its statutory opposite, the section 4(a)(2) private placement. What must be done, then, is an offering that, although technically under section 4(a)(1), has some of the basic characteristics of a section 4(a)(2) transaction. For those reasons, private resales of control or restricted securities often are referred to as section 4(a)(1½) transactions.

In the case of restricted securities, the seller needs to avoid assuming the status of an underwriter. Rule 144A establishes a safe harbor for certain private resales of restricted securities, by providing that the seller in a transaction qualified under the rule will not be deemed to be an underwriter. If the seller is a dealer, rule 144A(c) provides also that the dealer will be deemed not to be a participant in a distribution of the securities covered by the rule. The rule is available only if the buyer is a "qualified institutional buyer" or an institution that the seller and any person acting on its behalf reasonably believe to be a "qualified institutional buyer." The rule is not available, however, for the resale of securities (1) that, at the time of their issuance, were of the same class of securities listed on a national securities exchange or quoted in a U.S. automated inter-dealer quotation system or (2) that were issued by one of enumerated types of companies that are or are required to be registered under the Investment Company Act of 1940. For transactions to be covered by rule 144A, the seller and any person acting on its behalf must take reasonable steps to ensure that the purchaser is aware that the seller may rely on the exemption from the registration requirements provided by the rule. Also, in the case of securities issued by certain companies (basically those that are not subject to the reporting requirements of the Exchange Act), the rule provides that, upon request, the purchaser has a right to obtain from the seller, and the seller and the purchaser have a right to obtain from the issuer, prior to the sale, certain basic information about the issuer. Although rule 144A originally permitted offers, as well as sales, only to those reasonable believed to be "qualified institutional buyers," the JOBS Act required the Commission to amend the rule to permit general solicitation.

For private resales of restricted securities that fall outside rule 144A, the seller must structure the transaction so that the seller is (1) not an underwriter and (2) cannot be made an underwriter by actions of the purchaser. Analytically, that would seem to involve offering and selling only to persons who can meet the requirements for purchasing in a private placement. It further involves structuring the transaction in such a way that the new purchasers cannot resell in a nonexempt transaction, since that will likely destroy the exemption or exemptions that supported sales earlier in the chain. That mainly involves having the new purchaser agree to contractual restrictions, of the type used in private placements, and ensuring that the certificates representing the securities that are sold are legended against resale without an exemption.

The situation is somewhat different in the case of control securities. In that case, the seller must ensure that the purchaser is not an underwriter. Theoretically, at least, it seems that the purchaser would not have to meet any requirements (such as investment sophistication), except those that go to the question of underwriter status. At a minimum, the seller would want to obtain a representation that the purchaser is not purchasing with a view to distribution and, in addition, would want to insist on the same type of contractual restrictions and legends on certificates that are needed in the case of restricted securities.

Chapter 8

LIABILITY FOR VIOLATION OF THE SECURITIES ACT

As will be seen in this chapter, the Securities Act has an arsenal of weapons for use against violators. And, like any good arsenal, the Securities Act is made up of weapons designed for differing uses.

Criminal and Other Governmental Actions

The Securities Act can be viewed as a criminal statute. For example, section 5, the centerpiece registration provision provides: "Unless a registration statement is in effect as to a security, it shall be unlawful. . . ." The main antifraud provision, section 17(a), begins the same way: "It shall be unlawful. . . ." Of more general effect is section 24, the penalties provision. It makes the willful violation of any provision of the Act, or of any of its rules, a felony punishable by up to five years imprisonment and a $10,000 fine.

"Willful" does not mean what it may seem at first. As Judge Friendly said in construing the same term in the Exchange Act: "A person can willfully violate an SEC rule even if he does not know of its existence."[1] Referring to the question of what is required in the case of a violation of the section 5 registration requirements, the Commission has said in an administrative action:

> [A]s is well settled, a finding of willfulness . . . does not require a finding of intention to violate the law. It is sufficient that registrants be shown to have known what they were doing. Registrants [in this case], of course, knew that no registration statement had been filed and the [press] release [violating Securities Act section 5] was intentionally composed and publicized.[2]

"Willfulness" can take on a different cast in a criminal action because of the issue of scienter. Even so, the willfulness requirement offers scant shielding for a violator. In an important criminal case involving alleged violations of section 17(a), in which one issue was whether a transaction involved a security, the Ninth Circuit said:

> We think that the government is required to prove specific intent only as it relates to the action constituting the

---

[1] *United States v. Peltz*, 433 F.2d 48, 54 (2d Cir.1970).

[2] *In re Carl M. Loeb, Rhoades & Co.*, 38 S.E.C. 843, 854 n. 21 (1959).

fraudulent, misleading or deceitful conduct, but not as to the knowledge that the instrument used is a security under the Securities Act. The government need only prove that the object sold or offered is, in fact, a security; it need not be proved that the defendant had specific knowledge that the object sold or offered was a security.[3]

The Securities Act, as well as the other securities statutes, is tricky in one other respect involving its criminal provisions. In an earlier chapter, the difficulty of avoiding the jurisdictional means requirement of the Securities Act (use of the mails or some means or instrument of interstate commerce) was discussed. Because the Securities Act prohibitions are tied to uses of jurisdictional means, each separate use of those means is a separate violation. Since the average securities transaction involves multiple uses of jurisdictional means, a violator almost always faces a multiple-count indictment. Plus, when an antifraud provision is involved, the indictment usually includes multiple counts for violations of the federal mail fraud and wire fraud statutes, along with one or more counts under the general conspiracy statute.

The Securities Act does not give the Commission the power to bring criminal actions. It does, however, give the Commission a variety of other powers. Section 20(b) allows the Commission to seek injunctive relief whenever it appears that the Act, or any rule under the Act, has been or is about to be violated. That authority is a powerful tool, one that has created much of the case law interpreting the Securities Act. Moreover, Exchange Act section 21(d)(5) provides the possibility of equitable relief in the context of all federal securities laws. It reads: "In any action or proceeding brought or instituted by the Commission under any provision of the securities laws, the Commission may seek, and any Federal court may grant, any equitable relief that may be appropriate or necessary for the benefit of investors." There is no way to predict the case law that may develop over time under this provision.

The Securities Act also gives the Commission authority to bring court actions seeking civil penalties, as well as the power to issue its own cease-and-desist orders. The latter authority is found in section 8A, which allows the Commission to issue a cease-and-desist order whenever it finds, after notice and opportunity for a hearing, that someone has violated, is violating, or is about to violate the Securities Act or one of its rules. Section 8A also permits the Commission to issue officer and director bars, with respect to service with Exchange Act reporting companies, against those who have violated Securities Act section 17(a)(1) or any of its

---

[3] *United States v. Brown*, 578 F.2d 1280, 1284 (9th Cir.1978).

rules. These bars may be conditional or unconditional, and temporary or permanent. (A comparable provision is found in Exchange Act section 21C.)

The Commission's power under the Securities Act to seek civil penalties is found in section 20(d). (Exchange Act sections 21(d)(3), 21A, and 21B cover the Commission's power in this area under that Act.) Under section 20(d), the Commission may ask a district court to impose such a penalty in most cases when it believes that someone has violated the Securities Act, a rule under the Securities Act, or one of the Commission's section 8A cease-and-desist orders. The maximum civil penalty a court can impose under section 20(d) (read along with rule of practice 1004, which relates to the adjustment of civil monetary penalties) varies with culpability and with the risk to the public presented by the violator's actions, with the maximums in various circumstances running from $7,500 to $150,000 for natural persons and $75,000 to $725,000 for others (unless, in any case, the gross amount of the gain to the violator as a result of the violation is greater than those amounts, in which event the penalty can be as high as the amount of the gain).

Pursuant to section 308 of the Sarbanes–Oxley Act of 2002, where the Commission obtains, under any of the securities laws, an order requiring disgorgement of ill-gotten profits (or disgorgement is provided for in a settlement), and the Commission also obtains a civil penalty against the same person, then "on the motion or at the direction of the Commission" the civil penalty shall be added to a disgorgement fund for the benefit of victims.

Under rule 9 of the Commission's rules of informal and other procedures, the Commission may, on a case-by-case basis, reduce the amount of penalty it seeks against a "small entity" (which includes a "Small Business" as defined by the Commission). Under the rule, the Commission considers a number of issues in making this determination, including the willfulness and egregiousness of the conduct, the violator's history of legal or regulatory violations, and the financial ability of the entity to pay the penalty.

In addition to imposing a civil penalty in an action brought by the Commission under section 20(d), a court may, under section 20(e), prohibit a person who has violated section 17(a)(1) from acting as an officer or director of a company that has securities registered under section 12 of the Exchange Act or that is required by Exchange Act section 15(d) to file Exchange Act reports (basically these Exchange Act provisions define publicly held companies, and section 17(a)(1) prohibits the employment of "any device, scheme or artifice to defraud" in connection with the offer or sale of securities). Under section 20(g), a court may, in a

Commission injunctive action, bar persons from participating in an offering of penny stock if their alleged misconduct related to an offering of penny stock. These bars may be conditional or unconditional, and temporary or permanent.

In *Central Bank of Denver, N.A. v. First Interstate Bank of Denver, N.A.*,[4] the Supreme Court determined that a private plaintiff cannot maintain an aiding-and-abetting action under Exchange Act rule 10b–5. By the Court's reasoning, it seemed clear that the same outcome was to be expected under other sections of and rules under both the Securities Act and the Exchange Act. Congress subsequently amended Exchange Act section 20 and Securities Act section 15 to give the Commission authority to bring aiding-and-abetting actions in connection with the violation of either Act or any rule or regulation thereunder. As to criminal actions for aiding and abetting, there is no issue, because 18 U.S.C. § 2 creates aiding-and-abetting liability for all federal criminal offenses.

Civil Liability

Under the Securities Litigation Uniform Standards Act of 1998, most class actions involving fraud or defects in disclosure relating to the securities of most publicly held companies must be brought in federal court under federal law. The Securities Act contains a number of provisions that may lead to civil liability.

Section 11

Securities Act section 11 provides a civil remedy in the case of a registration statement that contains "an untrue statement of a material fact or omit[s] to state a material fact required to be stated therein or necessary to make the statements therein not misleading." Joint and several liability under that section may fall on a number of persons, including the issuer; its chief executive, financial, and accounting officers; each director; each underwriter; and each accountant or other expert who has taken responsibility for some portion of the registration statement. Under section 11(f), however, the liability of outside directors is determined in accordance with Exchange Act section 21D(f), which generally distributes liability proportionally by responsibility and requires a violation to be knowingly committed before joint and several liability attaches. Until 2010, Rule 436(g) conferred an exemption from liability for credit rating agencies, which could be named (with their consent) in a registration statement as having assigned a disclosed rating. The Dodd-Frank Act removed the exemption, with the result that at least some credit rating agencies now refuse to be

---

[4]   511 U.S. 164 (1994).

named. This means that disclosure of ratings takes place outside of the registration statement.

A purchaser of a registered security may sue under section 11, regardless of whether he or she purchased the security in the registered offering or later in the trading markets (the theories of some to the contrary notwithstanding). The only limitation, besides being able to trace one's securities back to the registered offering, is that the purchaser must bring suit before the statute of limitations has run. Proof of causation is not a requirement for recovery, nor is proof of reliance in the usual situation.

The effect of those factors on defendants is softened somewhat by other factors. Damages cannot exceed the difference between the offering price in the registered offering and the value of the securities at the time of suit (or the price at which the plaintiff disposed of them earlier). Further, no underwriter can be held responsible for damages in excess of the aggregate public offering price of the securities underwritten by it.

A more general softening effect comes from the defenses available under section 11. Each defendant other than the issuer has a defense, called a due diligence defense, that provides an escape from liability. Those defenses take two basic forms, depending, first, upon whether a particular defendant is an "expert" and, second, upon whether the portion of the registration statement that is the subject of the complaint is "expertized" (under section 11(a)(4), an expert is a person whose profession gives authority to his or her statements, such as accountants). Of all the possible permutations, the due diligence defense requires the least when a nonexpert defendant is sued for a problem in an expertized part of the registration statement. In that situation, ignorance is sufficient to escape liability. Basically, the defendant needs to show that he or she had no reasonable ground to believe, and did not believe, that the expertized part of the registration statement contained a material misstatement or omission. More is required of an expert, and also of a nonexpert when a nonexpertized portion of the registration statement is the subject of a complaint. In those cases, the defendant must have had, after reasonable investigation, reasonable ground to believe, and he or she must have believed, that the statements in the portion of the registration statement in question were true and that there was no material omission.

The biggest interpretative problem involving section 11 is determining what constitutes a reasonable investigation. The Commission's one rule directly on point, rule 176, lists a few relevant circumstances (such as the office held, when the defendant is an officer, and the presence or absence of another relationship to the issuer when the defendant is a director) to consider in making that determination. Regrettably, case law also is sparse.

The leading case, *Escott v. BarChris Construction Corp.*,[5] involved a situation in which the defendants fell far short of what might be considered a reasonable investigation, which left the court little opportunity to draw the line separating acceptable from unacceptable conduct. The court, however, did make at least two things clear. First, the closer the involvement of a defendant, and the higher his or her position, the more a court expects. Second, those conducting a due diligence investigation must look for facts to support statements in a registration statement. Merely asking questions of corporate officers is not enough.

Despite the scarcity of case law on the subject, there is no uncertainty concerning what in general must be done in a due diligence investigation. The starting point is the registration statement itself, and here two steps are required. The information in the registration statement must be verified, and the issuer and its affairs must be examined in an attempt to uncover what must be added to the registration statement to prevent it from containing a material omission.

As a practical matter, extensive due diligence investigations cannot be done individually for each possible defendant. The managing underwriter and counsel for the underwriters decide on an allocation between them of the due diligence work, and they do an investigation for all the underwriters. The more correct analysis, it would seem, would be in terms of delegating the due diligence work, rather than the responsibility, under standard rules of agency law. The same procedure could be utilized on the issuer's side of the transaction by the issuer's law firm.

At the beginning of this section, it was mentioned that a misstatement or omission must be material to lead to section 11 liability. The "bespeaks caution" doctrine can, however, save a defendant from liability, because sufficient cautionary language in a disclosure document can render alleged omissions or misrepresentations immaterial as a matter of law (general boilerplate cautions are not enough). Most courts limit the bespeaks caution doctrine to situations that include forward-looking statements, but this is not universal.

Picking up on the "bespeaks caution" doctrine, Congress in 1995 added section 27A to the Securities Act. This section provides, to Exchange Act reporting companies and some other persons, a safe harbor for certain forward-looking statements that are

---

[5] 283 F.Supp. 643 (S.D.N.Y.1968).

accompanied by cautionary statements meeting the section's requirements. This section should be read along with rule 175, which also relates to liability for certain forward-looking statements.

Section 12

Section 12 rounds out the express civil remedies provided in the Securities Act. While section 11 relates only to civil liability in the context of registration statements, section 12 aims more broadly. Section 12(a) has two parts, each of which deals with entirely different situations. Except for drafting convenience, the two parts could just as well have been written as separate provisions.

Section 12(a)(1)

Section 12(a)(1) provides for civil liability when a person "offers or sells a security in violation of section 5," that is, when unregistered securities are offered or sold without an exemption. Under section 12(a)(1), a purchaser may not recover from an issuer, or any other seller (e.g., an intermediate seller if there has been a chain of purchases and sales), unless there is a direct link between the purchaser and seller. That limitation flows from the provision in section 12(a) that provides that a seller is "liable, subject to subsection (b), to the person purchasing . . . from him." Other than the requirement that the suit be commenced before the statute of limitations has run, there is generally nothing else standing in the way of a plaintiff's obtaining rescission of his purchase, with recovery of interest, or damages when he has sold his securities at a loss.

Courts have interpreted the term "seller" relatively broadly. The leading case is *Pinter v. Dahl*,[6] a 1988 Supreme Court case. Under *Pinter*, the term "seller" encompasses not only persons who pass title to securities. As stated by the Court, "liability [as a statutory 'seller'] extends [to a] person who successfully solicits the purchase, motivated at least in part by a desire to serve his own financial interests or those of the securities owner."

Section 12(a)(2)

Section 12(a)(2) is a very different kind of provision from section 12(a)(1). It provides that any person who offers or sells a security (except a government security), by "means of a prospectus or oral communication" that includes a material misstatement or omission, is liable to his or her purchaser for rescission or damages (subject to the loss causation provisions found in section 12(b)).

---

[6] 486 U.S. 622 (1988).

Note that the "bespeaks caution" doctrine and the safe harbor for forward-looking statements provided in section 27A and rule 175, discussed in connection with section 11, are also applicable to section 12(a)(2). Section 12(a)(2) also provides that a plaintiff cannot win if he or she knew about the misstatement or omission complained of. Under section 13's statute of limitations, an action under section 12(a)(2) must be brought within one year after discovery of the misstatement or omission, or after its discovery should have been made by the exercise of reasonable diligence. In any event, the action must be brought within three years after the sale.

Many decades after the Securities Act was passed, some courts began finding for the first time that section 12(a)(2) applies only to initial sales of securities by issuers (or affiliates) and not to secondary trading transactions. This reached its zenith in *Gustafson v. Alloyd Co., Inc.*,[7] decided by the Supreme Court, 5–4, in 1995. This case involved the sale of a business, and the issue, as stated by the Court, was "whether [the section 12(a)(2)] right of rescission extends to a private, secondary transaction, on the theory that recitations in the purchase agreement are part of a 'prospectus.'" The Court found that the purchase agreement was not a prospectus, because in its view "the word 'prospectus' is a term of art referring to a document that describes a public offering of securities by an issuer or controlling shareholder," and on that basis the Court found that section 12(a)(2) did not apply to the transaction. In the Court's reasoning, liability under section 12(a)(2) "cannot attach unless there is an obligation to distribute [a] prospectus . . . (or unless there is an exemption)." The Court also said that "[t]he intent of Congress and the design of the statute require that [12(a)(2)] liability be limited to public offerings."

It is important to realize here that Justice Ginsburg, in her dissent, properly reads the Court's opinion as extending beyond registered public offerings: "I understand the Court's definition of a public offering to encompass both transactions that must be registered under § 5 and transactions that would have been registered had the securities involved not qualified for exemption under § 3." This follows because offerings under section 3 are considered "limited public offerings." It also follows from the Court's parenthetical quoted above, "(or unless there is an exemption)," since this statement clearly relates to exempt offerings.

In predicting how wide the application of Gustafson ultimately could be, beyond the strict holding of the case, there is a great deal in the opinion that requires consideration. Among these matters is

---

[7] 513 U.S. 561 (1995).

the fact that much of the logic of the opinion hinges on the Court's understanding of the structure of the Securities Act. In this connection, it should be noted that the Court explains that part of the structure made up of sections 11 and 12(a)(2) by the following statement: "Section 11 provides for liability on account of false registration statements; § [12(a)(2)] for liability based on misstatements in prospectuses." From this statement it seems clear that the Court did not know that the bulk of a registration statement consists of a prospectus and that virtually all cases involving false or misleading statements will involve the prospectus part of a registration statement. Because of this evident failure of understanding, the Court has these two sections covering the same thing. That could not have been intended by the drafters or by Congress.

It is noteworthy that when the Commission, in 2005, adopted provisions allowing the use of "free writing prospectuses," it specified that these writings would constitute "prospectuses" under section 2(a)(10) and would be deemed to relate to public offerings. Moreover, when in 2012 Congress adopted Securities Act section 3(b)(2), effectively directing the Commission to liberalize regulation A's exemption from registration, it provided that any person offering or selling a security exempt by reason of the liberalization is subject to Section 12(a)(2).

As in the case of section 12(a)(1), a plaintiff-purchaser can collect, as a matter of primary liability, only from a person who has "sold" to him. But, also as with section 12(a)(1), courts have stretched the requirement to allow plaintiffs the targets provided by *Pinter v. Dahl*, which is discussed in the preceding section of this chapter.

Although a plaintiff can prevail under section 12(a)(2) without proving knowledge or awareness of improper activity on the part of a defendant, the section provides that a defendant can defeat a claim by showing that he did not know, and in the exercise of reasonable care could not have known, of the material misstatement or omission that gives rise to the claim. That defense is reminiscent of the due diligence defense provided under section 11. The question is, how similar are they? The leading case has read them to be essentially equivalent,[8] but what the final answer may be is uncertain.

While there are situations, under the *Gustafson* case and otherwise, where both section 11 and section 12(a)(2) may apply to the same defendant in a situation involving disclosure problems in a registration statement, one thing that should be clear is that

---

[8] *Sanders v. John Nuveen & Co.*, 619 F.2d 1222, 1228 (7th Cir.1980).

there should be no liability under section 12(a)(2) if the defendant escapes liability under section 11. Congress focused with care and specificity on the rules for finding liability when there is a material misstatement or omission in a registration statement. That being the case, someone who falls within the specifically tailored liability provisions of section 11 should not be subjected to different rules under the Act's more general liability provision. Otherwise, it must be questioned why the drafters bothered to work out section 11 in all its intricate detail.

Section 12(b)

Congress in 1995 added subsection (b), relating to loss causation, to section 12. Under this subsection, if a defendant proves that any or all of the amount otherwise recoverable under section 12(a)(2) arose from something other than the defective disclosure complained of, then that amount is not recoverable.

Section 4A(c)

Section 4A(c) provides for recovery from an issuer by way of rescission (or recissory damages) by purchasers in an exempt crowdfunding transaction if the issuer, by means of any written or oral communication, makes an untrue statement of material fact or omits to state a material fact required to be stated or necessary in order to make the statements made not misleading. This is obviously quite similar to the liability imposed under Section 12(a)(2). The similarity is enhanced by (1) the requirement that the purchaser must not have known of the untruth or omission, (2) the availability of a reasonable care defense, (3) incorporation by reference of the lack of loss causation defense available under Section 12(b), and (4) invocation of the statute of limitations contained in Section 13. Critical differences are the fact that the new provision makes no reference to a "prospectus" and that the term "issuer" includes directors, partners, and specified officers of issuers, as well as anyone who offers or sells a security in the transaction.

Section 15

Section 15 is an important part of the liability scheme of the Securities Act. It provides that anyone who controls a person liable under section 11 or 12 is jointly and severally liable to the same extent as the controlled person, with one exception: the controlling person can escape liability provided he or she "had no knowledge of or reasonable ground to believe in the existence of the facts by reason of which the liability of the controlled person is alleged to exist." "Control" is in general a broad concept, and the language used in section 15 to describe the means by which control can exist parallels the general meaning of the term:

> Every person who, by or through stock ownership, agency, or otherwise, or who, pursuant to or in connection with an agreement or understanding with one or more other persons by or through stock ownership, agency, or otherwise, controls any person liable under section 11 or 12. . . .

The exact limits of the concept of "control" in this context are uncertain and vary by circuit, but the concept easily can include major shareholders, directors, and officers. It is important to note, however, that culpability for the actions complained of typically play an important role in litigation under section 15. Some courts require a showing of culpability by the plaintiff, while others require a lack of culpability to be raised by the defendant as an affirmative defense.

Section 17(a)

For reasons that will become clear shortly, it is important to set forth section 17(a) in full:

> Section 17. (a) It shall be unlawful for any person in the offer or sale of any securities by the use of any means or instruments of transportation or communication in interstate commerce or by the use of the mails, directly or indirectly—
>
> (1) to employ any device, scheme, or artifice to defraud, or
>
> (2) to obtain money or property by means of any untrue statement of a material fact or any omission to state a material fact necessary in order to make the statements made, in the light of the circumstances under which they were made, not misleading, or
>
> (3) to engage in any transaction, practice, or course of business which operates or would operate as a fraud or deceit upon the purchaser.

As indicated at the beginning of this chapter, section 17(a) is a criminal provision. It is discussed here because some courts have over the years found that an implied private right of action exists under it.

Those familiar with Exchange Act rule 10b–5 will notice a close resemblance between it and section 17(a). The reason is that when the Commission drafted rule 10b–5, it copied the numbered subdivisions of section 17(a) almost word for word. The most obvious difference in the language of the two provisions is that section 17(a) covers fraud in the sale of securities, while rule 10b–5 covers fraud in the purchase or sale of securities.

In *Aaron v. SEC*[9] the Supreme Court held that scienter must be proven under rule 10b–5 in an action by the Commission seeking an injunction, and it already had held that scienter was required in criminal and private rule 10b–5 actions. With respect to section 17(a), however, the Court held that the Commission need only show scienter when it brings an action under section 17(a)(1), not when it does so under section 17(a)(2) or (3). Under those latter subsections, a showing of negligence is sufficient. The reason for the differing results under the rule and the section is that section 17(a) was passed by Congress, and it must be interpreted in a way that effectuates the will of Congress. Rule 10b–5, on the other hand, is merely a rule of the Commission, and to discern the intent of Congress with respect to it, one must look to congressional intent with respect to section 10(b). In *Aaron*, then, the Supreme Court looked at Securities Act section 17(a) and Exchange Act section 10(b) and discerned two different congressional intents.

With *Aaron*, the issue of whether an implied right of action exists under section 17(a) took on major importance, since for the first time plaintiffs would often prefer that section to rule 10b–5. The Supreme Court has never spoken on the issue, but at the time of or shortly after *Aaron*, four courts of appeals had found that a private right of action exists under section 17(a). Now, each of those circuits has reversed course, and most courts that have decided the issue have found that the right does not exist. The Sixth Circuit has, however, confirmed a private right of action exists under section 17(a).[10] To appreciate the issues involved in deciding whether such an action in fact exists, it is necessary to look at the rules, developed by the Supreme Court since the mid-1960s, for determining the existence of an implied private right of action under federal statutes. It is especially worthwhile to spend some time on those rules, since the question of implied rights of action arises in many securities law contexts.

In the most influential early case, *J.I. Case Co. v. Borak*,[11] the Supreme Court used an expansive analysis to decide that a private right of action exists under Exchange Act section 14(a):

> The purpose of § 14(a) is to prevent management or others from obtaining authorization for corporate action by means of deceptive or inadequate disclosure in proxy solicitation. . . . While [the language of the section] makes no specific reference

---

[9] 446 U.S. 680 (1980).

[10] *Craighead v. E.F. Hutton & Co.*, 899 F.2d 485 (6th Cir.1990).

[11] 377 U.S. 426 (1964).

to a private right of action, among its chief purposes is the "protection of investors," which certainly implies the availability of judicial relief where necessary to achieve that result.

As might be expected under a test whose touchstone is the protection of investors, courts were quick to imply private rights of action in the years following *Borak*.

That expansive era of implying rights of action continued for about a decade, until *Cort v. Ash*.[12] In *Cort*, the Supreme Court established four factors as relevant in determining the existence of an implied remedy:

1. Is the plaintiff of the class for whose especial benefit the statute was enacted?

2. Is there any indication of legislative intent, explicit or implicit, either to create such a remedy or to deny one?

3. Is it consistent with the underlying purposes of the legislative scheme to imply such a remedy for the plaintiff?

4. Is the cause of action one traditionally relegated to state law, in an area basically the concern of the states?

Compared to *Borak*, which focused only on the third of those factors, *Cort* obviously was more restrictive.

Four years later, the Supreme Court refined its analysis in *Touche Ross & Co. v. Redington*,[13] where the Court indicated that each of the four factors does not carry equal weight, but rather that the central inquiry is legislative intent. In 1982, the focus on legislative intent took an interesting turn. In *Merrill Lynch, Pierce, Fenner & Smith, Inc. v. Curran*,[14] the Court chose to focus on the intent of Congress at the time it passed comprehensive amendments to a particular statute in 1974. Noting that prior to those amendments "the federal courts routinely and consistently had recognized an implied private cause of action," the Court reasoned that leaving "intact the statutory provisions under which the federal courts had implied a cause of action is itself evidence that Congress affirmatively intended to preserve that remedy."

The next year the Court dealt with a different kind of implied right of action question. In *Herman & MacLean v. Huddleston*,[15] the issue was whether the implied right of action under rule 10b–5 could be pursued in a situation clearly covered by Securities Act

---

[12] 422 U.S. 66 (1975).

[13] 442 U.S. 560 (1979).

[14] 456 U.S. 353 (1982).

[15] 459 U.S. 375 (1983).

section 11. With seeming ease, the Court determined that it could. According to the Court, the resolution of the issue turned "on the fact that the two provisions involve distinct causes of action and were intended to address different types of wrongdoing." Thus, the Court found it to be "hardly a novel proposition" that the Securities Act and the Exchange Act prohibit some of the same conduct.

In any private right of action that might exist under section 17(a)(1), which relates to fraudulent conduct of various sorts, the Sarbanes–Oxley Act of 2002 lengthens the applicable limitations period. Under section 804 of Sarbanes–Oxley, the statute of limitations for all private rights of action for securities fraud is the earlier of two years after the discovery of the facts constituting the violation or five years after the violation. This provision arguably would apply to section 17(a)(3) as well.

Indemnification and Contribution

Section 11(f)(1) of the Securities Act specifically grants the right of contribution to any person liable under the section, except when the person seeking contribution is, and the person from whom contribution is sought is not, guilty of fraudulent misrepresentation. (When dealing with the liability of outside directors under section 11, note that section 11(f)(2) brings the proportionate liability provisions of Exchange Act section 21D(f) into play. One issue covered is contribution.) Contribution also has been found to be available in a private suit under section 17(a).[16] The reasoning underlying that result in the case of section 17(a), including "the general drift of the law today ... toward the allowance of contribution among joint tortfeasors," applies with equal force to section 12. Also, it is instructive to note that the Supreme Court has found contribution to be available in suits brought under Exchange Act rule 10b–5.[17] There should, therefore, be little question that contribution is generally available in Securities Act suits.

Indemnification is a more difficult problem. As indicated in Chapter 4, the Commission has long been dissatisfied with the idea that officers, directors, and other persons controlling an issuer might be indemnified by the issuer for Securities Act liability. The Commission's position is that such indemnity is against public policy and, therefore, it believes that any provision granting it is unenforceable.

---

[16] *Globus v. Law Research Serv.*, 318 F.Supp. 955 (S.D.N.Y.1970), *aff'd*, 442 F.2d 1346 (2d Cir.1971).

[17] *Musick, Peeler & Garrett v. Employers Ins. of Wausau*, 508 U.S. 286 (1993).

The Commission's stance on the public policy issue makes it more likely, of course, that a court will take such a position itself. And, in fact, courts have brought into question indemnification against Securities Act liability. In *Globus v. Law Research Service, Inc.*,[18] the Second Circuit had before it a case involving an underwriter seeking indemnification from an issuer under a provision in an underwriting agreement. The jury found that the underwriter had actual knowledge of misstatements leading to Securities Act liability, and the district court accordingly found that, in such circumstances, it would be against public policy to allow indemnification. The Second Circuit agreed, but emphasized it was considering "only the case where the underwriter has committed a sin graver than ordinary negligence." Since *Globus*, some other courts have held that there is no implied right of action for indemnification under the Securities Act or the Exchange Act, and some have refused to enforce the indemnification provisions in an underwriting agreement irrespective of the culpability of those seeking indemnification.

---

[18] 418 F.2d 1276 (2d Cir.1969).

Chapter 9

COMMISSION'S GENERAL EXEMPTIVE AUTHORITY AND REGISTRATION AND REPORTING UNDER THE EXCHANGE ACT

The next several chapters cover the Securities Exchange Act of 1934. Since much of what is discussed in these chapters applies only to companies that have securities registered under that Act, Exchange Act registration is the natural starting point for the discussion. One of the major consequences of registration, periodic reporting to the Commission, is intertwined with registration, since it involves the updating of information provided to the Commission at the time of registration. For that reason, it is also examined in this chapter. First, however, it is important to say something about the Commission's general exemptive authority.

Commission's General Exemptive Authority

In connection not only with this chapter, but with all chapters dealing with the Exchange Act, it should be noted that, as part of the National Securities Markets Improvement Act of 1996, Congress added section 36 to the Exchange Act. Under this section, "the Commission, by rule, regulation, or order, may conditionally or unconditionally exempt any person, security, or transaction, or any class or classes of persons, securities, or transactions, from any provision or provisions of this title or of any rule or regulation thereunder." Section 36 contains only two caveats. First, any exemption must be "necessary or appropriate in the public interest, and consistent with the protection of investors." Second, the authority of the Commission does not extend to Exchange Act section 15C, which relates to government securities brokers and dealers. An important element of the Commission's authority under section 36 is that the Commission can exercise this authority by order or ad hoc.

Also to be considered in connection with section 36 is section 3(f), which was added to the Exchange Act at the same time as section 36. When engaged in rulemaking, or the review of a rule by a self-regulatory organization such as a securities exchange, section 3(f) requires the Commission to consider "whether the action will promote efficiency, competition, and capital formation," at any time it is "required to consider or determine whether an action is necessary or appropriate in the public interest."

Exchange Act Securities Registration

The Exchange Act requires the registration of securities under two distinct circumstances. First, an issuer must register securities when the securities are to be traded on a securities exchange. Second, an issuer must register securities when it meets certain tests with respect to number of shareholders and amount of assets.

Exchange Act section 12(g)(1) now requires registration if an issuer (a) has total assets exceeding $10,000,000 and (b) a class of equity security "held of record" by either 2,000 or more persons or 500 or more unaccredited investors. Section 12(g)(5) and (6) add two additional complications. First, securities owned by persons receiving them through employee compensation plan transactions exempt from registration under the Securities Act will not be counted toward section 12(g)'s "held for record" tests. Second, the Commission is required to adopt rules excluding from section 12(g) calculations securities acquired pursuant to the new "crowdfunding" exemption from Securities Act registration. The issuer must make the registration filing within 120 days after the end of the first fiscal year on the last day of which it meets those requirements. Companies that are not required to register securities under section 12(g)(1) may register them nevertheless, if they wish. Over the years, a number of companies have registered securities voluntarily to meet the current public information requirement of Securities Act rule 144(c), and thus make that rule available to shareholders who wish to sell securities under it. Some companies have also registered voluntarily in response to a proxy fight, in order to subject proxy solicitations of their shareholders to Exchange Act regulation.

Companies that wish to have their securities trade on an exchange must register the securities under section 12(b). The statutory framework for requiring that registration is somewhat roundabout. It starts with section 12(a), which makes it unlawful for any securities professional to effect a transaction in any security (except an exempted security) on a national securities exchange "unless a registration is effective as to such security for such exchange." Section 12(b) then provides the mechanism for registration, which involves filing an application with the exchange and with the Commission.

Section 12(b) serves as the starting point for establishing what disclosures must be included in the registration application. That section also grants the Commission authority to prescribe the details of that disclosure. Section 12(g)(1) gives the Commission that same power with respect to registrations under that section, and the Commission has adopted the same forms for registering securities under either section 12(b) or section 12(g)(1). Form 10 is the general form. Issuers that are already Exchange Act reporting companies because of the provisions of Exchange Act section 15(d), which is discussed below, may use the very simple form 8–A.

Exchange Act registration forms have much in common with Securities Act registration forms, because there is a great sameness in the general disclosures required for registration under each Act. Commonality also arises because the registration statement forms under each Act use regulation S–K as the repository of detailed disclosure requirements, with each form consisting mainly of references to the items in the regulation with which a registering company must comply.

It is confusing that both the Securities Act and the Exchange Act provide for the registration of securities. The consequences of registration under the two Acts are entirely different. Registration under the Securities Act allows the securities that are registered to be sold in a particular transaction. In that case, it is only technically incorrect to say that the transaction itself is what is registered. The consequences of Exchange Act registration are that the issuer of the registered securities is subject to that Act's periodic reporting requirements and to certain other requirements, for example with respect to proxy solicitations, which will be discussed in later chapters. In the case of the Exchange Act, it is only technically incorrect to say that the issuer is what is registered.

Periodic Reporting Under the Exchange Act

By registering securities under Exchange Act section 12, an issuer becomes a "reporting company." That is, it becomes subject to the periodic reporting requirements of section 13(a). Under that section, the Commission has power to require the filing of virtually any document or report it wishes. An exception to the Commission's broad grant of power was added, however, by the JOBS Act and limits the financial information that must be presented by emerging growth companies. Moreover, Congress in some instances has directed how the Commission's power to require disclosure is to be used. For instance, the Sarbanes–Oxley Act of 2002 added Section 13(j), mandating that the Commission adopt rules regarding disclosure of material off-balance sheet transactions and certain officer certification requirements. More recently, the Dodd-Frank Act of 2010 required the adoption of rules calling for disclosures with respect to use of "conflict minerals" (tantalum, tin, gold, or tungsten mined in the Democratic Republic of Congo and surrounding countries) and with respect to payments made to governments to further commercial development of oil, natural gas, or minerals.

Regulation 13A outlines the filings required by the Commission under section 13(a). For the typical issuer, these filings are on form 10–K for annual reports, form 10–Q for quarterly reports, and form 8–K for reports upon the occurrence of certain materially important events. The disclosures that form 8–K requires have grown over the years and can be expected to grow further, and the form also allows any information to be filed on the form that an issuer wishes. Some securities lawyers advise issuers to file every press release of any significance on a form 8–K, for example. In fact, a form 8–K filing is sometimes the only way small companies can publicly disseminate information as a practical matter, since their developments often do not interest the financial press.

A report on form 8–K is typically short and limited to providing the information called for by a triggering event or volunteered by the issuer. A form 10–Q report usually consists mainly of quarterly financial statements. A form 10–K report is much like the form 10 registration statement that is used to register securities under the Exchange Act. In each case, the forms consist primarily of references to the detailed disclosure requirements collected in regulation S–K.

There is one other way in which companies become subject to the reporting requirements of the Exchange Act. Under section 15(d), read along with regulation 15D, a company that has registered securities under the Securities Act is subject to the same section 13 filing requirements as are companies that have securities registered under Exchange Act section 12. As a practical matter, the usual impact of section 15(d) is simply earlier compliance with the periodic reporting requirements of the Exchange Act. Companies that register equity securities under the Securities Act typically meet the requirements of section 12(g)(1) upon completion of the offering. A company does not, however, have to register securities under those provisions until 120 days after the end of the first fiscal year on the last day of which it meets the requirements.

Some of the more interesting questions concerning periodic reporting relate to the liabilities that may flow from material misstatements or omissions in Exchange Act filings. Since the Exchange Act can be thought of as a criminal statute, the first concern may be criminal liability. With that in mind, here is the Act's penalty provision:

Section 32. (a) Any person who willfully violates any provision of this title (other than section 30A), or any rule or regulation thereunder the violation of which is made unlawful or the observance of which is required under the terms of this title, or any person who willfully and knowingly makes, or causes to be made, any statement in any application, report, or document required to be filed under this title or any rule or regulation thereunder . . . , which statement was false or misleading with respect to any material fact, shall upon conviction be fined not more than $5,000,000, or imprisoned not more than 20 years, or both, except that when such person is a person other than a natural person, a fine not exceeding $25,000,000 may be imposed; but no person shall be subject to imprisonment under this section for the violation of any rule or regulation if he proves that he had no knowledge of such rule or regulation.

It is important to note that since that provision deals with violations of the Exchange Act and its rules generally, much of what is discussed below is applicable to problems other than those arising in the context of periodic reporting.

A comparison of section 32 with Securities Act section 24 shows that the Exchange Act's penalty provision is somewhat easier on violators. There are at least two important differences. First, in a criminal prosecution under the Securities Act, willfulness must be shown. As discussed in the preceding chapter, in the context of a Securities Act prosecution for false or misleading statements, to show willfulness the government need not prove that the defendant knew of the existence of the statutory section or involved in the violation. All that is necessary is proof that the defendant knowingly committed a wrongful act. On the other hand, in a similar case brought under Exchange Act section 32, the government must prove that the defendant acted "willfully and knowingly." To satisfy that requirement, the government must establish that the defendant knew of the existence of the section or rule allegedly violated. Second, under Exchange Act section 32, but not Securities Act section 24, a defendant can avoid imprisonment (but not a fine), by proving a lack of knowledge of the allegedly violated rule or regulation.

Section 18 provides an express civil remedy for false or misleading statements in Exchange Act filings. That section is not plaintiffs' first choice for relief, however, because of a number of requirements and limitations. First, under section 18, plaintiffs must show that they purchased or sold securities in reliance on a defective filing. Second, to show damages, plaintiffs must prove that the price at which they purchased or sold was affected by the defective filing. Third, defendants can defeat a claim when they can establish that they acted in good faith and without knowledge that the filing was defective. Fourth, courts can require an undertaking for costs and can assess costs, including attorneys' fees, against any party. As a result of their dissatisfaction with section 18, plaintiffs who sue on the basis of a false or misleading statement typically sue under rule 10b–5.

Note that in an action under section 18, or indeed in any private right of action case under the Exchange Act, the protections afforded defendants by Exchange Act sections 21D and 21E apply. These sections relate in part to (i) the requirement of loss causation, (ii) limitations on damages, (iii) proportionate liability, and (iv) a safe harbor for certain forward-looking statements. One would also want to consider the effect of the "bespeaks caution" doctrine and the situation with controlling person and aiding-and-abetting liability for Exchange Act violations. (Each of these issues, and some other liability issues also relevant here, are discussed below, in Chapter 12, which relates to securities fraud and related issues under rule 10b–5 and under the Sarbanes–Oxley Act of 2002.)

EDGAR

Filings of both Exchange Act registration statements and periodic reports must be made under the Commission's Electronic Data Gathering, Analysis and Retrieval System (EDGAR).

Foreign Corrupt Practices Act

Exchange Act section 13(b) contains record-keeping requirements that are intimately related to periodic reporting. The most controversial of these requirements are sections 13(b)(2) and (3), which were added by the Foreign Corrupt Practices Act of 1977. Under section 13(b)(2), every Exchange Act reporting company is required to:

(A) make and keep books, records, and accounts, which, in reasonable detail, accurately and fairly reflect the transactions and dispositions of the assets of the issuer; and

(B) devise and maintain a system of internal accounting controls sufficient to provide reasonable assurances that—

(i) transactions are executed in accordance with management's general or specific authorization;

(ii) transactions are recorded as necessary (I) to permit preparation of financial statements in conformity with generally accepted accounting principles or any other criteria applicable to such statements, and (II) to maintain accountability for assets;

(iii) access to assets is permitted only in accordance with management's general or specific authorization; and

(iv) the recorded accountability for assets is compared with the existing assets at reasonable intervals and appropriate action is taken with respect to any differences.

Section 13(b)(3) exempts issuers from those requirements when they act in cooperation with certain federal officials in connection with "matters concerning the national security of the United States"cthat is, when they provide cover for clandestine operations.

Impact of Twenty-First Century Legislation

The first years of the twenty-first century were marked by significant financial turmoil. The Enron, WorldCom and other scandals (in large part relating to accounting irregularities) spawned the Sarbanes–Oxley Act of 2002. The financial panic beginning in 2008 gave rise to the Dodd-Frank Act of 2010. The recession lingering after the panic prompted the JOBS Act of 2012 (and public sentiment at the same time led to the adoption of the Stop Trading on Congressional Knowledge Act). Each of these Acts was, at the time of its adoption, billed as "the most sweeping change in financial regulation since the Great Depression." In the case of the Dodd-Frank and JOBS Acts, most of the changes made to securities regulation—as opposed to other types of financial regulation—were amendments to portions of the Securities and/or Exchange Acts that could be, and are, described in other portions of this book. This is also true of many of the changes made by Sarbanes–Oxley. Some of Sarbanes–Oxley's innovations, however, require additional explanation, as does Dodd-Frank's expansion and, in the case of emerging growth companies, the JOBS Act's relaxation of certain of those innovations.

As noted earlier in this chapter, Sarbanes–Oxley mandated passage of rules relating to officer certifications. These related both to the accuracy of periodic reports and the efficacy of internal controls. The rules passed by the Commission are not the complete story on officer certification, however. Sarbanes–Oxley amended the general criminal provisions in title 18 of the United States Code by adding a new section 1350. This section requires chief executive and chief financial officers of Exchange Act reporting companies to certify, with each periodic report containing financial statements, that the report "fully complies with the requirements of [the Exchange Act] and that information contained in the periodic report fairly presents, in all material respects, the financial condition and results of operations of the issuer." The new criminal provision also sets heavy penalties for false certifications. The penalty for certifying compliance of the report with section 1350, knowing the report is not in compliance, is up to $1 million or 10 years imprisonment, or both. If the false certification is also "willful," the penalties increase to us to $5 million or 20 years imprisonment, or both. As a result, many chief executive and chief financial officers are, among other things, requiring lower-level officers and others within the issuers to make certifications to them covering the matters that have to be certified to the Commission.

Sarbanes–Oxley also contained provisions designed to improve the audit process. One of these requires auditor certification of management's internal controls; another mandates auditor rotation. The JOBS Act excuses emerging growth companies from both of these requirements. Even emerging growth companies, however, must comply with other audit-related innovations (as well as other Sarbanes–Oxley requirements). These include Exchange Act section 10A(m) and Sarbanes–Oxley section 303. Section 10A(m) relates in various ways to audit committees of publicly held companies and states a requirement that each audit committee member be an independent member of the board of directors. Sarbanes–Oxley section 303 makes it unlawful, in contravention of the Commission's rules, fraudulently to influence the conduct of audits for the purpose of making financial statements materially misleading. (Section 303 is particularly notable insofar as it specifically indicates that there is no private right of action for violation of this provision.)

Additional Sarbanes–Oxley provisions called for the Commission to pass rules relating to codes of ethics for financial officers, and disclosures of financial experts on audit committees. Pursuant to the resulting rules, although companies are not required to adopt ethics codes or to have financial experts on their audit committees, they are required to describe any circumstances under which they have chosen not to do so.

Sarbanes–Oxley made other changes that relate more tangentially to Exchange Act reporting but are discussed here because they have become of much interest to securities lawyers. First, section 13(k) was added to the Exchange Act. This section basically makes it unlawful for any issuer, directly or indirectly, to extend or maintain credit, or to arrange to extend credit, in the form of a personal loan, for any director or executive officer, with specified exceptions. These include loans on market terms and certain home loans. The problem for lawyers is determining just what may or may not be considered maintaining or extending credit, or making arrangements for extending credit. Minor examples are allowing an officer to bill overnight delivery or telephone charges to his or her company, for convenience and to take advantage of the company's discount, with the charges to be repaid when the company receives the vendor's invoice. A much more troubling example is the so-called cashless exercise of stock options.

Moreover, Sarbanes–Oxley gave the Commission the authority to recoup for an issuer certain executive compensation. Basically, it calls for the return of bonuses or other incentive or equity-based compensation in the event of an accounting restatement due to material noncompliance with any financial reporting requirement as a result of misconduct. This "clawback" approach was augmented by a Dodd-Frank provision requiring public companies to adopt policies compelling the return of certain overpayments made to executives on the basis of financial results that require restating (whether or not misconduct was involved).

Chapter 10

PROXY REGULATIONS

Proxy voting by shareholders is a necessity for most publicly held corporations. State corporation laws require annual meetings, and typically such corporations cannot satisfy quorum requirements unless most shareholders are represented by proxy holders. For that reason, management usually solicits proxies from a corporation's shareholders at least annually, and more often when a special shareholders' meeting is needed. In addition to that ordinary use of proxies, those attempting to take over the management of a corporation sometimes solicit proxies from shareholders to gather needed votes. Once that solicitation begins, management intensifies its proxy solicitation efforts, and a proxy contest develops.

Exchange Act Section 14 and the Proxy Rules

At the heart of the Exchange Act's scheme for the regulation of proxy solicitations is section 14(a):

> It shall be unlawful for any person, by the use of the mails or by any means or instrumentality of interstate commerce or of any facility of a national securities exchange or otherwise, in contravention of such rules and regulations as the Commission may prescribe as necessary or appropriate in the public interest or for the protection of investors, to solicit or to permit the use of his name to solicit any proxy or consent or authorization in respect of any security (other than an exempted security) registered pursuant to section 12 of this title.

Although the drafters used essentially the standard formula for invoking the jurisdictional means requirement, there is in fact no such requirement in section 14(a). The addition of the words "or otherwise" in the jurisdictional means clause makes the entire clause surplus. Section 14(a) is a classic administrative law provision. It embodies no substantive regulation but simply gives the Commission the power to pass rules. The section then provides that the rules have the force of law.

Section 14(b) makes it unlawful for securities firms, banks, and others exercising fiduciary powers, to violate the Commission's proxy rules with respect to registered and certain other securities that are "carried for the account of a customer"Cthat is, securities that are beneficially owned by a customer but that are owned of record by the securities firm, bank, or someone else. Pursuant to rules 14a–13, 14b–1, and 14b–2, the Commission has established a system under which proxy and related materials are sent to beneficial owners so that they can decide what action should be taken.

Section 14(c) is a gap-closing measure. The proxy statement required by the Commission under authority of section 14(a) fills a niche in the Commission's overall scheme of disclosure. Not all companies under the Commission's jurisdiction need to solicit proxies, however. In some cases, one or a few insiders own sufficient securities to constitute a quorum. To prevent the void in disclosure that would exist if such companies could avoid sending security holders the information mandated by section 14(a) and its rules, section 14(c) requires that substantially equivalent information be filed with the Commission and sent to security holders any time management does not solicit proxies, consents, or authorizations in connection with a meeting.

How the Proxy System Works

Section 14(c) is not the only gap-filling measure in the proxy system. Actually, the entire statutory scheme serves that purpose. The thrust of the proxy system is the mandate of full disclosure in connection with shareholders' meetings, and such meetings are the primary concern of state corporation law. The proxy system's relation to the buying or selling of securities, which is a central concern of the Exchange Act, is indirect. In a more perfect world, proxy regulation would be handled in state corporation statutes.

State law is generally silent on the subject of disclosure in proxy solicitations. Typically, the only regulation of such disclosure is provided by the availability, in very limited circumstances, of actions for common-law fraud or breach of fiduciary duty. Although those actions provide some protection against false disclosures, they are of less help to a shareholder whose proxy is solicited on the basis of little or no disclosure.

To give effect to section 14(a), the Commission adopted regulation 14A. The rules that constitute that regulation provide detailed instructions for the preparation, filing, and provision to security holders of proxy materials. The formal disclosure document that must be filed and given to security holders is called a proxy statement. Rule 14a–101 details the information that must be included in that statement. The rule is voluminous and has much in common with Securities Act and Exchange Act registration statement forms.

Under rule 14a–6, preliminary copies of the proxy statement and form of proxy may or may not have to be filed with the Commission at least ten days before they are used, depending on what matters are to be acted upon at the meeting. No such filings are required, for example, in the case of proxy materials for the most mundane annual meetings. In any case, however, definitive copies of each of those documents must be filed with the Commission not later than the date they are first used. Besides also providing details of filing requirements in specialized situations, rule 14a–6 deals with filing fees.

Proxy statements (and information statements required by section 14(c)) are not the only communications governed by the proxy rules. The proxy form itself is covered, as is, with some exceptions, any "other communication to security holders under circumstances reasonably calculated to result in the procurement, withholding or revocation of a proxy." The scope of that last provision is very broad.

So as to allow shareholders to discuss corporate matters among themselves, and make public statements about those matters, without becoming subject to the proxy rules, the Commission, in rule 14a–1, has excluded from the definition of solicitation, in most circumstances, public communications by shareholders as to how they intend to vote and their reasons for their decision. In rule 14a–2, the Commission also has exempted from the proxy rules (except the rule prohibiting false or misleading statements) activities that would constitute solicitations, so long as the shareholders or other people involved (1) are not affiliated with management, (2) do not have an individual interest in the proposal to which the solicitation relates, and (3) do not seek proxy authority or provide to anyone proxy or other forms, such as consents, relating to voting. Another useful exemption permits non-management solicitation of up to ten persons.

The Commission also has adopted rule 14a–2(b)(6), further expanding the ability of shareholders to communicate without being characterized as engaging in proxy solicitation. They may participate in electronic shareholder forums, provided that such participation occurs more than 60 days prior to the date announced for an annual or special meeting of the shareholders of the relevant company. (Where an announcement is made less than 60 days before a meeting, the exemption will pertain for only two days after the announcement.) A communicating party must not solicit proxy authority while relying on the exemption, but may later engage in a solicitation complying with regulation 14A. Importantly, although the focus of the expansion was the facilitation of intra-shareholder communication, management also may participate.

Although everyone who seeks proxy authority is subject to the proxy rules, the rules are different for solicitations conducted by management than for other solicitations. The greatest difference is that proxy statements sent by management in connection with a typical annual meeting must be accompanied or preceded by an annual report that meets detailed requirements (or specified financial statements, in the case of certain small business issuers). The annual report, together with the proxy statement, provides the security holders with basic information concerning the issuer and its recent financial history, along with specific information on matters to be voted on at the annual meeting. One of the most important matters at the annual meeting is the election of directors, and a substantial portion of the proxy statement consists of information concerning management's candidates for election to the board. The proxy statement also contains extensive disclosures regarding management compensation. The motivation for requiring that disclosure is to discourage executives from paying themselves too handsomely.

The Dodd-Frank Act of 2010 added new section 14A to the Exchange Act, providing that the proxy statements of companies registered under the Act must include a resolution providing for an advisory vote by shareholders on the executive compensation of certain named executive officers. This vote generally is referred to as "say on pay." A separate resolution must address the frequency with which say on pay must occur, with the permissible variation between one and three years (this is known as "say on frequency"). A separate advisory resolution (known as "say on parachutes") is called for in the event special compensation—so-called "golden parachute" compensation—is to be granted in connection with a merger or similar transaction and has not already been included in a say on pay vote. The JOBS Act of 2012, however, provides that emerging growth companies (described in Chapter 4) need not comply with these requirements, and also limits the disclosures those companies must make with respect to executive compensation.

Dodd-Frank made other notable changes related to executive compensation and/or proxy regulation. First, stock exchanges must mandate that listed companies have compensation committees the members of which meet certain independence standards. Second, an issuer's proxy statement must disclose the reasons that the company has selected one person to serve as both Chairman of the Board and Chief Executive Officer (or, if it has chosen to have different individuals serve in those positions, to justify that choice). Third, and very importantly, brokers now are prohibited from using discretionary authority to vote proxies with respect to executive compensation, the election of directors, or other matters designated by the Commission. The Commission has designated say-on-pay, say-on-frequency, and say-on-parachutes as three of those matters.

Proxy filings are subject to the requirements of the Commission's Electronic Data Gathering, Analysis and Retrieval System, known as EDGAR, which mandates the electronic filings of proxy statements and most other material filed with the Commission.

Proposals of Security Holders

A security holder may solicit proxies from fellow security holders. If a security holder does so, compliance with the general regulatory scheme is required. The cost of compliance, however, could be prohibitive. In light of that, the Commission adopted rule 14a–8, which requires management to include in its proxy statement proposals made by security holders, along with supporting statements (up to 500 words, including the proposal itself), when certain conditions are met. Those conditions cover such things as timeliness, amount of securities held, and, most important, the subject of the proposal. An issuer may refuse to include a proposal on a number of grounds. Some of those grounds are that the proposal: (1) under the laws of the registrant's state of incorporation is not a proper subject for action by security holders, (2) deals with a matter relating to the conduct of the ordinary business operations of the registrant, or (3) relates to an election to office. When a proxy statement includes a proposal of a security holder, the proxy form must provide security holders with a mechanism for telling the proxy holder how to vote on the proposal. If management wishes to exclude a security holder's proposal, it must make a filing with the Commission in which, among other things, it states its reasons. As a practical matter, these filings take the form of no-action letter requests. As a result, much "law" on rule 14a–8 can be found in the responses of the Commission's staff to those requests and in staff legal bulletins 14, 14A, and 14B, which relate to proposals of security holders. In the last of these bulletins, the Commission made it harder than it had been for companies to exclude security holders' proposals from their proxy statements.

It is fair to say that the Commission has not been entirely consistent in its interpretation of some of the ground for excluding shareholder proposals. These notably include the meaning of "matter relating to the conduct of ordinary business operations" and "related to an election to office." With respect to the latter, the Dodd-Frank Act empowered the Commission to adopt rules allowing certain shareholders (basically, groups that have held three percent of voting power for at least three years) to include director nominees in the company's proxy materials. What the Commission in fact has done is amend rule 14a–8 to limit the previous broad exclusion for proposals relating to elections to office. As amended, the rule now provides that a proposal can be excluded if it:

(1) Would disqualify a nominee who is standing for election;

(2) Would remove a director from office before his or her term expired;

(3) Questions the competence, business judgment, or character of one or more nominees or directors;

(4) Seeks to include a specific individual in the company's proxy materials for election to the board of directors; or

(5) Otherwise could affect the outcome of the upcoming election of directors.

False or Misleading Statements

Most litigation in the proxy area has involved rule 14a–9(a), which states regulation 14A's antifraud prohibitions:

> No solicitation subject to this regulation shall be made by means of any proxy statement, form of proxy, notice of meeting or other communication, written or oral, containing any statement which, at the time and in the light of the circumstances under which it is made, is false or misleading with respect to any material fact, or which omits to state any material fact necessary in order to make the statements therein not false or misleading or necessary to correct any statement in any earlier communication with respect to the solicitation of a proxy for the same meeting or subject matter which has become false or misleading.

In 1964 the Supreme Court held, using a free-wheeling approach from which it has retreated, that an implied private right of action exists for violations of rule 14a–9.[1] Since that time, virtually all of the interesting cases involving the rule have been brought by private plaintiffs. A discussion of some of those cases as they relate to various elements in a private antifraud action follows.

Materiality

Under rule 14a–9, and all other antifraud rules, a misstatement or omission must be material before it gives rise to a cause of action. The current standard of materiality, used in all securities law contexts, was set forth by the Supreme Court in a

---

[1] *J.I. Case Co. v. Borak*, 377 U.S. 426 (1964).

rule 14a–9 case, *TSC Industries, Inc. v. Northway, Inc.*: "An omitted fact is material if there is a substantial likelihood that a reasonable shareholder would consider it important in deciding how to vote."[2] Elaborating on the standard, the Court indicated that the standard contemplates a showing of a substantial likelihood that, under all the circumstances, the omitted fact would have assumed actual significance in the deliberations of the reasonable shareholder. Understanding the substantial-likelihood standard itself is relatively easy. It is sometimes difficult, however, to predict what misstatement or omission a court will determine fits under the standard.

The "bespeaks caution" doctrine needs to be considered when deciding whether a particular misstatement or omission is material. Under that doctrine, a misstatement or omission can be rendered immaterial if it appears in the context of a document that contains sufficient cautionary language that the document "bespeaks caution." Also, forward-looking statements in proxy materials are covered by the general safe harbor provisions contained in Exchange Act section 21E, so long as the requirements of that section are met, and subject to specified exclusions.

Causation

The Supreme Court has declared that causation is a required element in private right of action cases under rule 14a–9. The interesting question is how to prove causation. The seminal case in the area is *Mills v. Electric Auto–Lite Co.*,[3] which involved a merger that required a two-thirds vote of shareholders. Since management of the defendant corporation controlled approximately 54 percent of the stock, it needed to gain the votes of less than another 13 percent of the shareholders. After management obtained the votes and effected the merger, shareholders complained that management's proxy statement had been defective. The district court and the court of appeals agreed, leaving as the main question whether the defects had caused the submission of sufficient proxies for the merger to be approved.

Both the court of appeals and the Supreme Court determined that "[r]eliance by thousands of individuals, as here, can scarcely be inquired into." Taking that principle as a starting point, each court devised an alternative method of approaching the question of causation. The Supreme Court's method came down to this:

> Where there has been a finding of materiality, a shareholder has made a sufficient showing of causal relationship between

---

[2] 426 U.S. 438, 449 (1976).

[3] 396 U.S. 375 (1970).

the violation and the injury for which he seeks redress if, as here, he proves that the proxy solicitation itself, rather than the particular defect in the solicitation materials, was an essential link in the accomplishment of the transaction.

The Court implied that, for practical reasons, it substituted that approach for direct proof on the question of how shareholders would have voted if the proxy materials had not been defective.

Actually, the reliance of shareholders in *Mills* could have been examined with fair precision by having a research firm survey a random sample of shareholders. There is no doubt about what such a survey would have shown: A majority of noninstitutional shareholders voted for the merger without reading the proxy statement. Thus, the merger would have gone through virtually regardless of what the statement had said. That should make no difference. As a discussion in Chapter 2 of the disclosure policy behind the securities acts indicates, the primary purpose of disclosures required in proxy statements is not to inform investors. The statements should be viewed mainly as a means of forcing proxy solicitors to structure transactions so that the details of the transactions can stand the spotlight of disclosure, even when the spotlight is lit effectively only for the use of plaintiffs' lawyers after the completion of a transaction.

Mills requires a decision by a court on whether a particular proxy solicitation is an essential link in the accomplishment of the particular transaction. The opinion in *Cole v. Schenley Industries, Inc.*[4] is an indication of how far a circuit court has been willing to go to find such a link. In that case, Glen Alden Corp., which held approximately 84 percent of the voting stock in Schenley Industries, Inc., decided to merge Schenley into a subsidiary of Glen Alden. For reasons that are not clear, the decision was made to solicit proxies from the minority shareholders, even though Glen Alden had enough votes to put the merger through. The Second Circuit determined that the minority shareholders had four options at that point: "(1) accept Glen Alden's offer, (2) seek appraisal rights under Delaware law, (3) threaten to seek appraisal rights in an attempt to force Glen Alden to improve its offer, and (4) seek to enjoin the merger." The court further reasoned that, because of the cash outlay that would have been required, the merger might not have been consummated had enough shareholders demanded appraisal rights. It concluded that in view of the options open to shareholders, "the proxy solicitation was an essential part of the merger."

It is interesting to note that in *Cole*, and like situations, each shareholder would have had those options, at least as a technical

---

[4]   563 F.2d 35 (2d Cir.1977).

matter, regardless of whether management solicited proxies. If providing information to shareholders by means of the proxy statement makes the proxy solicitation an "essential link in the accomplishment of the transaction," a court should find that providing an information statement, as required by section 14(c) in cases in which management does not solicit proxies, also creates such a link. Since at least an information statement in connection with a shareholders' meeting is always required of companies subject to the proxy rules, under that reasoning the rule 14a–9 causation requirement would be, as a practical matter, in many cases virtually empty of substance.

When the Supreme Court got its post-*Mills* chance to speak on the issue of what it takes to form an "essential link" in the accomplishment of a transaction, it showed an inclination not to be expansive. The case was *Virginia Bankshares, Inc. v. Sandberg,*[5] which the Court decided in 1991. In that case, the votes of minority shareholders were not needed to put through a merger, because they owned only 15 percent of a corporation's stock. Nevertheless, the corporation solicited their proxies, and a dissenting minority shareholder later sued under rule 14a–9, arguing that the proxy solicitation was an essential link in the accomplishment of the merger. Two theories were involved. The first theory was that the corporations involved in the merger would not have gone through with it save for the approval of the minority shareholders, because of a desire to avoid bad shareholder or public relations. The second theory was that minority shareholder approval was sought so as to protect the merger from voidability on conflict-of-interest grounds. Adopting either of these theories would, the Court said, expand the rule 14a–9 private right of action beyond the ambit of *Mills*, and the Court announced its unwillingness to do that after reviewing legislative history and prior cases on implied private rights of action. Because of the particular state laws applicable to the merger, however, the case did not present minority shareholders with the same kinds of possible remedies as exist in a case such as *Cole*. Therefore, the Court left open the question of whether shareholders have a rule 14a–9 cause of action in a case where failure to disclose material information has caused them to lose an opportunity to seek a state remedy that would have been open to them.

In addition to the general form of causation referred to above, which is called transaction causation, courts began requiring loss causation in cases under rule 14a–9. In 1995, Congress codified the loss causation requirement in Exchange Act section 21D(b)(4),

---

[5] 501 U.S. 1083 (1991).

which provides: "In any private action arising under [the Exchange Act], the plaintiff shall have the burden of proving that the act or omission of the defendant alleged to violate [the Act] caused the loss for which the plaintiff seeks to recover damages."

Degree of Fault Required

The Supreme Court has never determined the degree of fault required to support a finding of liability under rule 14a–9. Courts of appeals have gone both ways on the question, with the choice being between negligence and scienter. Negligence is the choice of the Second Circuit. In reaching that conclusion, in *Gerstle v. Gamble–Skogmo, Inc.*,[6] the court discussed why scienter is required in a rule 10b–5 action (because of language in section 10(b) indicating a congressional intent to limit the scope of the section and its rules to actions involving fraud or deception) and then differentiated the situation under rule 14a–9. "In contrast," said the court, "the scope of the rulemaking authority granted under section 14(a) is broad, extending to all proxy regulation 'necessary or appropriate in the public interest or for the protection of investors' and not limited by any words connoting fraud or deception."

Several years after *Gerstle*, the Sixth Circuit examined the issue of whether to require scienter or only negligence in a case in which an accounting firm was sued for defects in a client's proxy statement.[7] The court determined that scienter was required to support such a claim and based its conclusion on two grounds. First, it differentiated between the accountants and their clients who issue proxy statements, making the case for differing treatment because accountants do not benefit from the proxy vote and are not in privity with the shareholders. Second, it read the legislative history of section 14(a) as pointing to the requirement of scienter for such outsiders as accountants. Interestingly, the Sixth Circuit's analysis of that history supports the imposition of a scienter requirement in all rule 14a–9 cases.

Other Liability Issues

Exchange Act section 20 provides that controlling persons are jointly and severally liable for any violation of the Exchange Act or its rules committed by the company or other person they control, "unless the controlling person acted in good faith and did not directly or indirectly induce the act or acts constituting the violation or cause of action." This section also prohibits various other actions, including hindering, delaying, or obstructing an Exchange Act filing, without just cause, by a director, officer, or security owner of

---

[6] 478 F.2d 1281 (2d Cir.1973).

[7] *Adams v. Standard Knitting Mills, Inc.*, 623 F.2d 422 (6th Cir.1980).

the filer. Section 20 also covers the Commission's authority to bring aiding-and-abetting liability actions for Exchange Act violations. Aiding-and-abetting liability, and certain other liability relevant here, are discussed in Chapter 12, which relates to securities fraud and related issues under rule 10b–5 and under the Sarbanes–Oxley Act.

In 1995 Congress added section 21D to the Exchange Act. Subsection (e) relates to a limitation on damages and subsection (f) to proportionate liability. The limitation on damages applies in private actions where the plaintiff seeks to establish damages by reference to the market price of a security. Basically, section 21D(e) provides that such damages cannot exceed the difference between the plaintiff's purchase or sale price and the mean trading price (as defined) "during the 90-day period beginning on the date on which the information correcting the misstatement or omission that is the basis for the action is disseminated to the market."

The proportionate liability provision in section 21D(f) is complex. Some of its basic aspects are that in private actions under the Exchange Act, (i) a defendant generally is liable solely for the portion of a judgment that corresponds to the percentage of responsibility of that defendant, as determined as provided in section 21D; (ii) a defendant is liable for damages jointly and severally only when the trier of fact specifically determines that the defendant knowingly committed a violation of the securities laws; and (iii) a defendant has a right of contribution, based on proportionate liability.

Along with the other 1995 amendments, Congress added section 21E to the Exchange Act. This section provides, to Exchange Act reporting companies and some other persons, a safe harbor for certain forward-looking statements that are accompanied by cautionary statements meeting the section's requirements.

Chapter 11

TENDER OFFERS

In a tender offer, a company that wishes to acquire another company goes to the target company's shareholders, for example by advertisements in the *Wall Street Journal*, and asks the shareholders to tender the shares they own of the target in exchange for some consideration, typically cash or stock in the acquiring company.

From the time tender offers first became a popular tool for corporate takeovers in the 1960s, they have been enmeshed in controversy. Some people view them in Darwinian terms as helpful weapons in an economic struggle for the survival of the fittest. Those who hold that view see better managed corporations wresting control of other corporations from less competent managers, to the benefit of shareholders and consumers. Others see tender offers mainly as wasteful diversions of capital, credit, and management energy-diversions away from the efficient production of goods and services and toward the ego satisfaction of a few rapacious men.

The controversy over the societal value of tender offers is mirrored by a controversy over the proper regulatory approach to take toward them. Tender offers in which the acquiring company offers its securities in exchange for shares in the target (often called "stock tender offers") always have been subject to the registration requirements of the Securities Act. Prior to 1968, however, tender offers in which the target's shareholders were offered cash (generally called "cash tender offers") were unregulated. That changed in 1968 when Congress passed the Williams Act, which amended the Exchange Act by the addition of three types of provisions:

1. Those requiring various disclosures;

2. Those mandating certain provisions that must be a part of all tender offers; and

3. One prohibiting various kinds of fraudulent conduct in connection with tender offers.

Not long after the passage of the Williams Act, the states began to involve themselves in the regulation of tender offers. Most states passed legislation to that end. Typically, that legislation has been designed to discourage tender offers.

155

Williams Act

The Williams Act added to the Exchange Act sections 13(d), 13(e), 14(d), 14(e), and 14(f). Section 13(d) is aimed at tender offers only indirectly. It requires a person who owns beneficially more than 5 percent of a class of equity security registered under the Exchange Act to provide certain information to the issuer, to the Commission, and to each exchange on which the security is traded, within ten days after the acquisition of securities that triggers the reporting requirement. Exchange Act regulation 13D–G details the disclosure requirements. The resulting disclosure document, schedule 13D, is designed to give management of the issuer information concerning potential tender offerors. That information includes the number of shares beneficially owned by the reporting person, the source of funds used to purchase the shares, and, if the purpose of the purchase of shares is to acquire control of the issuer, any plans of the reporting person to liquidate the issuer, to sell its assets, to engage it in a merger, or to effect any other major change in its structure. Under section 13(d), amendments to that schedule must be filed upon the occurrence of material changes in the disclosed information. (In specified circumstances, shareholders are allowed to file a schedule 13G, the requirements of which are less than those of schedule 13D.) The other Williams Act provision in section 13 is section 13(e). It gives the Commission the power to regulate repurchases by issuers of their own equity securities. The Commission has done this by extensive rulemaking, including the requirement to file, in specified circumstances, schedule 13E–3 and schedule TO, which require substantially more disclosure than schedule 13D.

The heart of the Williams Act is section 14(d). Under that provision, it is unlawful to make a tender offer for an Exchange Act-registered equity security if success in the offer would result in beneficial ownership of more than 5 percent of the class, unless certain filings are made. The filings consist of disclosures reminiscent of those required in a schedule 13D filed under section 13(d), plus any documents used to solicit or advertise for tenders. The main disclosure document must be filed with the Commission not later than the time the tender offer is announced, and all other documents must be filed by the time they are first used. Copies of all filings must be sent to the issuer not later than the time they are first published or sent or given to shareholders.

Section 14(d) also contains substantive regulation on three points. First, the section provides that securities deposited in response to a tender offer may be withdrawn within seven days after the date of the original tender offer, and after sixty days have elapsed following that date. By rule 14d–7, the Commission has extended the withdrawal right to cover the entire period of the tender offer. Second, section 14(d) says that when a tender offer is for less than all the securities of a class, a tender offeror must purchase tendered securities pro rata, according to the number of securities tendered by each security holder during the first ten days the offer is open. By rule 14d–8, the Commission has extended the pro rata purchase requirement to cover securities tendered at any time during the period of the tender offer. Third, when a tender offeror increases the tender offer price after some holders have tendered, section 14(d) provides that all tendering security holders must be paid the higher price.

The Williams Act's antifraud provision is section 14(e). It provides:

> It shall be unlawful for any person to make any untrue statement of a material fact or omit to state any material fact necessary in order to make the statements made, in the light of the circumstances under which they are made, not misleading, or to engage in any fraudulent, deceptive, or manipulative acts or practices, in connection with any tender offer or request or invitation for tenders, or any solicitation of security holders in opposition to or in favor of any such offer, request, or invitation.

Unlike the other Williams Act provisions, section 14(e) relates not only to tender offers for specified types of securities, but to tender offers for any kind of security. . . . Notice, too, that section 14(e) also covers so-called "mini-tender offers," which are tender offers for not more than five percent of a class of security that, if they were for a higher percentage, would be covered by the other provisions of the Williams Act.

Section 14(f) is a specialized provision that calls for certain disclosures to the Commission and to security holders when a majority of a corporation's directorships are to be filled, otherwise than at a meeting of security holders, following an acquisition of securities that is subject to the requirements of section 13(d) or 14(d). The usual trigger of that provision is the filling of vacant directorships by sitting directors, which generally is allowed under state corporation law.

What Is a Tender Offer

Congress used the term "tender offer" in the Williams Act without definition. The Commission has the power to provide a definition by rule, but has chosen not to do so, presumably because it does not want to lose the flexibility provided by the statute. In the years since the passage of the Williams Act, however, the Commission and the courts have worked toward a definition. That effort has reached its most refined form in the case of *Wellman v. Dickinson*,[1] in which the court accepted eight factors, suggested by the Commission, as characteristic of a tender offer:

> (1) active and widespread solicitation of public shareholders for the shares of an issuer; (2) solicitation made for a substantial percentage of the issuer's stock; (3) offer to purchase made at a premium over the prevailing market price; (4) terms of the offer are firm rather than negotiable; (5) offer contingent on the tender of a fixed number of shares, often subject to a fixed maximum number to be purchased; (6) offer open only for a limited period of time; (7) offeree subjected to pressure to sell his stock; and (8) public announcements of a purchasing program concerning the target company precede or accompany rapid accumulation of large amounts of the target company's securities.

The *Wellman* articulation of factors has been accepted by other courts, including the Ninth Circuit in *SEC v. Carter Hawley Hale Stores, Inc.*[2] In that case, the court made it clear that all eight of the Wellman factors do not have to be present in a particular situation before it is recognized as a tender offer. "[R]ather, they provide some guidance as to the traditional indicia of a tender offer."

In *Hanson Trust PLC v. SCM Corp.*,[3] the Second Circuit recognized the *Wellman* factors as relevant for the purposes of determining whether a particular solicitation amounts to a tender offer, but rejected as unwise and unnecessary the notion that they should be made a "litmus test." Rather, the court said:

> [T]he question of whether a solicitation constitutes a "tender offer" within the meaning of § 14(d) turns on whether, viewing the transaction in the light of the totality of circumstances, there appears to be a likelihood that unless the pre-acquisition filing strictures of that statute are followed there will be a substantial risk that solicitees will lack information needed to make a carefully considered appraisal of the proposal put before them.

Still other courts have used another well-known test that grew out of a district court opinion in *S–G Securities, Inc. v. Fuqua Investment Co.*[4] That test is much simpler than the test in *Wellman*, but it is limited in that it only relates to specialized situations that do not fit the mold of classic tender offers. That test holds that a tender offer exists, for the purposes of section 14(d), when there is:

---

[1] 475 F.Supp. 783 (S.D.N.Y.1979).

[2] 760 F.2d 945 (9th Cir.1985).

[3] 774 F.2d 47 (2d Cir.1985).

[4] 466 F.Supp. 1114 (D.Mass.1978).

(1) a publicly announced intention by the purchaser to acquire a substantial block of the stock of the target company for purposes of acquiring control thereof, and

(2) a subsequent rapid acquisition by the purchaser of large blocks of stock through open market and privately negotiated purchases.

In *Carter Hawley Hale*, the Ninth Circuit rejected that test on a number of bases. The court indicated that the test is "vague and difficult to apply" and "offers little guidance to the issuer as to when his conduct will come within the ambit of [one Commission rule rather than another]."

It is unclear what test, if any, for determining the existence of a tender offer ultimately will be adopted by the Supreme Court or agreed to by any particular court. What is clear is that, considering the fact that the Commission clearly desires continued flexibility in determining the existence of a tender offer, it is ill-advised to conclude too quickly that a transaction that involves the acquisition of securities is not a tender offer simply because it does not fall within one or the other of the currently existing tests. When the Commission confronts what it considers abuses in that general area, it can be expected to expand the tender offer boundaries in whatever direction suits its purposes.

Issues in Williams Act Litigation

Although a wide range of issues can be raised in litigation under the Williams Act, two have been of the most interest. One involves the question of who may bring suit under the various statutory provisions, particularly sections 13(d) and 14(e). The other relates to what type of conduct is proscribed by section 14(e). Those two issues are discussed below.

Who May Bring Suit?

In the event of a Williams Act violation, the Commission can, under section 21 of the Exchange Act, bring an enforcement action in a district court seeking an injunction or it can, under section 21C, issue a cease-and-desist order on its own. The Justice Department can seek a criminal indictment when it believes willfulness was involved in a breach. As in many other areas of the securities laws, the interesting issue involves whether private individuals may bring suit and, if so, which persons have standing.

Section 13(d)

Under section 13(d), the largest issue, now settled into a clear majority-minority situation, is whether an implied private right of action exists under which an issuer can sue shareholders who have violated the disclosure requirements of the section. In the classic action, a shareholder has acquired a substantial block of the issuer's stock, but has either failed to file the required schedule 13D or has filed one that allegedly is defective. In those cases, the issuer typically seeks an injunction against further violations, in addition to an injunction that either requires the sale of the securities or prohibits the shareholder from voting them.

The best-known section 13(d) case fits that mold. It is *Rondeau v. Mosinee Paper Corp.*,[5] which the Supreme Court decided in 1975. In that case, the Court had to decide whether a district court had correctly refused to issue the requested injunction. Because of the facts in the case (involving a late filing of a schedule 13D due to a lack of familiarity with the securities laws), the Supreme Court upheld the denial. It is important to note, however, that the defendant did not challenge the plaintiff's right to bring the action, and the Court did not question the existence of the right.

In the years following *Rondeau*, a number of courts of appeals have decided (or proceeded on the assumption) that issuers have a private right of action under section 13(d) when they seek injunctive relief. *Indiana National Corp. v. Rich*[6] is one of the most persuasive of those cases, since it contains a reasoned analysis of the issue based on the Supreme Court cases on implied rights of action. Nevertheless, some courts have refused to find that a private right of action exists under section 13(d), at least in certain circumstances including requests for damages.

Section 14(e)

There is some small question, as a technical matter, as to whether a private right of action really exists under section 14(e). There are also the questions of who may bring the action and what remedy may be sought, damages or only an injunction. The leading case, *Piper v. Chris–Craft Industries, Inc.*,[7] touched on each of those questions, but answered only one—may an unsuccessful tender offeror sue the target or a competing offeror for damages?

In answering that question the Supreme Court looked first to the legislative history, which it concluded "shows that the sole purpose of the Williams Act was the protection of investors who are confronted with a tender offer" and which offers "no hint ... that Congress contemplated a private cause of action for damages by one of several contending offerors against a successful bidder or by a

---

[5] 422 U.S. 49 (1975).

[6] 712 F.2d 1180 (7th Cir.1983).

[7] 430 U.S. 1 (1977).

losing contender against the target corporation." Specifically left open in *Piper* was the question of whether the target or its shareholders have an implied right of action under section 14(e) for relief of any kind, and whether a tender offeror may sue under that section for injunctive relief rather than damages.

Piper does provide some help on the question of standing to sue for injunctive relief in that it quotes with approval Judge Friendly's comment in the first section 14(e) case to the effect that "in corporate control contests the stage of preliminary injunctive relief, rather than post-contest lawsuits, 'is the time when relief can best be given.' "[8] A number of courts have examined the question of whether a tender offeror may bring a section 14(e) action for injunctive relief. Each court has decided that the action may be brought. There seems to have been little doubt over the years that target corporations can sue tender offerors when they seek an injunction, and in fact the Second Circuit so held the year after the Williams Act was passed, in *Electronic Specialty Co. v. International Controls Corp.*[9] In addition to holding that target corporations have a right to sue under section 14(e), the Second Circuit determined in *Electronic Specialty* that shareholders of the target also have that right.

In 1985, the Supreme Court decided *Schreiber v. Burlington Northern, Inc.*,[10] a section 14(e) case brought by a target shareholder. The Court took the case to resolve a split in the circuits over whether misrepresentation or nondisclosure is a necessary element in an action under section 14(e). The existence of a private right of action under that section was not an issue in the case, and the Court did not discuss it. Considering its interest in questions relating to implied rights of action, however, it is unlikely the Court would have accepted the case for review if it had substantial doubts regarding the right of target shareholders to sue under section 14(e).

Conduct Proscribed by Section 14(e)

The last Williams Act topic discussed here is the type of conduct proscribed by section 14(e). That section of the Williams Act is phrased in the disjunctive, speaking first about making "any untrue statement of a material fact or the omission to state a material fact ... " and then—separated by the word "or"—speaking about engaging "in any fraudulent, deceptive, or manipulative acts or practices." Prior to *Schreiber*, the Sixth Circuit had found that a defendant could be held liable for conduct that was manipulative even when the conduct did not contain an element of misstatement or

---

[8]　409 F.2d 937, 947 (2d Cir.1969).

[9]　*Id.*

[10]　472 U.S. 1 (1985).

nondisclosure. The Second, Third, and Eighth Circuits, on the other hand, had handed down opinions with the opposite conclusion. In *Schreiber*, the Supreme Court went with the weight of authority and brushed aside the argument that the disjunctive "or" should in fact be read disjunctively. It concluded:

> All three species of misconduct, i.e., "fraudulent, deceptive, or manipulative," listed by Congress are directed at failures to disclose. The use of the term "manipulative" provides emphasis and guidance to those who must determine which types of acts are reached by the statute; it does not suggest a deviation from the section's facial and primary concern with disclosure or congressional concern with disclosure which is the core of the Act.

Schreiber serves as a reminder that words in a statute mean what courts say they mean and nothing more.

One of the more interesting section 14(e) developments was the adoption by the Commission in 1980 of rule 14e–3. That rule generally makes it illegal to purchase or sell, or cause to be purchased or sold, securities that are or are to be the subject of a tender offer (or certain related securities) when a person "is in possession of material information relating to such tender offer which information he knows or has reason to know is nonpublic and which he knows or has reason to know has been acquired" from the tender offeror or the target, or from someone connected with either. The rule also makes it illegal for insiders to tip others with material information about tender offers. Rule 14e–3 serves as an adjunct to rule 10b–5, which is the main Exchange Act weapon against the purchase or sale of securities on the basis of material, nonpublic information. Rule 14e–3 is especially important in this respect because, at least as interpreted to date, it may be violated without the existence of a related violation of a fiduciary or other such duty, as is required in a rule 10b–5 case. In *United States v. O'Hagan*,[11] however, the Supreme Court only upheld the Commission's authority to pass rule 14e–3 with respect to the kind of conduct to which the case related (straightforward insider trading by a lawyer who owed fiduciary obligations to the bidder). The Court specifically declined to state whether the Commission's authority to pass such a rule under section 14(e) is greater than its authority under section 10(b), leaving open the question of whether rule 14e–3 would be held valid in the case of, for example, someone in a public place who innocently overheard a conversation by officers of a prospective bidder.

---

[11] 521 U.S. 642 (1997).

Other Liability Issues

Exchange Act section 20 provides that controlling persons are jointly and severally liable for any violation of the Exchange Act or its rules committed by the company or other person they control, "unless the controlling person acted in good faith and did not directly or indirectly induce the act or acts constituting the violation or cause of action." This section also prohibits various other actions, including hindering, delaying, or obstructing an Exchange Act filing, without just cause, by a director, officer, or security owner of the filer. Section 20 also covers the Commission's authority to bring aiding-and-abetting actions for Exchange Act violations. (The situations with aiding-and-abetting liability, and with certain other liability issues under the Exchange Act, are discussed below in Chapter 12, relating to securities fraud and related issues under rule 10b–5 and under the Sarbanes–Oxley Act of 2002. In that chapter the "bespeaks caution" doctrine is also discussed, and it is equally relevant to tender offer disclosures.)

In 1995 Congress added section 21D to the Exchange Act. Subsection (e) relates to a limitation on damages and subsection (f) to proportionate liability. The limitation on damages applies in private actions where the plaintiff seeks to establish damages by reference to the market price of a security. Basically, section 21D(e) provides that such damages cannot exceed the difference between the plaintiff's purchase or sale price and the mean trading price (as defined) "during the 90-day period beginning on the date on which the information correcting the misstatement or omission that is the basis for the action is disseminated to the market."

The proportionate liability provision in section 21D(f) is complex. Some of its basic aspects are that in private actions under the Exchange Act, (i) a defendant generally is liable solely for the portion of a judgment that corresponds to the percentage of responsibility of that defendant, as provided in section 21D; (ii) a defendant is liable for damages jointly and severally only when the trier of fact specifically determines that the defendant knowingly committed a violation of the securities laws; and (iii) a defendant has a right of contribution, based on proportionate liability.

Also in 1995, Congress provided a loss causation requirement in Exchange Act section 21D(b)(4). This section provides: "In any private action arising under [the Exchange Act], the plaintiff shall have the burden of proving that the act or omission of the defendant alleged to violate [the Act] caused the loss for which the plaintiff seeks to recover damages."

Along with the other 1995 amendments, Congress added section 21E to the Exchange Act. This section provides, to Exchange Act reporting companies and some other persons, a safe harbor for certain forward-looking statements that are accompanied by cautionary statements meeting the section's requirements.

Chapter 12

FRAUD AND RELATED ISSUES UNDER RULE 10b–5, SARBANES–OXLEY, AND THE STOCK ACT

How It All Started and Where It's Gone

The Commission adopted rule 10b–5 in 1942 to close a gap in the antifraud provisions of the securities laws. The Commission's regional administrator in Boston discovered that a company president was inducing the company's shareholders to sell their shares to him at a low price by telling the shareholders the company was doing badly, while in fact the company was doing very well. The regional administrator reported that to the Commission's main office staff. The general antifraud provision then available, Securities Act section 17(a), was of no help because it covers fraud only in the sale of securities, not in their purchase. To solve that problem, the staff drafted rule 10b–5 by putting the numbered subdivisions of Securities Act section 17(a) (which describe various kinds of prohibited conduct) together with language from Exchange Act section 10(b) (which makes it unlawful by jurisdictional means to use, "in connection with the purchase or sale of any security, any manipulative or deceptive device or contrivance" in violation of any rule of the Commission). That day the staff presented the proposal to the Commissioners, who passed it without comment, except for Sumner Pike, who said, "Well, we are against fraud, aren't we?"

Here is the resulting rule:

Rule 10b–5. Employment of Manipulative and Deceptive Devices

It shall be unlawful for any person, directly or indirectly, by the use of any means or instrumentality of interstate commerce, or of the mails or of any facility of any national securities exchange,

(a) To employ any device, scheme, or artifice to defraud,

(b) To make any untrue statement of a material fact or to omit to state a material fact necessary in order to make the statements made, in the light of the circumstances under which they were made, not misleading, or

(c) To engage in any act, practice, or course of business which operates or would operate as a fraud or deceit upon any person, in connection with the purchase or sale of any security.

The first big event in the history of rule 10b–5 was the 1946 decision in *Kardon v. National Gypsum Co.*,[1] in which a district court found that an implied private right of action exists under the rule. From that time until the 1960s, the use of the rule grew slowly. Its use then began to soar, partially as a result of two cases, *In re Cady, Roberts & Co.*,[2] decided by the Commission in 1961, and *SEC v. Texas Gulf Sulphur Co.*,[3] handed down by the Second Circuit in 1968. The increased use of the rule was aided by an expansive interpretation by the courts that continually pushed out its boundaries. That is seen in discussions in this chapter of cases decided between 1968 and 1975. In 1975 and 1976, the Supreme Court issued two opinions that put the brakes on the continued expansion of the rule. Those were *Blue Chip Stamps v. Manor Drug Stores*[4] and *Ernst & Ernst v. Hochfelder*,[5] each of which is discussed below. The rule's history since those cases is characterized by refinements that generally make the rule less useful to private plaintiffs.

Developments since 1975 notwithstanding, rule 10b–5 clearly occupies the preeminent position among the antifraud provisions in the securities laws. The best known use of the rule has been in insider trading cases, typically those in which an officer, director, or other person who has a fiduciary relationship with a corporation buys or sells the company's securities when in the possession of material, nonpublic information. But the rule is also used in at least five other situations:

1. When a corporation issues misleading information to the public, or keeps silent when it has a duty to disclose;

2. When an insider selectively discloses material, nonpublic information to another party, who then trades securities based on the information (generally called "tipping");

3. When a person mismanages a corporation in ways that are connected with the purchase or sale of securities;

---

[1] 69 F.Supp. 512 (E.D.Pa.1946).

[2] *In re Cady, Roberts & Co.*, 40 S.E.C. 907 (1961).

[3] 401 F.2d 833 (2d Cir.1968).

[4] 421 U.S. 723 (1975).

[5] 425 U.S. 185 (1976).

4. When a securities firm or another person manipulates the market for a security traded in the over-the-counter market; and

5. When a securities firm or securities professional engages in certain other forms of conduct connected with the purchase or sale of securities.[6]

All but the last two uses of the rule will be examined in this chapter. The last two uses will be discussed in Chapter 14, which deals with the regulation of the securities business.

Although the preeminence of rule 10b–5 does not seem to have challenged, section 807 of the Sarbanes–Oxley Act amended title 18 of the United States Code to add a new section 1348, which relates to securities fraud in connection with securities of Exchange Act reporting companies. This provision, along with some other provisions of Sarbanes–Oxley, is discussed below.

General Requirements

The "In Connection With" and "Manipulative or Deceptive" Requirements

To be subject to rule 10b–5, the conduct prohibited by the rule must be "in connection with the purchase or sale of a security." In cases involving public dissemination of false or misleading information "in a medium upon which an investor would presumably rely," courts have tended to find that the "in connection with requirement" may be satisfied by a showing of materiality.[7] Under the "means of dissemination plus materiality" standard, " . . . it is irrelevant that the misrepresentations were not made for the purpose or the object of influencing the investment decision of market participants."

In cases not involving public dissemination, the "in connection with" requirement has presented some real challenges. The leading case in that area is *Superintendent of Insurance of New York v. Bankers Life & Casualty Co.*[8] The facts and allegations in that case are complex. Briefly stated, an insurance company sold the stock of one of its subsidiaries to purchasers who, through a series of transactions, allegedly raised the funds to pay for the stock (1) by causing the corporation they purchased to sell bonds it owned and (2) by misappropriating the proceeds from the sale of the bonds. The board of directors of the corporation allegedly was deceived into

---

[6] Jacobs, *The Role of Securities Exchange Act Rule 10b–5 in the Regulation of Corporate Management*, 59 CORNELL L. REV. 27, 29 (1973).

[7] See, *e.g.*, *Semerenko v. Cendant Corp.*, 223 F.3d 165 (3d Cir.2000).

[8] 404 U.S. 6 (1971).

authorizing the sale of the bonds by a misrepresentation involving what would happen to the cash from the sale.

Later the Superintendent of Insurance, suing on the corporation's behalf, brought a rule 10b–5 action against a number of persons allegedly involved in the scheme by which the bonds were sold and the funds misappropriated. The district court dismissed the complaint, and the court of appeals affirmed. With very little discussion, the Supreme Court reversed and found that the complaint stated a cause of action under the rule. Although the Court noted that "Congress by 10(b) did not seek to regulate transactions which constitute no more than internal corporate mismanagement," the corporation allegedly was injured, the Court said, "as an investor through a deceptive device which deprived it of any compensation for the sale of its [bonds]." Tying the conduct to the "in connection with" requirement, the Court indicated that the corporation allegedly "suffered an injury as a result of deceptive practices touching its sale of securities as an investor."

The looseness of the "touching" formulation, and the almost summary way in which the Supreme Court disposed of the case, seemed to send a clear signal to lower courts that they were to continue to interpret rule 10b–5 expansively. The lower courts responded affirmatively, at least until the Supreme Court sent contrary signals in Blue Chip Stamps in 1975 and Hochfelder in 1976. In 2002, the Supreme Court returned specifically to address the "in connection with" requirement once again. In *SEC v. Zandford*.[9] Zandford, a securities salesperson, convinced an elderly man, in poor health, to open a brokerage account for himself and his disabled daughter. Zandford sold securities he had bought for the account and then stole most of the proceeds. The Commission sued Zandford under rule 10b–5, seeking an injunction and recovery of all stolen funds. The Fourth Circuit reasoned that Zandford's sales of securities were incidental to his scheme to defraud, and therefore not in connection with the sale of securities.

The Supreme Court reversed, saying "[I]t is enough that the scheme to defraud and the sale of securities coincide."[10] The Court distinguished cases in which, after a lawful transaction had been consummated, a broker decided to steal the proceeds and did so, and in which a thief simply invested the proceeds of a routine conversion in the stock market.

Subsequent to *Bankers Life* and prior to *Zandford*, lower courts grappled with application of the "in connection with" requirement in cases basically involving corporate mismanagement. In the current

---

[9] *SEC v. Zandford*, 535 U.S. 813 (2002).

[10] *Id.* at 1903–04.

discussion, post-*Hochfelder* cases are more important. Of those, two "in connection with" cases that reach different conclusions on similar facts are particularly instructive. They are *Ketchum v. Green*[11] and *Brown v. Ivie.*[12]

Each of those cases involved what might be termed internal corporate struggles. In *Ketchum*, the plaintiffs and most of the defendants were shareholders in a close corporation. The two plaintiffs owned approximately 45 percent of the stock and served both as directors and as chairman of the board and president. The defendants controlled almost 48 percent of the stock. At the annual meeting in question, however, the plaintiffs had majority control because they held proxies from other shareholders. At that meeting, following the recommendations of a nominating committee, the shareholders unanimously re-elected the incumbent directors. The re-elected board then met to elect officers. The nominating committee had nominated all the officers for re-election, and the plaintiffs expected to be re-elected. Instead, the board elected others to the offices previously held by the plaintiffs and moved to terminate the plaintiffs as employees of the corporation.

Under a stock retirement agreement to which the plaintiffs were subject, terminated employees were required to resell their stock to the corporation, and they were required to do so at a price one-third as high as it would have been in the event of a sale forced by death, retirement, or disability. Rather than sell their stock to the corporation, the plaintiffs sued under rule 10b–5, among other causes of action that alleged various types of misconduct, and claimed that the defendants had, in the words of the Third Circuit, "fraudulently induced them to vote for their own demise" by concealing their plans to remove the plaintiffs as employees. The major legal issue was the "in connection with" requirement.

The Third Circuit noted that, "[a]lmost without exception, [federal courts] have found compliance with the 'connection' requirement even where fraudulent conduct is implicated only tangentially in a securities transaction" and that "[c]ommentators have suggested that the 'touch' language of the *Bankers Life* opinion could be interpreted to cover practically all disputes relating to intra-corporate management." Nevertheless, the court upheld the district court's dismissal of the case, finding that it "involves little more than allegations pertaining to an internal corporate conflict." As viewed by the Third Circuit, "the essence of the plaintiffs' claim concerned their dismissal as officers," rather than their forced sale of securities. The court also viewed the alleged misconduct as far

---

[11] 557 F.2d 1022 (3d Cir.1977).

[12] 661 F.2d 62 (5th Cir.1981).

removed from the securities sale and only tangentially related to it: "It . . . is evident that the alleged misrepresentations on the part of the defendants were undertaken with the objective of inducing the expulsion of the plaintiffs as officers and employees—not to foster the surrender of their stock."

Brown v. Ivie involved a similar situation. The plaintiff and the two defendants were officers, directors, and equal owners of a corporation. An agreement among them provided that any shareholder no longer employed by the corporation was required to sell his shares to the corporation at book value, but the agreement evidently was unenforceable. The plaintiff alleged that the defendants induced him to sign a new agreement, containing the same terms as the old agreement, by misrepresenting their reasons for wanting a new agreement and by failing to tell him they intended to use the agreement to force him to sell his stock. Seven days after the plaintiff signed the new agreement, the defendants terminated the plaintiff's employment and insisted that he sell his stock to the corporation for book value.

As in *Ketchum*, the plaintiff sued and the district court dismissed. But in *Brown* the Fifth Circuit reversed, distinguishing *Ketchum* by finding that the alleged facts "demonstrate a more direct causal connection between the fraud and the sale of securities than was present in *Ketchum*." The plaintiff's allegation that "the defendants fraudulently induced him to sign the 1979 agreement, thereby guaranteeing that they would obtain his stock at book value," was an important factor. "Thus," said the court, "accepting the fraud as alleged, there is a direct connection between it and the execution of the . . . agreement obligating [the plaintiff] to sell his stock for less than fair value."

There are a number of ways to explain the *Ketchum* and *Brown* cases. First, of course, their facts simply can be distinguished, as was done in *Brown*. On the other hand, the differing outcomes can be viewed as a result of the fact that the plaintiff's lawyers in *Brown* were able to draft their complaint with one eye on their facts and the other on the opinion in *Ketchum*.

Interestingly, some of the more important rule 10b–5 cases that involve the question of corporate mismanagement do not discuss the "in connection with" requirement directly. Since they are so closely related to the cases discussed above, however, it is best to consider them here. The most important such case is *Santa Fe Industries, Inc. v. Green*,[13] which involved the applicability of rule 10b–5 in the context of a freeze-out merger. Minority shareholders who were forced out of a corporation by a merger sued under the rule rather

---

[13] 430 U.S. 462 (1977).

than pursue the appraisal remedy given them under Delaware law. In the suit the plaintiffs sought to have the merger set aside or recover the fair value of their shares. The merger involved was a short-form merger that did not require the vote of the plaintiff-shareholders, and it allegedly was accomplished without notice to them.

The district court dismissed the complaint, but the Second Circuit reversed and found that the plaintiffs' claim of gross undervaluation of their stock was sufficient by itself to state a rule 10b–5 claim and that, even without misrepresentation, the merger constituted a violation of the rule if accomplished without notice to the shareholders and without any corporate purpose. The Supreme Court reversed on the ground that the rule does not prohibit conduct that is neither manipulative nor deceptive and that the merger, if accomplished as alleged, did not involve either manipulation or deception. Citing *Bankers Life*, the Court noted that it "adhere[d] to the position that 'Congress by § 10(b) did not seek to regulate transactions which constitute no more than internal corporate mismanagement.'" Since *Santa Fe*, courts of appeals have found rule 10b–5 claims to exist in merger situations when deception or manipulation has been involved.

Fault Required

The case of *Ernst & Ernst v. Hochfelder*[14] was part of the Supreme Court's mid-1970s assault on rule 10b–5. It involved the question of whether scienter or merely negligence is required to support a verdict for a private rule 10b–5 plaintiff. In *Hochfelder*, the Court found that scienter is required, and did so with an analysis confirming that the old, expansive days of rule 10b–5 were over. It did, however, leave open two questions: (1) is scienter required to be proved in an enforcement action by the Commission? and (2) is recklessness sufficient by itself to constitute scienter? The first of those questions was answered affirmatively by the Supreme Court in the 1980 case of *Aaron v. SEC*.[15] Virtually all courts that have addressed the second question have found that recklessness constitutes scienter.

As part of the Private Securities Litigation Reform Act of 1995, Congress added section 21D to the Exchange Act. Section 21D(b)(2) provides that: "In any private action arising under this Act in which the plaintiff may recover money damages only on proof that the defendant acted with a particular state of mind, the complaint shall, with respect to each act or omission alleged to violate this Act, state

---

[14] 425 U.S. 185 (1976).

[15] 446 U.S. 680 (1980).

with particularity facts giving rise to a strong inference that the defendant acted with the required state of mind." The Supreme Court now has ruled that an inference is strong "only if a reasonable person would deem the inference of scienter cogent and at least as compelling as any opposing inference one could draw from the facts alleged."[16]

Materiality

As indicated in Chapter 10, the substantial likelihood standard of materiality, set forth by the Supreme Court in the rule 14a–9 case of *TSC Industries, Inc. v. Northway, Inc.*,[17] is used in all securities law contexts. So far as rule 10b–5 is concerned, the Supreme Court expressly adopted that standard in *Basic Inc. v. Levinson*.[18] Rephrased to fit rule 10b–5, the standard in simplified form may be put like this: A fact is material if there is a substantial likelihood that a reasonable investor would consider it important in making a decision to buy or sell a security. Explaining this test, the Court in *TSC Industries* and in *Levinson* said that "there must be a substantial likelihood that the disclosure of [an] omitted fact would have been viewed by the reasonable investor as having significantly altered the 'total mix' of information made available."

In *Levinson*, the Court had to consider the application of that standard in the context of incorrect disclosures by an issuer about preliminary merger discussions, and as the Court said there, "[t]he application of this materiality standard [in this context] is not self-evident." The problem, as the Court stated it, is that where a corporate development "is contingent or speculative in nature, it is difficult to ascertain whether the 'reasonable investor' would have considered the [correct] information significant at the time." The Court's solution is a fact-specific inquiry in each situation to determine what a reasonable investor likely would do with a particular bit of information if the information were presented. The Court indicated that when dealing with contingent or speculative information or events, materiality "will depend . . . upon a balancing of both the indicated probability that the event will occur and the anticipated magnitude of the event in light of the totality of the company activity," which balancing has come to be called the probability/magnitude test.

If a misstatement or omission is alleged to exist in a disclosure document, whether in the context of mergers or otherwise, the "bespeaks caution" doctrine needs to be considered in determining

---

[16] *Tellabs, Inc. v. Makor Issues & Rights, Ltd.*, 551 U.S. 308 (2007).

[17] 426 U.S. 438, 449 (1976).

[18] 485 U.S. 224 (1988).

whether the misstatement or omission is material. Under that doctrine, a misstatement or omission can be rendered immaterial as a matter of law if it appears in the context of a document that contains sufficient cautionary language that the document "bespeaks caution."

Picking up on the "bespeaks caution" doctrine, Congress in 1995 added section 21E to the Exchange Act. This section provides, to Exchange Act reporting companies and some other persons, a safe harbor for certain forward-looking statements that are accompanied by cautionary statements meeting the section's requirements.

Additional Requirements for Private Plaintiffs

All litigation brought under rule 10b–5 must address the "in connection with," "manipulative or deceptive," "scienter," and "materiality" requirements described above. Litigation brought by private plaintiffs presents additional issues.

Reliance and Causation

Reliance and causation are complex subjects under rule 10b–5. The best starting point is *Affiliated Ute Citizens v. United States*,[19] decided by the Supreme Court in 1972. In that case, the Court had to struggle with reliance and causation in the context of face-to-face dealings between officers of a bank who engaged in stock transactions with members of the Ute tribe. The major allegations were the failure of the bank officers to disclose material information. The Court found that "[u]nder the circumstances of this case, involving primarily a failure to disclose, positive proof of reliance is not a prerequisite to recovery. All that is necessary is that the facts withheld be material. . . . [The] obligation to disclose and this withholding of a material fact establish the requisite element of causation in fact." (It would have been better if the Court had spoken in terms of the establishment of a rebuttable presumption of reliance, which is how courts have quite properly read the case.) Two years after *Affiliated Ute*, the Second Circuit, in *Shapiro v. Merrill Lynch, Pierce, Fenner & Smith, Inc.*,[20] extended the *Affiliated Ute* presumption to a rule 10b–5 situation that involved anonymous market transactions. In *Stoneridge Investment Partners, LLC v. Scientific-Atlantic, Inc.*, however, the Supreme Court ruled that the reliance requirement cannot be satisfied unless a defendant's deceptive words or acts have been communicated to the public.[21]

---

[19] 406 U.S. 128 (1972).

[20] 495 F.2d 228 (2d Cir.1974).

[21] 552 U.S. 148 (2008).

In cases coming after *Affiliated Ute*, most courts have been careful to distinguish nondisclosure situations, which clearly are covered by the *Affiliated Ute* presumption, from those involving misstatements. In those latter situations, courts typically require a showing of reliance. That requirement is not what it may seem, however, because of what is known as the "fraud on the market theory." That theory was nicely articulated in the Ninth Circuit case of *Blackie v. Barrack*:

> A purchaser on the stock exchanges . . . relies generally on the supposition that the market price is validly set and that no unsuspected manipulation has artificially inflated the price, and thus indirectly on the truth of the representations underlying the stock price—whether he is aware of it or not, the price he pays reflects material misrepresentations.[22]

Under that theory, which was accepted by the Supreme Court in *Basic Inc. v. Levinson*,[23] a presumption of reliance may arise in a misstatement case even in the absence of any proof that a plaintiff relied individually on a defendant's misstatement. As of the time of this writing, however, the Court had agreed to hear a case asking it to reject the "fraud on the market" theory.[24]

The type of causation discussed so far is called transaction causation. In addition to transaction causation, courts began requiring loss causation, which the Seventh Circuit in *Bastian v. Petren Resources Corp.*[25] has described as "the standard rule of tort law that the plaintiff must allege and prove that, but for the defendant's wrongdoing, the plaintiff would not have incurred the harm of which he complains." In 1995, Congress codified the loss causation requirement in Exchange Act section 21D(b)(4).

The "Purchaser–Seller" Requirement

Early in the life of rule 10b–5, the Second Circuit established the requirement that a private plaintiff had to be a purchaser or seller of securities to have standing to sue under the rule. That standing requirement, generally called the *Birnbaum* rule after the case from which it came,[26] universally has been accepted by the other courts of appeals. Although there have been some exceptions to the rule, such as the forced-seller exception, in which a plaintiff who is scheduled to give up his or her shares in a merger is allowed to sue while he or she

---

[22] 524 F.2d 891, 907 (9th Cir.1975).

[23] 485 U.S. 224 (1988).

[24] *Erica P. John Fund, Inc. v. Halliburton Co.*, 718 F.3d 423 (5th Cir. 2013), *cert. granted* __U.S. __ (2013).

[25] 892 F.2d 680, 685 (7th Cir.1990).

[26] *Birnbaum v. Newport Steel Corp.*, 193 F.2d 461 (2d Cir.1952).

still holds the shares, there is no general disagreement concerning the applicability of the requirement.

Over two decades after the initiation of the *Birnbaum* rule, the Supreme Court decided its first "purchaser-seller" requirement case, *Blue Chip Stamps v. Manor Drug Stores*.[27] In that case, offerees in a Securities Act registered offering sued under rule 10b–5 and alleged that the prospectus through which they were offered shares "was materially misleading in its overly pessimistic appraisal of Blue Chip's status and future prospects" and that "Blue Chip intentionally made the prospectus overly pessimistic in order to discourage [purchases]." The alleged facts were of the once-in-a-lifetime variety, and made sense only because Blue Chip had been required under an antitrust consent decree to make the offering of its stock at a favorable price to persons allegedly injured by anticompetitive activities.

The district court dismissed the claim, but the court of appeals found a limited exception to the *Birnbaum* rule and reversed. Justice Rehnquist, writing for the majority of the Supreme Court, did much more than deny the limited exception. In the opinion he discussed at length the evils that would arise in the absence of the "purchaser-seller" requirement, such as the chance for "vexatious litigation" in which questions such as whether a plaintiff would have purchased or sold securities, and the amount the plaintiff would have purchased or sold, are answerable only in a trial on the basis of oral testimony. Much of Justice Rehnquist's displeasure was directed at so-called strike suiters, who bring groundless but troublesome suits to force settlements. What is interesting about that opinion is that it had little to do with the case at hand, since the members of the plaintiff class were all easily identifiable recipients of the benefits of the antitrust consent decree, each of whom was offered only a specified number of shares. Reading between the lines, the opinion appears an essay on the evils of a rule 10b–5 allowed to go too far.

A later Supreme Court case on the "purchaser-seller" requirement is *Wharf (Holdings) Ltd. v. United International Holdings, Inc.* In that case, the Court brushed aside an argument, which was premised on a discussion in *Blue Chip Stamps*, that oral contracts for the sale of securities may not serve as the basis for "purchaser" status if the prospective seller has no intent to perform.

In order to avoid the limitations imposed by the Private Securities Litigation Reform Act of 1995 (portions of which are described elsewhere in this chapter), many lawyers began bringing class action suits in state courts. In response, Congress enacted the Securities Litigation Standards Act of 1998, which added section

---

[27] 421 U.S. 723 (1975).

28(f) to the Exchange Act. This section covers most class actions involving fraud or problems with disclosure relating to the securities of most publicly held companies, and it requires that such actions be brought in federal court under federal law. The Supreme Court has held that the preemptive effect of this legislation extends even to cases sought to be instituted by holders of securities who lack standing under *Blue Chip Stamps* (thus depriving them of any remedy).[28]

Insider Trading: Persons Subject to Trading Constraints

Traditional Insiders, Misappropriators, and Tippees

The question of who is subject to the trading constraints of rule 10b–5—that is who must disclose material non-public information or refrain from trading—has been one of the most interesting aspects of the rule. In the seminal case on the subject, *In re Cady, Roberts & Co.*,[29] the Commission began its analysis with a focus on the fact that the prohibitions of the rule were phrased in terms of their applicability to "any person." Although the Commission then laid an analytical base for determining who has obligations under the rule, that base was virtually lost in the period of the rule's growth. In the most influential case, *SEC v. Texas Gulf Sulphur Co.*, for example, the Second Circuit largely ignored that analytical base and baldly stated the proposition of who is subject to the rule's constraints on trading: "*[A]nyone* in possession of material inside information must either disclose it to the investing public, or [refrain from trading]."[30]

In the years following *Texas Gulf Sulphur*, securities lawyers and courts tended to view the trading constraints of rule 10b–5 as broadly as the Second Circuit did in that case. Then, however, the Supreme Court decided *Chiarella v. United States*.[31] In *Chiarella*, an employee of a financial printing company that printed documents relating to planned tender offers purchased shares in the target companies before the tender offers were announced publicly. He then sold those shares at a profit after the announcements caused the market prices to rise. The employee was indicted, tried, and convicted for violating rule 10b–5, and his conviction was upheld by the Second Circuit.

The district court's instructions were based on the well-accepted, broad conception of who is subject to rule 10b–5's trading constraints:

---

[28] *Merrill Lynch, Pierce, Fenner & Smith, Inc. v. Dabit*, 547 U.S. 71 (2006).

[29] 40 S.E.C. 907 (1961).

[30] 401 F.2d at 848 (emphasis added).

[31] 445 U.S. 222 (1980).

In effect, the trial court instructed the jury that petitioner owed a duty to everyone; to all sellers, indeed, to the market as a whole. The jury simply was told to decide whether petitioner used material, nonpublic information at a time when "he knew other people trading in the securities market did not have access to the same information."

That, the Court said, would not do. In the view of the Supreme Court, a duty to disclose information or abstain from trading does not fall on "anyone," because the mere possession of material inside information does not trigger that duty. Something more is necessary. It followed, therefore, that since the jury instructions were overly broad, the conviction could not stand.

Regrettably, *Chiarella* offered little guidance for understanding who is subject to the trading constraints of rule 10b–5. It did offer some assistance however:

> In its brief to this Court, the United States offers an alternative theory to support petitioner's conviction. It argues that petitioner breached a duty to the acquiring corporation when he acted upon information that he obtained by virtue of his position as an employee of a printer employed by the corporation. The breach of this duty is said to support a conviction under § 10(b) for fraud perpetrated upon both the acquiring corporation and the sellers.

This is called the "misappropriation theory," and as might be expected, lawyers bringing rule 10b–5 cases after *Chiarella* seized on it.

The most important of the circuit court cases considering the theory originated in the Second Circuit. Before the end of 1984, that Circuit had provided an opinion in every possible type of rule 10b–5 case: criminal, enforcement action, and private right of action. In criminal cases and enforcement cases brought by the Commission, the Second Circuit had no trouble finding against the defendant on the misappropriation theory.

It was a different story, however, when the court handled the issue in a private right of action case, *Moss v. Morgan Stanley Inc.*[32] In finding against the plaintiffs, the court's reasoning came down to this: In a private right of action rule 10b–5 suit, as opposed to a suit brought by the government on behalf of all the people, the plaintiff must show that the defendant violated a duty owed to the plaintiff.

It bothered many people that *Moss*, if followed generally, would allow inside traders to escape civil liability in most situations. As a

---

[32] 719 F.2d 5 (2d Cir.1983).

result of that case, Congress in 1988 added section 20A to the Exchange Act. That section undid the *Moss* result by stating explicitly that those who violate the Act's insider-trading rules are liable to anyone who contemporaneously trades any securities of the same class (with the key word "contemporaneously" being undefined).

In *United States v. O'Hagan*,[33] the Supreme Court was confronted with a criminal case involving a traditional example of insider trading under the misappropriation theory—trading by a lawyer who worked for a law firm that represented a bidder in a tender offer. The Court upheld the theory, with the majority not appearing to be troubled in the least by what some have considered strained or overly legalistic arguments about the jurisprudential underpinnings of the theory.

Rule 10b5–2 addresses the circumstances under which there is a duty based on a "relationship of trust and confidence" sufficient to find liability under the misappropriation theory as approved in *O'Hagan*. According to the rule (which is not exclusive), such a duty exists if (1) "a person agrees to maintain information in confidence;" (2) the person communicating the material nonpublic information and the recipient "have a history, pattern, or practice of sharing confidences," resulting in a reasonable expectation of confidentiality; or (3) the person communicating the material nonpublic information and the recipient are spouses, parents, or siblings. Family members may, however, prove that because of the particular facts and circumstances of their relationship, no duty of trust and confidence existed.

The Supreme Court has decided another case that helps complete the discussion of who is subject to the trading constraints of rule 10b–5, *Dirks v. SEC*.[34] A former officer of Equity Funding of America, Ronald Secrist, had approached Raymond Dirks, a New York securities analyst, with extraordinary information. According to Secrist, Equity Funding's assets were substantially overstated as a result of massive corporate fraud. At the urging of Secrist, Dirks investigated and found corroboration for Secrist's story. Dirks asked the *Wall Street Journal* to publish a story on the allegations of fraud, but the paper declined because of the risk of libel. During the two weeks Dirks conducted his investigation, he disclosed to clients and other investors information he had obtained about Equity Funding. Some of those investors sold Equity Funding securities during that period, evidently as a result of Dirks's information.

After the Equity Funding fraud came to light a short time later, the Commission determined that Dirks had aided and abetted

---

[33] 521 U.S. 642 (1997).

[34] 463 U.S. 646 (1983).

violations of rule 10b–5 "by repeating the allegations of fraud to members of the investment community who later sold their Equity Funding stock." Dirks appealed to the Court of Appeals for the District of Columbia Circuit, and that court affirmed.

After reiterating its finding in *Chiarella* that "a duty to disclose under § 10(b) does not arise from the mere possession of nonpublic market information," the Supreme Court indicated that "[s]uch a duty arises rather from the existence of a fiduciary relationship." In a discussion of that duty and what might constitute a breach of it in the context of a tipping case, such as *Dirks*, the Court went on to say:

> In determining whether a tippee is under an obligation to disclose or abstain, it . . . is necessary to determine whether the insider's "tip" constituted a breach of the insider's fiduciary duty [, and the test for that] is whether the insider personally will benefit . . . from his disclosure. . . .

> . . . This requires courts to focus on objective criteria, *i.e.*, whether the insider receives a direct or indirect personal benefit from the disclosure, such as a pecuniary gain or a reputational benefit that will translate into future earnings. . . . The elements of fiduciary duty and exploitation of nonpublic information also exist when an insider makes a gift of confidential information to a trading relative or friend.

Turning to the facts in *Dirks*, the Supreme Court determined that Secrist and the other insiders who gave information to Dirks "were motivated by a desire to expose the fraud." Thus, the insiders breached no fiduciary duty to the Equity Funding shareholders and, "[i]n the absence of a breach of duty to shareholders by the insiders, there was no derivative breach by Dirks" for aiding and abetting.

Two aspects of *Dirks* bear discussion. First, when the Supreme Court described the duty that may subject a person to the trading constraints of rule 10b–5 as a fiduciary duty, it used a term that is largely empty of specific content. As Justice Frankfurter said, "[T]o say that a man is a fiduciary only begins analysis; it gives direction to further inquiry."[35] It would be wrong to expect the question of whether a person is subject to rule 10b–5's trading constraints to turn on whether the person fits a mold typically labeled "fiduciary."

Second, it is to be expected that few traders will escape the constraints of rule 10b–5 because of the requirements articulated in *Dirks*. Only the extraordinary situation will allow a trader to slip past those requirements. In most cases, a tipping insider will derive a personal benefit from the tipping, either a benefit that will translate into future earnings or the more ethereal benefit derived from

---

[35] *SEC v. Chenery Corp.*, 318 U.S. 80, 85–86 (1943).

making a gift of inside information. Further, the Court in *Dirks* outlined an additional means by which traders may be brought within the constraints of the rule:

> Under certain circumstances, such as where corporate information is revealed legitimately to an underwriter, accountant, lawyer, or consultant working for the corporation, these outsiders may become fiduciaries of the shareholders. . . . When such a person breaches his fiduciary relationship, he may be treated more properly as a tipper than a tippee.

Among the many issues not yet addressed by the Supreme Court is the question of whether the insider (or the insider's illicit tippee) is entirely precluded from trading without disclosing material non-public information once he or she possesses it. In *SEC v. Adler*[36] the Eleventh Circuit adopted the "use test" as the standard to be used in insider trading cases brought by the Commission, and in *United States v. Smith*,[37] the Ninth Circuit did so for criminal actions. With this test, it had to be shown that the defendant used inside information in trading, not merely that he or she traded while in possession of the inside information. In response to the "use test," the Commission adopted rule 10b5–1. Under this rule, it is enough to show that a defendant was aware of material inside information when trading. The rule does provide, however, some exceptions that are designed to allow persons to trade, while aware of inside information, in limited circumstances. The most interesting is when a trade is made pursuant to a written plan of trading that meets specified requirements.

Federal Employees

One issue that had percolated for years is whether rule 10b–5 trading constraints properly applied, or should apply, to the securities transactions of government employees in possession of nonpublic information acquired in their official capacities. In 2012, the Stop Trading on Congressional Knowledge ("STOCK") Act became law. The STOCK Act was intended, in part, to make it clear that section 10(b) and rule 10b–5 prohibit members and employees of Congress, as well as employees of the executive and judicial branches of government, from engaging in securities transactions while aware of material nonpublic information derived from federal employment. This was accomplished by an amendment to Section 21A (which otherwise deals with civil penalties for insider trading). The amendment provides that, for purposes of section 10 and rule 10b–5, federal government employees are in a position of trust and

---

[36] 137 F.3d 1325 (11th Cir.1998).

[37] 155 F.3d 1051 (9th Cir.1998).

confidence owed to the government and the citizens of the United States with respect to all information they acquire in their official capacities.

Issuers' Duty to Disclose

So long as a publicly-held company is not trading in its own securities, it is said that there is no general duty, under Rule 10b–5 or otherwise, that requires it to disclose material inside information. In the absence of an explicit mandate in a given situation, or some special circumstance, a company may disclose material information or not, as suits its purposes.

It is useful, however, to consider the explicit disclosure mandates, which now are quite broad. These include, of course, the periodic and other reports discussed in Chapter 9. In this connection it is worth noting that section 13(l) of the Exchange Act, added by the Sarbanes–Oxley Act, imposes a continuous duty to disclose information concerning material changes in the issuer's financial condition or operations, all in accordance with Commission rules. The Commission's response to its mandate under section 13(l) was to increase substantially the items required to be reported on form 8–K and to shorten the time within which that form must be filed. The resulting duty of disclosure obviously is extremely significant.

Another explicit disclosure mandate is found in Regulation FD. Regulation FD imposes a duty upon issuers intentionally to reveal material information only through public disclosure. Selective (nonpublic) disclosures thus are prohibited, although communications with groups not reasonably expected to trade on the information, such as the press, customers, suppliers, and rating agencies, are exempt. If an issuer learns it unintentionally has made a material selective disclosure, it is required to make public disclosure of the same information within 24 hours. "Public" disclosure includes the filing of an Exchange Act Report on Form 8–K, or other means designed to reach the public "on a broad, nonexclusionary basis" (such as a press release). Regulation FD is not intended to give rise to liability to private plaintiffs.

Beyond the requirement to make those mandated disclosures, lawyers representing public companies usually find themselves questioning the need for disclosure in two distinct circumstances. The first is when they believe such disclosure may be necessary in order to update or correct earlier information released by the company, and the second is when management responds to questions put by securities analysts, reporters, major shareholders, or others. In the first circumstance, most securities lawyers would agree that public companies have a duty to correct, and perhaps to update, prior disclosures that are still "alive." Here the rub comes from two directions: From one side comes the issue of whether a reasonable investor can still rely on a prior disclosure, or whether enough time has passed, or sufficient external developments have occurred, so that the old disclosure is no longer material. From another side comes the problem of telling just what kind of prior disclosure requires modification or correction because of a particular new development. There are few sure answers to questions such as those, because most such answers are still in the minds of judges and cannot be learned except by litigating specific facts before them.

Stransky v. Cummins Engine Co., Inc.[38] is nicely instructive on one court's view of the duty to update or correct earlier information. In this case, the Seventh Circuit carefully distinguished between the duty to correct and the duty to update. With respect to information that is incorrect when released, the court said "[t]he company then must correct the prior statement within a reasonable time." (Presumably, however, the court would require the correction only if the information were still "alive," so that the misstatement remained material.) While noting that some believe there is a duty to update, the court rejected that notion, finding that "forward-looking statements can lead to liability only if they were unreasonable in light of the facts known at the time . . . or they were not made in good faith."

The Third Circuit, however, has reached a different conclusion on the duty to update. In *Weiner v. The Quaker Oats Co.*,[39] the court found that, when issuing an annual report, the defendant company had a duty to update prior predictions "if it expected the predictions to change markedly in the ensuing year."

When management decides how to respond to questions put by securities analysts, reporters, major shareholders, or others it also faces a difficult problem. The Commission has written that "[w]henever an issuer . . . responds to an inquiry . . . concerning rumors, unusual market activity, possible corporate developments or any other matter, the statement must be materially accurate and complete."[40] That inarguably is correct, but of little help. Of somewhat more help is the Commission's footnote, found in the same paragraph, indicating that if an issuer wishes to avoid disclosure, it can do so by responding, "No comment." That statement is particularly helpful, in fact, because the Supreme Court cited it with approval in *Basic Inc. v. Levinson*,[41] saying there that such statements generally are "the functional equivalent of silence." If an

---

[38] 51 F.3d 1329 (7th Cir.1995).

[39] 129 F.3d 310 (3d Cir.1997).

[40] *In re Carnation, Exchange Act Release No. 22,214* (July 8, 1985).

[41] 485 U.S. 224 (1988).

issuer chooses that response, however, it must be sure that silence is what it is communicating, lest it find itself in trouble for being incomplete or otherwise misleading. For example, if an issuer always denies rumors that are false but says "No comment" when rumors are at least half true, it will not take long for analysts and the financial press to learn the code.

Damages and Penalties

Considering the abundance of rule 10b–5 cases, it might be expected that damage issues would be completely resolved. They are not. The measure of damages generally applied is the out-of-pocket measure, which is the difference between the price paid or received for securities and their actual value at the time of the purchase or sale.

Where this measure is sought, Section 21D(e) comes into play. This provision applies in any private action brought under the Exchange Act where the plaintiff seeks to establish damages by reference to the market price of a security. Basically, Section 21D(e) provides that such damages cannot exceed the differences between the plaintiff's purchase or sale price and the mean trading price (as defined) "during the 90-day period beginning on the date on which the information correcting the misstatement or omission that is the basis for the action is disseminated to the market." Other measures of damages are sometimes used, however, including (1) rescissionary damages, under which a plaintiff is entitled to a return of the amount paid, reduced by whatever is realized when the security is sold and by any income received on the security, (2) benefit-of-the-bargain damages, and (3) damages measured by the disgorgement approach.

In 1984, Congress amended the Exchange Act to add civil penalties for insider trading. Exchange Act section 21A allows the Commission to seek, and a federal court to impose, such penalties, both on inside traders and on persons who control inside traders. The penalty is in the discretion of the court, but may be as high as three times the profit gained, or loss avoided, as a result of insider trading, except in the case of controlling persons, whose penalties can be as high as $1,425,000 regardless of profit gained or loss avoided (when read along with the Commission's rule of practice 1004, which relates to the adjustment of civil monetary penalties). The toughness of the penalty on controlling persons is mitigated, however, by the fact that, to be subject to a penalty, the Commission must show that the controlling person "knew or recklessly disregarded the fact that [the] controlled person was likely to engage in the . . . violations and failed to take appropriate steps to prevent [the violations]." In order to enhance the Commission's ability to uncover insider trading, section 21A also provides for the payment of bounties, of up to 10 percent of the penalty, to persons who provide information that leads to the imposition of a penalty.

Interestingly, however, when Congress toughened the Exchange Act's civil penalties provision in 1988, it also opted to provide disgorgement as the measure of damages in civil liability cases covered by new Exchange Act section 20A (basically actions by persons who traded in the market contemporaneously, as opposed to actions brought by persons to whom the inside trader owed some pre-existing duty). Congress also softened the impact of section 20A by providing that damages under that section are to be diminished by any amounts required to be disgorged in a civil penalties action brought under section 21A.

Note that sections 21A and 20A are provisions that are specific to insider trading cases. Other penalties that may be invoked in connection with an action under rule 10b–5 are, to put it mildly, complex. First, of course, are the criminal penalties discussed in Chapter 9 (up to $5 million in fines and 20 years in prison for natural persons and up to $25 million in fines for other than natural persons). The following discussion deals with the penalties that the Commission may seek in litigation brought in federal court and the penalties the Commission may impose in its own administrative proceedings.

Section 21(d)(3) grants the Commission authority to seek court-ordered civil penalties under all provisions of the Exchange Act and its rules (other than for acts already subject to the civil penalty provision in section 21A relating to insider trading). Under section 308 of the Sarbanes–Oxley Act, these amounts can be added to a disgorgement fund for the benefit of victims if the Commission also has obtained an order requiring disgorgement. Section 21(d)(5) permits the Commission to seek equitable relief (which includes disgorgement) under any provision of the federal securities laws. Under section 21(d)(2), the courts specifically are given the power to prohibit persons who violate Exchange Act section 10(b) from serving as an officer or director of a company that has securities registered under section 12 of the Exchange Act or that is required under Exchange Act section 15(d) to file Exchange Act reports. Section 21(d)(6) authorizes court-ordered bars against participation in offerings of penny if the defendant's alleged misconduct related to an offering of penny stock.

The Commission has received progressively more significant ability to impose penalties in its own administrative proceedings. Thus, section 21B now gives the Commission the basic power to impose civil penalties. The amount of possible penalty escalates in tiers, depending on the nature of the conduct involved, to a high of

$725,000 for certain acts or omissions by other than natural persons (when read along with Rule of Practice 1004). Section 21C provides the Commission authority to issue cease-and-desist orders when it finds, after notice and an opportunity for a hearing, that someone is violating, has violated, or is about to violate any provision of the Exchange Act or any of its rules. This section also gives the Commission the power to order an accounting and disgorgement in cease-and-desist proceedings and the power in cease-and-desist proceedings to issue officer and director bars, with respect to service with Exchange Act reporting companies, against those who have violated Exchange Act section 10(b) or any of its rules. The Commission may, under section 21(d)(3), seek court-ordered civil penalties for violations of its own cease-and-desist orders.

Under rule 9 of the Commission's rules of informal and other procedures, the Commission may, on a case-by-case basis, reduce the amount of penalty it seeks or assesses against a "small entity" (which includes a "Small Business" as defined by the Commission). Under the rule, the Commission considers a number of issues in making this determination, including the willfulness and egregiousness of the conduct, the violator's history of legal or regulatory violations, and the financial ability of the entity to pay the penalty.

Statute of Limitations

The issue of what statute of limitation applies in the case of a rule 10b–5 implied private right of action was confused for decades. Since the Exchange Act contains no overtly governing provision, courts originally had to borrow from the securities statute in the forum state or from the statute of limitation in that state governing common-law fraud. The length of those periods varies dramatically, from one year to six or more years.

The Supreme Court changed all that in *Lampf, Pleva, Lipkind, Prupis & Petigrow v. Gilbertson*,[42] which it decided in 1991. In that case the Court concluded that, in picking a limitation period for an implied right of action, a court should look first to the statute of origin for a period to borrow, and that a court should borrow from state law only when the statute of origin contains no relevant provision. Looking at the Exchange Act, the Court found that the limitation period specified in section 9(e) should apply to rule 10b–5 actions or, in other words, that suit must be filed "within one year after the discovery of the facts constituting the violation and within three years after such violation." The Court also determined that the doctrine of equitable tolling is inconsistent with the three-year

---

[42] 501 U.S. 350 (1991).

limitation. One critically important aspect of the decision is the fact that the Court applied its decision retroactively.

The story changed again with the passage of the Sarbanes–Oxley Act of 2002. Sarbanes–Oxley section 804 amended 28 U.S.C. § 1658 to provide that, with respect to proceedings commenced on or after July 30, 2002:

> [A] private right of action that involves a claim of fraud, deceit, manipulation, or contrivance in contravention of a regulatory requirement concerning the securities laws . . . may be brought not later than the earlier of:
>
> (1) 2 years after the discovery of the facts constituting the violation; or
>
> (2) 5 years after such violation.

In other words, Congress in Sarbanes–Oxley lengthened the limitation period, replacing a one-year/three-year statute with a two-year/five-year statute. In *Merck & Co. v. Reynolds*, the Supreme Court held that the "two years after discovery" measure begins to run at the earlier of (i) the time the plaintiff actually discovered, or (ii) the time at which a reasonably diligent plaintiff should have discovered, the facts constituting a violation—including facts relating to the defendant's scienter.[43]

The rules, however, appear to be different when the issue has to do with actions brought by the Commission. The Ninth Circuit said in a rule 10b–5 case that the Commission is not bound by any statute of limitations when it brings a civil enforcement action,[44] while the District of Columbia Circuit found that the five-year statute of limitations in 28 U.S.C. § 2462 (covering federal civil penalties, fines, and forfeitures generally) applies to administrative proceedings held by the Commission.[45]

Secondary Liability and Conspiracy

Exchange Act section 20 provides that controlling persons are jointly and severally liable for any violation of the Exchange Act or its rules committed by the company or other person they control, "unless the controlling person acted in good faith and did not directly or indirectly induce the act or acts constituting the violation or cause of action." This section also prohibits various other actions, including hindering, delaying, or obstructing an Exchange Act filing, without just cause, by a director, officer, or security owner of the filer.

---

[43] 559 U.S. 633 (2010).

[44] *SEC v. Rind*, 991 F.2d 1486 (9th Cir.1993).

[45] *Johnson v. SEC*, 87 F.3d 484 (D.C.Cir.1996).

Until the 1993–94 Supreme Court term, there seemed to be no question that one could be charged with aiding and abetting a rule 10b–5 violation, both in private actions and in those brought by the government. There had been a multitude of such cases at all levels of the court system, during half a century. Then in *Central Bank of Denver, N.A. v. First Interstate Bank of Denver, N.A.*, the Supreme Court determined that a private plaintiff cannot maintain an aiding-and-abetting action under Exchange Act section 10(b). Under the Court's reasoning, which was based primarily on its interpretation of congressional intent, it was problematic whether the Commission had authority to bring actions for aiding and abetting violations of section 10(b). The uncertainty was cleared up when Congress in 1995 amended Exchange Act section 20 to provide that the Commission has authority to bring actions for aiding and abetting the violation of any section of the Exchange Act or of any of its rules or regulations.

Although private plaintiffs currently are forced to characterize defendants as primary violators (or controlling persons), their ability to do so successfully is subject to limits. In *Stonebridge Investment Partners, LLC v. Scientific-Atlantic, Inc.*, the Supreme Court held that only if a defendant has engaged in deceptive acts that have been communicated to the plaintiff (or, presumably, if the fraud-on-the-market theory is applicable, the public) may the action proceed.[46] Then, in 2011, the Court in *Janus Capital Group, Inc. v. First Derivative Traders*[47] heavily cited both *Central Bank* and *Stoneridge* in holding that, in the context of a private lawsuit, Rule 10b–5 liability for a misleading statement will attach only to those with "ultimate control" over the statement. The Court indicated that, in the ordinary case, attribution will be critical in determining ultimate control. Participation in drafting and dissemination of misleading statements attributed to others generally will not suffice to sustain a private right of action under Rule 10b–5.

In criminal actions, there has been no question but that aiding-and-abetting liability exists for section 10(b) violations, because a general statute provides for such liability in connection with all federal criminal offenses.

In *Dinsmore v. Squadron, Ellenoff, Plesent, Sheinfeld & Sorkin*, the Second Circuit, reasoning from *Central Bank of Denver*, found that there is no conspiracy cause of action in suits under rule 10b–5. The court pointed out, however, that alleged conspirators can be held liable if the requirements for primary liability are met.

---

[46] 552 U.S. 148 (2008).

[47] 131 S.Ct. 2296.

Contribution

An interesting question, unsolved until 1993, had been whether defendants in an implied private right of action suit under rule 10b–5 have a right to contribution from other defendants who have paid no damages or have paid less than their fair share. In *Musick, Peeler & Garrett v. Employers Insurance of Wausau*,[48] the Supreme Court put the issue to rest: There is a right of contribution in rule 10b–5 suits. Section 21D(f) of the Exchange Act, added in 1995, codifies that holding and provides that contribution is to be on the basis of proportionate liability, as detailed in that section.

Fraud and Related Issues Under the Sarbanes–Oxley Act

The Sarbanes–Oxley Act of 2002 made significant changes in the antifraud provisions of the securities laws, arguably challenging the preeminence of rule 10b–5. To begin with, Sarbanes–Oxley section 807 creates an entirely new securities fraud provision, which appears not in the securities laws but in the criminal code as 18 U.S.C. § 1348. It provides:

> Whoever knowingly executes, or attempts to execute, a scheme or artifice—
>
> (1) to defraud any person in connection with any security of [an Exchange Act reporting company]; or
>
> (2) to obtain, by means of false or fraudulent pretenses, representations, or promises, any money or property in connection with the purchase or sale of any security of [an Exchange Act reporting company];
>
> shall be fined under this title, or imprisoned not more than 25 years, or both.

Whether a private right of action exists under new section 1348 is an interesting question. Here it is important to consider Sarbanes–Oxley section 303, which makes it unlawful, in contravention of Commission rules, for certain persons fraudulently to influence the conduct of audits for the purpose of making financial statements materially misleading. Section 303 specifically indicates that there is no private right of action for violation of this provision. Plaintiffs' lawyers certainly will argue that if Congress had intended there to be no private right of action under section 1348, it would have done likewise with respect to this section. The argument has added strength when section 1348 is analogized to Exchange Act rule 10b–

---

[48] 508 U.S. 286 (1993).

5, under which there has long been found to exist a private right of action.

Several points about section 1348 are unresolved. It is unclear how the word "knowingly" will be interpreted in section 1348, although allowing recklessness to suffice is not unlikely, since recklessness is enough to constitute scienter under rule 10b–5. It also is unclear how broad the reach of section 1348(1) will be, since it refers simply to "a scheme or artifice . . . to defraud any person in connection with any security of [an Exchange Act reporting company]." The big difference here from rule 10b–5 is that the rule covers only fraud in connection with the purchase or sale of a security. This issue harks back to the time when the scope of rule 10b–5 was much in issue. Many courts expressed a broad view of such scope until the Supreme Court decided otherwise. Especially in light of this history, Congress may now be argued to have given the go-ahead to an exceedingly broad interpretation of section 1348(1), since almost any fraud relating to an issuer can be said to be in connection with its securities in some way. Many more issues will be raised, but a final one deserves mention here: whether and to what extent section 1348(2), which echoes rule 10b–5's "purchase or sale" requirement, covers broader conduct than rule 10b–5. The phrasing of the two provisions is very different, and this leads to the argument that Congress intended section 1348(2) to expand upon rule 10b–5.

Sarbanes–Oxley also contained a number of provisions that are outside the scope of this book—for example, those relating to the creation of the Public Company Accounting Oversight Board, analyst conflicts of interest, various matters concerning accountants and auditing, forfeiture of bonuses in certain circumstances, tampering with records or otherwise impeding investigations, the nondischargeability of certain debts in bankruptcy, the protection of whistle-blowers, and increased penalties for mail and wire fraud.

Chapter 13

LIABILITY FOR TRADING PROFITS UNDER SECTION 16(b) AND SARBANES–OXLEY

Section 16(b)

Exchange Act section 16(b) is designed to minimize the unfair use of inside information. Under that section, profits made by insiders from transactions involving equity securities of publicly held companies, when a purchase and a sale are made less than six months apart, must be disgorged and paid over to the issuer.

Before examining section 16(b), it is helpful to discuss section 16(a). That section requires beneficial owners of more than ten percent of any class of equity security (other than an exempted security) that is registered under the Exchange Act, and officers and directors of issuers of such securities, to file reports with the Commission and relevant securities exchanges concerning their holdings of all equity securities of such issuers. Section 16(a) sets the filing periods for initial reports to be filed upon becoming subject to the section (basically, at the same time a company registers an equity security under the Exchange Act or within ten days of becoming a person listed in the section, unless the Commission provides for a shorter period). It also establishes the filing period for reports of changes in ownership—which now stands at within two business days after the change. Section 16(a), however, does give the Commission power to extend the two day reporting requirement when the requirement is not feasible, which the Commission has done to a very limited extent. Rule 16a–3 details the reporting requirements. The rule provides that initial reports of ownership are to be made on the Commission's form 3, changes in ownership are to be reported on form 4, and an annual report is to be made on form 5. These are relatively short, fill-in-the-blanks forms. Rule 16a–3(k) requires issuers that maintain a website to post these forms on their website not later than the end of the next business day after filing.

Section 16(b) provides that:

(1) Any profit;

(2) By any person subject to the reporting requirements of section 16(a);

(3) Realized on any purchase and sale, or sale and purchase;

(4) Within any period of less than six months;

(5) Of any nonexempt equity security of an issuer that has an equity security registered under the Exchange Act, or of any security-based swap agreement involving any such equity security

"shall inure to and be recoverable by the issuer." An exception exists when the security was purchased in good faith in connection with a debt previously contracted. Under section 16(b), an issuer may sue to recover these so-called short-swing profits, or any security holder of the issuer may sue derivatively to recover the profits when, after request, the issuer fails to bring suit within sixty days or when it fails diligently to prosecute a claim once filed.

Many questions concerning section 16 are answered by the Commission's rules, which are extensive and highly detailed. The rules provide exemptions in some specialized situations. Some of the more interesting situations are covered in rules 16a–4, 16b–3, and 16b–6, which relate to so-called derivative securities (for example, options that can be exercised to buy equity securities at a fixed price) and to transactions between an issuer and its officers and directors (as opposed to market transactions). These rules are highly complex and are filled with twists and turns. One important aspect of these situations is that the grant of a derivative security, such as a stock option, is deemed to be a purchase of the underlying equity security, thus triggering (unless there is an applicable exemption) section 16(b) short-swing trading liability if the purchase can be matched with an appropriate sale within less than six months.

Most general questions that arise under section 16(b) can be grouped under one of five topics: (1) persons liable, (2) what constitutes a purchase or sale, (3) timing of purchases and sales, (4) who has standing to sue, and (5) calculation of profits. These topics will be discussed below. Before turning to those topics, it will be helpful briefly to mention one interesting point. Unlike most provisions in the Exchange Act, section 16(b) is not a criminal provision. It does not make short-swing trading illegal. Instead, the section merely provides that the profits from certain trades essentially belong to the issuer.

Persons Liable

On the question of persons subject to section 16(b), the statute speaks in terms of officers, directors, and greater than ten percent beneficial owners. As in so many areas of securities law, however, intricacies are buried beneath the surface.

Titles

One interesting issue relates to titles. For most purposes, of course, a person's status as an officer or director of a corporation depends on whether he or she has been elected an officer or director in accordance with the requirements of state corporation law and the corporation's by-laws. Things are not so simple under section 16(b). Two special definitions create complications:

> Section 3(a)(7). The term "director" means any director of a corporation or any person performing similar functions with respect to any organization, whether incorporated or unincorporated.

> Rule 16a–1(f). The term "officer" shall mean an issuer's president, principal financial officer, principal accounting officer (or, if there is no such accounting officer, the controller), any vice-president of the issuer in charge of a principal business unit, division or function (such as sales, administration, or finance), any other officer who performs a policy-making function, or any other person who performs similar policy-making functions for the issuer. Officers of the issuer's parent(s) or subsidiaries shall be deemed officers of the issuer if they perform such policy-making functions for the issuer. . . .

Deputization

"Deputization" is a legal concept that can be used to bring within the coverage of section 16(b) a person or firm who, although not a director, officer, or greater than ten percent holder, has his, her, or its interest in a corporation represented by a person who sits on the board of directors. Perhaps the most important deputization case was decided by the Second Circuit in 1969. It is *Feder v. Martin Marietta Corp.*,[1] the first court of appeals case to find the existence of deputization. In that case, the president of Martin Marietta served as a director of Sperry Rand Corp. during a period when Martin Marietta was purchasing large amounts of Sperry stock, which it sold shortly after the president resigned his directorship. The Second Circuit put much weight on the fact that the president was ultimately responsible for the operation of the corporation, including approval of all the corporation's investments, i.e., purchases of Sperry stock.

Beneficial Ownership

Under section 16(b), an insider must disgorge "profits realized *by him*" (emphasis added). In the usual transaction, it is no trouble to determine the profits that have accrued to a particular owner.

---

[1] 406 F.2d 260 (2d Cir.1969).

Sometimes, however, that is not the case. Take, for example, when shares are traded by a director's spouse or by an officer for the account of a minor child. Are any resulting profits "by" the insider?

In rule 16a–1(a)(2), the Commission indicated that for such determinations:

> [T]he term "beneficial owner" shall mean any person who, directly or indirectly, through any contract, arrangement, understanding, relationship or otherwise, has or shares a direct or indirect pecuniary interest in the equity securities, subject to the following. . . .

In the rule the Commission then provides that a pecuniary interest means "the opportunity, directly or indirectly, to profit or share in any profit derived from a transaction in the subject securities" and that the term "indirect pecuniary interest" in securities includes, among other possibilities, securities held by immediate family members who share the same home (with the proviso that "the presumption of such beneficial ownership may be rebutted").

Another interesting beneficial ownership issue arises under section 16 when two or more people agree to act together in buying, holding, voting, or selling securities. The question is whether the group is considered the beneficial owner of the relevant securities held by members of the group. Rule 16a–1(a)(1) says that, solely for the purpose of determining who is a section 16 "beneficial owner," that terms means "any person who is deemed a beneficial owner pursuant to section 13(d) of the Act and [its rules, with specialized exceptions]." The most helpful place to turn for further understanding is rule 13d–5(b)(1). It provides that when a group agrees "to act together for the purpose of acquiring, holding, voting, or disposing of equity securities of an issuer," the group is deemed to own beneficially all equity securities of that issuer that are beneficially owned by each member of the group.

The Second Circuit interpreted these rules in *Morales v. Quintel Entertainment, Inc.*[2] The case involved the acquisition of Quintel stock, by the three shareholders of Psychic Reader's Network, under a sales agreement between the two corporations. One of the three shareholders ended up owning less than three percent of Quintel's stock, although the three together owned more than ten percent. Thereafter the shareholder who owned less than three percent made a number of short-swing purchases and sales and was sued in a derivative action to recover profits he made on those trades. The Second Circuit used a straightforward reading of the Commission's

---

[2] 249 F.3d 115 (2d Cir.2001).

rules and remanded for the district court to determine whether the three shareholders had agreed "to act together for the purpose of acquiring, holding, . . . or disposing of" Quintel stock.

What Is a Purchase or Sale

Determining what constitutes a purchase or sale is easy in the usual context, but it is more difficult when unorthodox transactions are involved. In that regard, one case in particular is of the greatest importance. That case is *Kern County Land Co. v. Occidental Petroleum Corp.*,[3] which the Supreme Court decided in 1973. By a tender offer, Occidental Petroleum had acquired a substantial minority position in Kern County Land Co. As a defense against a threatened Occidental takeover, Kern County entered into a merger agreement that called for its merger with a subsidiary of Tenneco, Inc. Under the terms of the agreement, all Kern County shareholders would receive Tenneco preference stock upon the effectiveness of the merger. Occidental then arranged to sell to a Tenneco subsidiary an option to purchase all the Kern County stock that Occidental owned. Kern County submitted the merger agreement to a shareholders' vote, in which Occidental did not participate. Occidental did indicate, however, that if it were voting, it would vote in favor of the merger. The Kern County shareholders approved the merger, and the Tenneco subsidiary exercised its option to purchase Occidental's Kern County stock, cashing Occidental out of the rights it had under the merger agreement. As a result of that string of transactions, Occidental netted profits of almost $20 million.

Kern County promptly sued Occidental under section 16(b), alleging two alternative theories. One theory was that the execution of the option, which occurred within six months of Occidental's purchase of its Kern County stock, effected a sale of all the stock. The other theory was that Occidental sold its Kern County stock at the point when, pursuant to the merger agreement, it became bound to take the Tenneco preference stock in exchange for its shares of Kern County. The Supreme Court found that Occidental was entitled to summary judgment.

The Court brushed aside the argument that the granting of the option was a sale and focused simply on the fact that "an option to sell is not generally regarded as a 'sale.'" In response to the plaintiff's contention that a sale occurred upon the effectiveness of the merger, the Court noted that "[o]nce the merger and exchange were approved, Occidental was left with no real choice with respect to the future of its shares of [Kern County]." In connection with those points, the Court made it clear that a policy reason was behind its ultimate

---

[3] 411 U.S. 582 (1973).

decision that the section 16(b) action should be dismissed. In each case, the reason was that the transactions involved in the case were not ones that had given Occidental any opportunity for speculative abuse.

In most cases, however, courts apply section 16 objectively and refuse to get involved in a subjective analysis of the intent of, or even the real-world opportunity for insider trading by, persons subject to its constraints. Such an inquiry will not occur in cases involving run-of-the-mill, straight forward purchases and sales, but may take place when a case involves transactions that: (1) are unorthodox and (2) are not viewed by a court as involving the real chance of speculative abuse.

An interesting twist in the issue of what constitutes a purchase or sale concerns so-called derivative securities. Not considering the exceptions, derivative securities are defined in rule 16a–1(c) as "any option, warrant, convertible security, stock appreciation right, or similar right with an exercise or conversion privilege at a price related to an equity security, or similar securities with a value derived from the value of an equity security," so long as the exercise price is a fixed price. The twist is that, under rule 16b–6, an increase or decrease in one's position in a derivative security is deemed to be a purchase or sale of the underlying equity security, so that, for example, the receipt of a stock option to buy a company's common stock is likely to be treated as a purchase of the common stock. A corollary is that the exercise or conversion of a derivative security generally is not considered to be a purchase of the underlying security. For the purposes of section 16(b), then, the actual exercise of the usual stock option is a non-event. Expiration of options and pre-determined conversion price adjustments also appear to be non-events.

Timing of Purchases and Sales

Section 16(b) contains the following provision on the issue of timing: "This subsection shall not be construed to cover any transaction where [a ten percent-plus] beneficial owner was not such both at the time of the purchase and sale, or the sale and purchase." In general, that provision is clear enough. But the Supreme Court has decided two cases that deal with subtleties. In one, *Foremost-McKesson, Inc. v. Provident Securities Co.*,[4] the Court faced the question of "whether a person purchasing securities that put his holdings above the ten percent level is a beneficial owner 'at the time of the purchase' so that he must account for profits realized on a sale of those securities within six months." Based largely on its reading of the legislative history, the Court found that the purchase that

---

[4] 423 U.S. 232 (1976).

increases ownership above ten percent does not count for section 16(b) purposes—a holding now reflected in rule 16a–2(c).

In the other of these cases, *Reliance Electric Co. v. Emerson Electric Co.*,[5] the Supreme Court dealt with a situation in which an owner of 13.2 percent of a corporation's common stock sold all of the stock in two transactions, each within six months of the original purchase. In the first sale the owner reduced its interest to 9.96 percent, and in the second it sold out entirely. The two sales were two weeks apart and involved different purchasers, but they were part of a plan devised by the owner expressly to avoid section 16(b) liability for profits on the second sale. Since the two sales were "interrelated parts of a single plan," the district court found section 16(b) liability, regardless of the dates of the actual sales. The Supreme Court disagreed, however, based on the idea that "a 'plan' to sell that is conceived within six months of purchase clearly would not fall within '16(b) if the sale were made after the six months had expired.'" The Court did not see a valid basis for reaching "a different result where the 10% requirement is involved rather than the six-month limitation." This holding also has found its way into rule 16a–2(c).

The resolution of timing issues is somewhat different for officers and directors than for beneficial owners. As will be remembered, section 16(b) provides that it does not "cover any transaction where [a ten percent-plus] beneficial owner was not such, both at the time of the purchase and sale, or the sale and purchase," but the statute is silent on timing issues in the case of officers and directors. The Commission has filled the gap, however. In rule 16a–2(a) it provides that transactions occurring before a person becomes an officer or director are not subject to section 16 (except when an officer or director becomes subject to the section solely because his or her corporation has registered a class of equity securities under the Exchange Act). The story is different for transactions occurring after the termination of officer or director status. Such transactions are, under rule 16a–2(b), subject to section 16 if they can be matched within the required six-month period with a purchase or sale that occurred when the person was an officer or director (assuming no exemption is available).

Standing to Sue

On the subject of standing, section 16(b) provides that a plaintiff must be the "owner of [a] security of the issuer" at the time suit is "instituted." In *Gollust v. Mendell*,[6] the Supreme Court decided an interesting issue concerning the meaning of that provision: Can a

---

[5] 404 U.S. 418 (1972).

[6] 501 U.S. 115 (1991).

shareholder who has properly begun a section 16 action maintain that action after the shareholder's stock has been exchanged for stock in the parent corporation as a result of a merger? The main issue for the Court was whether one type of financial stake could be switched for another. With little discussion, the Court decided that it could.

Calculation of Profits

Section 16(b) provides no guidance on how to calculate profits. Theoretically, there are a number of possibilities. For example, a court could, for a particular period, subtract total sales prices from total purchase prices to arrive at total profits. Alternatively, a court could, for example, calculate profits by matching purchases and sales by stock certificate numbers when possible and, when that technique is impossible, use the "first in-first out" approach. Courts rejected those alternatives early on, however, in favor of an approach that gives the teeth of section 16(b) maximum bite.

The adopted approach, and the rationale behind it, were spelled out in a 1943 Second Circuit case, *Smolowe v. Delendo Corp.*:

> We must suppose that the statute was intended to be thoroughgoing, to squeeze all possible profits out of stock transactions, and thus to establish a standard so high as to prevent any conflict between the selfish interest of a fiduciary officer, director, or stockholder and the faithful performance of his duty. The only rule whereby all possible profits can be surely recovered is that of lowest price in, highest price out within six months. . . .[7]

The following are hypothetical purchases and sales that illustrate how that method works:

January 1	100 shares purchased at $10
February 1	200 shares purchased at $10
March 1	100 shares purchased at $11
April 1	100 shares purchased at $11
May 1	100 shares purchased at $12
June 1	100 shares purchased at $12
July 1	500 shares sold at $12
August 1	200 shares sold at $10
September 1	100 shares purchased at $7
October 1	100 shares purchased at $7
November 1	100 shares purchased at $7
December 1	100 shares sold at $8

---

[7] 136 F.2d 231, 239 (2d Cir.1943).

Profits are calculated by matching the highest sales price (500 shares sold at $12 on July 1) with the lowest purchase prices for a total of 500 shares (100 shares purchased on September 1, October 1, and November 1 at $7, and 200 shares purchased on February 1 at $10). The total sales price was, then, $6,000 (500 x $12) and the total purchase price $4,100 (300 x $7 = $2,100, plus 200 x $10 = $2,000), leading to a profit of $1,900. Once those matchings are accomplished, there are no other purchases and sales that can be matched to find a profit, and so all other transactions are ignored.

That matching illustrates the two aspects of profit calculation with which newcomers to section 16(b) often have trouble. First, transactions are broken down into whatever components are necessary to effect a matching that maximizes profits, share by share if necessary. For example, one purchase of 100 shares will be matched with 100 sales of one share each if that leads to the greatest profits. Second, the matchings for a multishare transaction that is broken into components can cover a period of just short of one year, not slightly less than six months. The only requirement is that, in each individual matching, the purchase and sale must be within six months of each other. For example, as indicated above, in the case of a 500-share sale on July 1, 200 shares involved in the matching were purchased on February 1 and 100 on November 1, even though February and November are more than six months apart.

Sarbanes–Oxley Blackout Trading Prohibition

Section 306 of Sarbanes–Oxley provides that, except as allowed by limited Commission rulemaking:

> it shall be unlawful for any director or executive officer of an issuer of any equity security (other than an exempted security), directly or indirectly, to purchase, sell, or otherwise acquire or transfer any equity security of the issuer (other than an exempted security) during any blackout period with respect to such equity security if such director or officer acquires such equity security in connection with his or her service or employment as a director or executive officer.

"Blackout period" is defined in detail. Basically the definition relates to periods during which ordinary beneficiaries of pension plans may not trade an issuer's securities. Section 306 also contains much detail with respect to, among other things, notices required to be given of blackout periods. One remedy provided by the section is disgorgement of profits and, as in the case of section 16(b), shareholders may sue to recover these profits, for the benefit of the issuer, in specified circumstances. The Commission has issued regulation BTR, which contains rules relating to trading during pension fund blackout periods.

Note an extremely important difference between section 306 and Exchange Act section 16(b). It is not unlawful to engage in short-swing trading under section 16(b)—the profits are merely to be disgorged to the issuer. Trading in violation of section 306, on the other hand, is unlawful. Therefore, in addition to disgorgement, traders are subject to criminal sanctions as well as non-criminal actions by the Commission.

Chapter 14

EXCHANGE ACT REGULATION OF THE SECURITIES BUSINESS

The Exchange Act contains a multitude of provisions that regulate the securities business. As its name implies, the Exchange Act regulates stock exchanges. It also regulates national securities associations (the Financial Industry Regulatory Authority ("FINRA") is the only such association registered under the Act) and other persons, businesses, and organizations involved in the securities business. Thus, for example, securities firms that act as brokers or dealers, and banks that act as transfer agents, also are regulated by the statute.

The Exchange Act's regulation of the securities business is highly specialized and involves only a small percentage of securities lawyers. Because of that specialization, only a selective examination of that regulation is warranted. Highlights of the following four areas are discussed below:

1. Regulation of stock exchanges and FINRA

2. Regulation of brokers and dealers

3. Margin requirements

4. Market manipulation and stabilization

Regulation of Stock Exchanges and FINRA

In its essence, section 5 of the Exchange Act requires the registration of securities exchanges, unless the Commission allows an exemption from the Act's registration requirements. Those requirements are detailed in section 6 and its rules, which provide for the filing of an application on Exchange Act form 1. Most of the requirements of section 6 relate to the substance of rules that an exchange is required to adopt. For example, an exchange's rules must "assure a fair representation of its members in the selection of its directors and administration of its affairs," must be "designed to prevent fraudulent and manipulative acts and practices," and must "provide that ... its members and persons associated with its members shall be appropriately disciplined for violation of the provisions of [the Exchange Act], the rules or regulations thereunder, or the rules of the exchange."

From the requirements for registration, it is easy to see that the drafters of the Exchange Act wanted registered exchanges to police themselves. Section 19 demonstrates the lengths to which that idea is taken. The section embodies a plan that involves self-regulation along with Commission oversight, which results in a high level of regulation and a minimal administrative burden on the Commission. As William O. Douglas described the Act's self-regulatory scheme, "[T]he exchanges take the leadership with Government playing a residual role. Government [keeps] the shotgun, so to speak, behind the door, loaded, well oiled, cleaned, ready for use but with the hope it [will] never have to be used."[1]

Under section 19, exchanges are required to file proposed rule changes with the Commission. After the Commission provides interested persons with the opportunity to be heard, it may either approve or disapprove a proposed rule change, or it may modify the change in any way it believes desirable. The Commission also is empowered to modify the rules of an exchange upon its own initiative. In addition, section 19 uses the same scheme in the case of disciplinary actions against a person who is subject to an exchange's rules: Exchanges make the initial decisions on discipline, but any final action by an exchange is subject to review by the Commission. Formal Commission action to override exchange-made decisions of any type is rare, however.

As originally drafted, the Exchange Act left the over-the-counter trading of securities generally unregulated. In 1938, however, Congress amended the Act to provide the same sort of self-regulatory scheme for that market as then existed for stock exchanges. The mechanism Congress chose was registration with the Commission of national securities associations and subjection of those associations to the Act's self-regulatory scheme. As indicated above, FINRA (formed in 2007 by the merger of the National Association of Securities Dealers, Inc. ("NASD") and the regulatory arm of the New York Stock Exchange) is the only securities association registered with the Commission.

Under Exchange Act section 15(b)(8) and (9), brokers and dealers required to be registered under the Act must be members of a registered securities association if they wish to trade in the over-the-counter market, with very limited exceptions.

It probably is worth noting that until fairly recently there were somewhat clear distinctions (both legal and practical) between traditional securities exchanges (such as the New York Stock Exchange) and "over-the-counter" markets. The "over-the-counter" markets—notably Nasdaq (which was pioneered by FINRA's predecessor, the NASD)—led the way in adopting electronic technology. Traditional exchanges, however, are increasingly relying on electronic communication, and Nasdaq itself has registered as a

---

[1] William O. Douglas, DEMOCRACY AND FINANCE 82 (1940).

national exchange. Other electronic trading systems have developed in competition with the traditional exchanges and Nasdaq; although historically regulated as broker-dealers, they now may choose to register either as broker-dealers or as exchanges. Those registering as broker-dealers typically will be members of FINRA.

New to the landscape of financial intermediaries are "funding portals," defined in Exchange Act section 3(a)(80). Pursuant to new section 4(a)(6) of the Securities Act, issuers may raise capital through exempt "crowdfunding" transactions facilitated either by these new entities or by brokers. Although funding portals are exempt from registering as brokers or dealers, they nonetheless must register with the Commission and become members of a registered national securities association. To qualify as a funding portal, the entity must be acting as an intermediary solely in crowdfunding transactions, must not offer investment advice or recommendations, and must not engage in solicitation with respect to securities offered on its website or portal. Funding portals also are prohibited from holding or otherwise handling investor funds.

Regulation of Brokers and Dealers

Exchange Act section 15(a) makes it unlawful to operate as a broker or dealer, through the means or instrumentalities of interstate commerce or the mails, unless Exchange Act registration is accomplished or an exemption is provided by the Commission. Obviously, securities firms are subject to that registration requirement, but other parties may also be covered, sometimes without realizing it. The issue may arise because the Exchange Act's definitions of "broker" and "dealer" include more than just traditional securities firms:

> Section 3(a)(4). The term "broker" means any person engaged in the business of effecting transactions in securities for the account of others, but does not include a bank.

> Section 3(a)(5). The term "dealer" means any person engaged in the business of buying and selling securities for his own account, through a broker or otherwise, but does not include a bank, or any person insofar as he buys or sells securities for his own account, either individually or in some fiduciary capacity, but not as a part of a regular business.

As discussed in the preceding section, securities firms that operate as brokers or dealers are subject to regulation by FINRA and perhaps by one or more exchanges. In addition, brokers and dealers come under the direct application of a wide variety of Exchange Act provisions and rules. For example, section 8 governs the lending of exchange-traded securities. Section 15(c)(1) and (2) prohibits a variety of forms of manipulative, deceptive, or fraudulent conduct. Rule 15c2–8 requires the delivery of Securities Act prospectuses on written request of customers and in some other circumstances. Rule 15c3–1 requires brokers and dealers to maintain specified amounts of net capital. And section 17 and its rules mandate in detail the keeping of records and the filing with the Commission of reports.

Although Congress has allowed the Commission substantial discretion in regulating broker-dealers, it still takes an active interest. For example, the Dodd-Frank Act both added Section 15(k) of the Exchange Act, authorizing the Commission to adopt a uniform fiduciary standard for investment advisers, brokers, and dealers when providing personalized investment advice, and directed the Commission to conduct a study on the wisdom of such an adoption. The JOBS Act less deferentially contained provisions effectively, and in some cases outright, repealing some of the (specific) former limits on broker-dealer conduct imposed by FINRA and the Commission.

In this context, one must not forget rule 10b–5. In addition to the applications of the rule as discussed in Chapter 12, it has applications of special interest to brokers and dealers. One of the more interesting applications of rule 10b–5 is its use to prohibit churning of customer accounts. Churning is the discretionary trading of a customer's securities for the purpose of generating commissions for the securities firm rather than profits for the customer. As stated by the Ninth Circuit,

> In order to establish a claim for churning, a plaintiff must show (1) that the trading in his account was excessive in light of his investment objectives; (2) that the broker in question exercised control over the trading in the account; and (3) that the broker acted with the intent to defraud or with the wilful and reckless disregard for the interests of his client.[2]

Proof of those elements is sufficient to establish a claim that rule 10b–5 has been violated.

The first element of a churning claim, excessive trading, is extremely subjective and involves proof and counterproof from expert witnesses who hold varying viewpoints on whether the trading was excessive. Typically, factors such as the rate at which the account is turned over, and the variations in turnover rate during the early and late stages in the life of an account, are examined against an arguable standard.

The second element, control over the account, may be easy to establish because, in the classic churning situation, a securities firm exercises formal discretionary authority over trades. The element of

---

[2] *Mihara v. Dean Witter & Co.*, 619 F.2d 814, 821 (9th Cir.1980).

control may also be proved by reference to the real facts of the relationship between the customer and the employee of the firm that handles the account, regardless of the legal power of the firm to trade without an order from the customer. In essence, the question is whether the firm in fact controlled the trading.

When the control element is proved, ambiguities concerning whether trades were excessive may well be resolved, at least as a practical matter, by how the trier of the facts decides the third element: intent to defraud or willful and reckless disregard for the interests of the client. It may be argued that that third element is, in fact, directly relevant to a determination of the existence of the first element. For example, it can be claimed that any trading done for the purpose of defrauding, rather than creating a return for, a client is excessive in light of the client's investment objectives.

"Day trading" is a strategy for speculating on short-term changes in market price generally involving buying and selling the same securities within a single day. FINRA rule 2130 requires member firms that promote day trading to establish accounts for would-be day traders only upon "reasonable grounds for believing that the day-trading strategy is appropriate for the customer." As part of the required process, firms must either approve an account for day trading or obtain a written agreement that it will not be so used. Member firms that promote day trading also must provide noninstitutional customers with risk disclosure statements.

Margin Requirements

Buying securities on excessive credit, or margin, was one of the problems that led to the stock market collapse that began in 1929. In many cases, customers who purchased securities used only a small percentage of their own money. As soon as security prices began to fall, large amounts of securities had to be dumped into a nonreceptive market to prevent losses by those who had lent most of the money for the purchase of the securities. Those sales then caused the market to fall even lower. The drafters of the Exchange Act were determined to prevent a recurrence of those conditions by establishing a system for regulating the amount of credit that can be used to purchase or carry securities.

The work of the drafters is found in section 7 of the Exchange Act. It provides that, initially upon the passage of the Act in 1934, the amount of credit that may be used to purchase or carry a non-exempted security is not to be more than the higher of:

(1) 55 per centum of the current market price of the security, or

(2) 100 per centum of the lowest market price of the security during the preceding thirty-six calendar months, but not more than 75 per centum of the current market price.

Congress realized that the amount of credit to be allowed, along with certain related matters, must be fine-tuned periodically. Therefore, in section 7, Congress gave power over those issues to the Board of Governors of the Federal Reserve System. Since 1934 the Board has controlled margin requirements through a series of regulations and amendments to those regulations. For many years, the legal margin rate has been 50 percent.

Nothing in the authority granted to the Board of Governors prevents the entities or individuals regulated from imposing stricter margin requirements than those mandated by the Board. For instance, FINRA has imposed stricter requirements on the accounts of "pattern day traders." For this purpose, "pattern day trading" generally is defined as the execution through a margin account of four intra-day purchases and sales within a period of five days.

Regulation of the Security-Based Swap Industry

In the Dodd-Frank Act of 2010, Congress sought to create a regulatory regime governing the market for swaps. The Commission was allocated responsibility for the part of the market known as "security-based swaps." In the words of the Commission, this means that the Commission regulates:

Dealers and major players in the security-based swap market;

Trading platforms and exchanges on which certain security-base swaps would be transacted;

Clearing agencies that generally step in the place of the original counterparties and effectively assume the risk should there be a default; and

Data repositories, which would collect data on security-based swaps as they are transacted by counterparties, make that information available to regulators, and disseminate data, such as the prices of security-based swap transactions, to the public.

Although this is a specialized area generally beyond the scope of this book, it is worth noting that the Commission is making progress in the area. A number of terms have been defined and rules have been proposed for, e.g., registration of security-based swap dealers. In addition, proposed Regulation SB SEF is designed to create a registration framework for security-based swap execution facilities

("SB–SEFs") and to establish rules for compliance with fourteen enumerated core principles. As part of the proposal, registered SB SEFs would be exempt from regulation as either exchanges or, subject to certain conditions, brokers

Market Manipulation and Stabilization

The Exchange Act and its rules provide a comprehensive scheme for the regulation of activities that disrupt the free movement of securities prices in accordance with supply and demand. Because of a historical anomaly, section 9 of the Act, which is entitled "Prohibition Against Manipulation of Security Prices," dealt only with securities listed on securities exchanges. So as not to leave the manipulation of securities prices in the over-the-counter market unchecked, the federal courts pressed into service two general antifraud provisions, Securities Act section 17(a) and Exchange Act rule 10b–5. Exchange Act sections 15(c)(1) and (2) also help prohibit manipulation in the over-the-counter market. Basically, the prohibitions against market manipulation ended up being essentially the same regardless of the market involved. The anomaly was addressed, however, in 2010, when section 9 was amended to include not only securities not registered on an exchange but also security-based swaps (security-based swap agreements were already included).

Section 9 contains a number of prohibitions. The one at the heart of market manipulation is found in section 9(a)(2), which essentially makes it unlawful for any person:

> To effect, alone or with one or more persons, a series of transactions in any security registered on a national securities exchange creating actual or apparent active trading in such security or raising or depressing the price of such security, for the purpose of inducing the purchase or sale of such security by others.

Although that prohibition relates to any person, and not only to those in the securities business, those in the securities business find the temptation of market manipulation closest to hand.

In light of the Exchange Act's strong general prohibition of market manipulation, it is interesting that one activity that is clearly manipulative—stabilization—is allowed specifically by the Exchange Act. The Commission, in Exchange Act Release No. 2,446 (Mar. 18, 1940), has described stabilization as "the buying of a security for the limited purpose of preventing or retarding a decline in its open market price in order to facilitate its distribution to the public."

How stabilization works is most easily seen in the case of a class of securities that are already publicly traded when the issuer wants to sell additional securities of the same class in an offering registered under the Securities Act. As a practical matter, the underwriters must offer the new securities to the public at essentially the same price at which securities of the class were trading just prior to the time the registration statement became effective, that is, at the market price. More important, the underwriters have to pay the issuer a price that is just far enough below the market price to allow the underwriters a fair profit when the securities are sold at the market price.

The problem for the underwriters is that the market price might drop if the usual market forces of supply and demand were allowed free rein during the period when the underwriters were selling the new securities. If the market price were to drop, the underwriters could not sell their securities without lowering their offering price. In the long run, of course, underwriters would refuse to take the risks involved in that type of underwriting, at least without additional compensation. During the period underwriters are distributing an offering of securities, however, the forces of supply and demand are not allowed to run free. Rather, the underwriters are allowed, under Exchange Act section 9(a)(6) and Exchange Act rule 104 of regulation M, to stabilize the market price for the class of securities they are selling.

Rule 104 is filled with detailed requirements and limitations. It allows the underwriters to buy in the trading markets, at prices allowed by the rule, any securities of the same class as those being underwritten. Typically, stabilizing is maintained until the offering is completed. That process usually takes one or two days, but an offering sometimes drags on for much longer. It is important to remember that, during the entire time stabilizing goes on, the price of the securities that are stabilized is artificially maintained—that is, the price is manipulated.

That manipulation can easily harm members of the trading public, who generally buy and sell securities on the assumption that prices are set in accordance with the law of supply and demand. For example, an investor who is contemplating the purchase of newly offered securities may check the current quotations for the security in the trading market and learn that it is trading at the public offering price. That investigation may provide false confidence that the market has valued the security at that price, particularly if it is done several days after the offering has begun, for if the offering has taken that long to complete, the new securities obviously are not being well received by the public. In that circumstance, the price likely will drop when the stabilizing bid is pulled, resulting in losses to anyone who bought in reliance on the apparent stability of the security's price in the market.

Because of the dangers of stabilization, the Commission requires that the prospectus disclose whether the underwriters intend to stabilize. Virtually without exception, prospectuses that offer stock, bonds, and some other securities include such disclosure. There are two main problems with the protections the legend offers. First, the average investor probably does not understand stabilization and its effect. Second, the average investor checking market quotations has no easy way of telling whether stabilization currently is going on.

Investors are not, however, the only ones who can suffer because of stabilization. The underwriters can fare even worse. Sometimes shareholders who own large amounts of securities wait to sell until a new offering is made, knowing that the underwriters will place a stabilizing bid. Then, as soon as stabilization begins, the shareholders dump their securities into the market. When that happens, the underwriters can end up buying a substantial amount of securities at the retail price.

Despite those shortcomings, it is hard to argue that stabilization should be prohibited. As indicated above, underwriting as it exists today could not be performed without stabilization, since the risks to the underwriters would be too great. If no other alternative were found, the costs of engaging underwriters would have to increase. Also, underwriters argue with substantial justification that bringing a new offering into a market in which securities of the same class are already trading itself introduces an abnormality, because of the sudden increase in supply it causes. To that extent, stabilization can be justified as an offset to a market abnormality. In the end, however, it probably is most correct merely to view stabilization as a necessary evil.

Chapter 15

INTERNATIONAL ASPECTS OF
SECURITIES LAW

Capital cannot be jurisdictionally contained. Issuers realize the benefits of reaching out to foreign investors, just as investors realize the benefits of holding international portfolios. Development of round-the-clock trading venues, as well as means of virtually instantaneous communication and expeditious fund transfers, seem to suggest that national borders are artificial constructs without obvious relevance to issuers' capital needs or investors' hunger for profits. This portrayal does not, of course, comport with regulatory reality. The Securities Act and the Exchange Act do, in fact, reach some transactions and not others, just as do the regulations of foreign nations. Although the precise metes and bounds of coverage are problematic, some aspects are quite clear.

Internationalization of the Securities Markets

There are a number of reasons why American issuers have increased their offshore offerings. Without a doubt, one of those reasons is that the burdens of foreign securities regulation are seen as significantly less than the burdens imposed by the United States. Ironically, foreign issuers also have increased their attempts to access American capital markets. These markets are both broader and deeper than those of other countries—a state of affairs often attributed to the United States' tradition of a strong scheme of securities regulation.

Naturally, securities that are initially distributed in a different country may not stay there. Thus, foreign investors may buy securities of an American issuer in an initial distribution but may also purchase such securities on the United States trading markets. They may attempt to sell their holdings in a foreign trading market or on an American one. All of the same permutations may apply in the case of Americans acquiring and disposing of the securities of foreign issuers and, for that matter, in the case of foreign investors dealing in the securities of issuers of non-American origin.

When and Where United States Laws Apply

When must foreign persons comply with the provisions of the Securities Act or the Exchange Act? Are there circumstances in which United States persons need not comply with the Securities Act or the Exchange Act because their conduct has so little to do with the

United States? An essential starting point in answering these questions is the definition of "interstate commerce." Under both the Securities Act and the Exchange Act, this term includes commerce or communication between any foreign country and any state.

Breadth of "Interstate Commerce"

Because "interstate commerce" includes commerce with foreign countries, an argument can be made that any transaction with "one end" in the United States can be reached under the United States' securities laws. In fact, given the broad construction of "interstate commerce," a single telephone call involving one party in the United States might invoke the jurisdiction of American securities laws. Certainly, then, one should not be surprised to find that if a foreign issuer launches a public offering to United States investors, it must comply with the registration requirements of the Securities Act (and will be liable for any disclosure problems or fraud).

Suppose, however, that a United States issuer wishes to offer its securities exclusively to foreign investors. In a move not dictated by the language of the Securities Act, the Commission has taken the position that the purpose of the federal securities laws is to protect *American* investors, and that an offering that is carefully directed offshore and reasonably tailored to stay there need not be registered. This position is discussed in more detail later in this chapter. As an introductory matter, however, the Commission's view is sufficient to alert us that United States securities laws will not be extended to their utmost literal coverage. The considerations prompting this restraint include notions of international comity, as well as an interest in conserving the Commission's own enforcement resources.

Importance of Context

Let us return to the case of the foreign issuer raising capital from American investors. As a variation, suppose that the foreign issuer is not specifically targeting United States residents but simply makes no particular attempt to exclude them from its offering. Suppose, for instance, that such an issuer holds a press conference in its home country, in order to discuss its public offering plans. Reports of the conference are foreseeably circulated in the United States— perhaps because a few expatriates have subscriptions to newspapers from their former homeland. The breadth of the concept of an "offer," introduced in Chapter 4, would ordinarily suggest that the readers now resident in the United States are offerees. The United States offers would be integrated with the public offering in the issuer's home country, and it would appear that registration in the United States would be required. Or would it? Although, as we shall see, the answer is "probably not," we would get a different answer if we asked whether a United States purchaser could claim a remedy under the antifraud provisions of either the Securities Act or the Exchange Act.

In fact, coverage of the United States securities laws is interpreted most narrowly when the need for registration under one of the Acts is at issue, and most broadly when the question presented involves liability for violation of one of the antifraud provisions of either the Securities Act or the Exchange Act. From the standpoint of international comity, this is quite sensible. Presumably, no foreign nation will have a strong interest in preserving the ability of its nationals to engage in fraud, nor any strong aversion to having its nationals protecting from the fraud of others. By contrast, foreign sovereigns may have their own schemes for registration and market regulation. Adding the requirements of the United States scheme might present outright conflicts and undue burdens on would-be securities transactions.

The difference in approach just described is well established, and in part has been exacerbated by the differing entities offering the relevant interpretations, as well as by the different purposes for which the interpretations have been offered. As noted above, the Commission has attempted to aid planners by defining the situations in which registration is and is not required. For predictable policy reasons, it has declined to take the most aggressive stance possible. The coverage of the United States antifraud laws typically is determined by the federal courts, and is considered only after the alleged wrongdoing occurs. The following sections present separate analyses for United States registration requirements and for the rules relating to fraud.

United States Registration Requirements

It is clear that Congress initially intended to reach offerings of foreign securities in the United States. Such offerings were common and contributed to the losses suffered by American investors before passage of the primary United States securities legislation in 1933 and 1934. Given the breadth of the "interstate commerce" and "offer" concepts, however, the Acts could be construed to cover much more.

Securities Offered Abroad

Regulation S

In 1964 the Commission issued Securities Act Release No. 4,708, announcing its belief that section 5 of the Securities Act does not apply to offerings reasonably designed to "come to rest" outside of the United States. In the years that followed, numerous offerings by American and foreign issuers took place in reliance on the Release. These offerings were directed to foreign nationals and restricted in various ways preventing, for a period of time, resales to American investors.

In 1990 the Commission adopted (and in 1998 significantly amended) regulation S to give additional guidance. Regulation S is a non-exclusive safe harbor from Securities Act registration for offers and sales taking place outside of the United States. Technically, it does not provide an exemption from registration. Rather, it expresses the Commission's view that registration for the protection of foreign investors is not within the principal purposes of the Securities Act.

Regulation S states that the terms "offer," "offer to sell," "sell," "sale," and "offer to buy" used in Securities Act section 5 are deemed to exclude offerings reasonably designed to preclude distribution and redistribution inside the United States or to United States investors. It then goes on to describe the terms of such offerings by both domestic and foreign issuers, and also provides a safe harbor for certain resales. Regulation S does not purport to address coverage of the antifraud provisions of either the Securities Act or the Exchange Act.

Regulation S is composed of Securities Act rules 901–905. These rules require that "no directed selling efforts" be made in the United States and that no offers be made to persons in the United States. They also require that sales take place on an established foreign securities exchange or designated offshore securities market, or that the buyer be offshore at the time the buy order originates. The rules are quite detailed and make use of a number of defined terms. One important focus of the rules is preventing securities placed under their auspices by domestic issuers from "trickling back" into the United States under circumstances suggesting initial abuse of the rules. For instance, equity securities placed offshore by domestic issuers are subject to a one-year "distribution compliance period." During this period, no offers or sales may be made to United States persons, and issuers are required to restrict transfers accordingly. Other restrictions also apply. Rule 905, added in 1998, also makes equity securities placed by domestic issuers under regulation S "restricted securities" for purposes of resale under rule 144, which is discussed in Chapter 7.

Pursuant to regulation S's own terms, domestic offerings and offshore transactions qualifying under the regulation can occur contemporaneously. In other words, the regulation contains its own safe harbor from integration.

Certain Press Communications

As part of the National Securities Markets Improvement Act of 1996, Congress directed the Commission to adopt rules clarifying the status of offshore press activities under the Securities Act. This action was stimulated by a concern that American journalists were being barred from press conferences, meetings, and receipt of press materials pertaining to proposed securities offerings and tender offers. The Commission obliged, responding in 1997 with new rules under both the Securities Act and the Exchange Act. These rules establish safe harbors for securities offerings by foreign issuers and selling security holders and for tender offers made by any bidder for a foreign private target.

The gist of rule 135e under the Securities Act is that all press activity qualifying for a safe harbor must occur offshore, must be open to foreign journalists as well as American journalists, and must relate to an offering that will take place at least partially offshore. To qualify, a meeting must be in a foreign country (with no telephone links to America) and written materials must be delivered on foreign soil. Written materials must bear appropriate legends and cannot be accompanied by any form of purchase order or coupon to indicate interest in the offering. Amended rule 14d–1 under the Exchange Act states similar conditions for press activity that will not be deemed to launch a tender offer in the United States for the securities of a foreign issuer. Neither rule covers paid advertisements.

The safe harbors for press contacts are, of course, only with respect to filing and procedural matters and do not relate to the requirements of the United States laws prohibiting fraud.

Website Postings

If offerors take adequate precautions to prevent United States persons from participating in an offshore Internet offering, the Commission will not view the offer as targeted at, and thus occurring in, the United States for registration purposes. In the case of website postings (but not more targeted forms of Internet communication), the Commission has provided specific guidance. In Securities Act Release No. 33–7516 (Mar. 23, 1998), it indicated an offshore Internet offer made by a non-United States offeror generally would not be regarded as targeted at the United States if (1) the website includes a prominent disclaimer that offers are being made in the United States (which might take the form of a statement that offers are being made only in other jurisdictions), (2) the offeror implements procedures reasonably designed to guard against sales to United States persons (such as confirming purchasers' residences before sale), and (3) the solicitation does not appear by its content to be targeted at United States persons (as might be the case if the investor's ability to avoid United States taxation were emphasized). In the case of United States offerors, these requirements must be augmented by password-type procedures reasonably designed to ensure that only non-United States persons can gain access to the offer. Under this kind of procedure, prospective investors would have to demonstrate to the issuer or intermediary that they were not United States persons before receiving the password.

Outside the Safe Harbors

Obviously, a cautious foreign issuer can plan an offering in reliance on Regulation S and, now, conduct its press contacts in accordance with the applicable safe harbor rules. It is just as obvious that some foreign issuers will engage in what they believe are offerings having nothing to do with the United States and therefore will fail to consult its safe harbors, much less adhere to them. We should return, then, to the earlier example of the foreign issuer holding the foreign press conference, reports of which are received by expatriates in newspapers from their foreign home towns. Let us assume that there is some reason the conference does not qualify for a safe harbor—perhaps because written materials were distributed without appropriate legends.

The stance taken by courts in dealing with these matters may fairly be summarized as follows: "[I]n the absence of a strong American interest, there is 'no reason to extend jurisdiction to cases where the United States activities . . . are relatively small in comparison to those abroad.'"[1] This means, of course, that United States courts are called upon both to assess the presence and strength of American interests as well as to evaluate the balance of American and offshore activities. In doing so, they have identified and discussed a number of factors, including the presence of alternative regulatory schemes and the reasonable expectations of the person arguably required to comply with United States law.

Securities of Foreign Issuers Offered in the United States

Exemptions from Securities Act Registration

A foreign issuer planning an offering to United States nationals must register under the Securities Act or find an applicable exemption. The exemptions from registration are, with two exceptions, available without respect to the issuer's nationality. The first exception is regulation A, which may be used only by domestic and Canadian issuers. The second is the crowdfunding exemption created by new section 4(a)(6), which is reserved for domestic issuers.

Not infrequently, foreign issuers will place securities with American institutional investors under section 4(a)(2) of the

---

[1] *Plessey Company plc v. General Electric Company plc*, 628 F.Supp. 477 (D.Del.1986).

Securities Act (the "private offering" exemption discussed in Chapter 6). They can, and often do, invoke the safe harbor of rule 506 (also discussed in that chapter), which calls for restrictions on resales of the securities involved. The institutions acquiring the securities may rely on the resale provisions of regulation S if they choose to attempt to dispose of the securities overseas. They may also sell pursuant to rule 144A, the safe harbor for resales to institutional investors. Rule 144, which deals generally with resales of restricted securities, also will be available when its terms are met.

Rules 801 and 802 were adopted by the Commission in 1999 to facilitate rights offers, exchange offers, and business combinations involving foreign private issuers. United States holders must own no more than ten percent of the securities subject to the transaction. To receive the benefit of the exemption, United States holders must be given equal treatment with foreign holders, and any information provided to holders of the securities must be provided to United States holders in English. There are other technical requirements, including that the following legend must appear prominently on any informational document disseminated to United States holders:

> This [rights offering, exchange offer, or business combination] is made for the securities of a foreign company. The offer is subject to the disclosure requirements of a foreign country that are different from those of the United States. Financial statements included in the document, if any, have been prepared in accordance with foreign accounting standards that may not be comparable to the financial statements of United States companies.

Securities Act Registration by Foreign Issuers

If registration is required, a foreign issuer may use one of a specially designed series of forms. These forms are denominated "F–1" and "F–3," and generally parallel the "S–1" and "S–3" forms used by domestic issuers. The foreign issuer's financial statements either may be reconciled with generally accepted accounting principles or prepared in accordance with international financial reporting standards ("IFRS") published by the International Accounting Standards Board. (Interestingly, although the Commission in 2008 issued a "roadmap" looking toward requiring IFRS-compliant financial statements from domestic filers as soon as 2014, the effort has stalled.) The Commission has entered into or is considering a number of multijurisdictional accords conforming the requirements for filings in multiple jurisdictions. For instance, specially designated forms permit certain Canadian issuers to satisfy United States registration requirements with Canadian disclosure documents.

Exchange Act Registration and Reporting by Foreign Issuers

In general, foreign issuers of securities traded on an exchange or quoted in an automated inter-dealer quotation system must register those securities under the Exchange Act using form 20–F. Form 20–F calls for the same level of disclosure as form F–1 under the Securities Act. Pursuant to rule 3a12–3(b), the securities of foreign issuers registered under the Exchange Act are exempt from proxy regulation under section 14, as well as short-swing trading regulation under section 16.

Exchange Act Section 12(g)(1) now requires registration within 120 days of the last day of the first fiscal year in which an issuer (a) has total assets exceeding $10,000,000 and (b) a class of equity security "held of record" by *either* 2,000 or more persons *or* 500 or more unaccredited investors. In light of the practical difficulties of extraterritorial enforcement of this requirement, section 12(g)(3) gives the Commission authority to exempt the securities of foreign issuers from section 12(g) "in the public interest and consistent with the protection of investors." Rule 12g–3–2 exempts a class of a foreign issuer's securities if that class has fewer than 300 holders resident in the United States. It also exempts a foreign issuer's securities if the issuer maintains a listing of its equity securities in their primary trading market outside the U.S. and electronically publishes certain disclosure documents in English. These exemptions do not address the requirement that an issuer register a security if it is traded on a U.S. national exchange (or, in the case of the second exemption, a security traded on the over-the-counter Bulletin Board).

Special Case of American Depositary Receipts

It is difficult to consider the topic of foreign securities offered in the United States without encountering the subject of American Depositary Receipts, or "ADRs." In recent years, ADRs have accounted for approximately 10 percent of the total value of the American public market in equity securities. In an ADR program, a United States bank agrees to act as depositary for a foreign issuer's securities. The bank issues ADRs, which are negotiable certificates representing ownership of some amount of the foreign issuer's securities, to American investors. The bank itself is the actual owner (typically through a foreign custodian) of the foreign issuer's securities. It receives dividends and passes them on in American dollars to the holders of the ADRs. It also forwards information and proxy materials received from the foreign issuer.

The Commission regards ADRs as securities issued by the United States bank maintaining the program, and it is the bank that must register them under the Securities Act. The amount of disclosure required depends on whether the ADR program is designed to raise capital for the foreign issuer or simply gives American investors access to securities that already have been issued. Exchange Act compliance, however, is a matter for the foreign issuer. Rule 12g–3, described in the preceding section, may excuse a foreign issuer whose ADRs are not traded on an exchange or automated quotation system from Exchange Act registration under section 12(g). If the foreign issuer's ADRs are traded on an exchange or automated quotation system, the foreign issuer must file a full form 20–F.

United States Antifraud Requirements

Federal courts do not define the international scope of the United States securities laws as coextensive with principles of international relations. In other words, they decline to assert the broadest application that might be tolerated by international law. Instead, they have sought to articulate the coverage of the federal securities laws in terms of (at least constructive) congressional intent.

Until 2010, it was possible to distill the wisdom of many of the judicial precedents on application of United States antifraud provisions in terms of two tests. The first was the "conduct" test; the second was the "effects" test. The "conduct" test was based on a principle of foreign relations law stipulating that a country can assert jurisdiction over significant conduct within its territory, and was adopted to protect the integrity of American security markets from reputational inroads. As described by the Second Circuit in *SEC v. Kasser*,[2] the test prevented the United States from becoming "a Barbary Coast . . . harboring international securities 'pirates.' " The "effects" test was based on a perception that a primary congressional purpose in adopting the securities laws is to protect American investors.

A great deal of the implied clarity of having two neatly labeled tests dissolved in application. For instance, is mailing documents into the United States conduct within the country or an effect within the country? More importantly, how much conduct and how much effect were enough to satisfy a judicial quest to comply with congressional intent? Courts generally assumed that could assert jurisdiction where either the "conduct" or "effect" approach so indicated. They also engaged in an "admixture" or "combination" approach.

The Supreme Court case of *Morrison v. National Australia Bank* was a game-changer as far as extraterritorial application of

---

[2]   548 F.2d 109 (2d Cir.1977).

Exchange Act section 10(b) and rule 10b–5 is concerned.[3] Courts applying the tests described above previously had viewed extraterritorial application of the two provisions as a question of subject matter jurisdiction. In *Morrison*, the Supreme Court noted that pursuant to section 27 of the Exchange Act, federal courts do have jurisdiction over all questions arising under the Act. Instead, it framed the inquiry exclusively as one of congressional intent with respect to which transactions section 10(b) was to cover. The Court concluded that section 10(b) reaches the use of a manipulative or deceptive device or contrivance *only* in connection with the purchase or sale of a security listed on an American stock exchange, or the purchase or sale of any other security in the United States.

The approach endorsed in *Morrison* has come to be known as the "transactional test." The case is subject to criticism for creating a number of ambiguities, including whether section 10(b) and rule 10b–5 should apply if a security cross-listed on both an American and foreign exchange were sold in a fraudulent overseas transaction.

Although *Morrison* involved a private plaintiff, the majority's logic seemed to extend to actions brought by the Commission and the Department of Justice as well. Less than a month after *Morrison* was decided, Congress amended section 27 of the Exchange Act to specify that U.S. federal courts have extraterritorial jurisdiction over actions brought by either the Commission or the United States involving allegations of fraud in violation of the Exchange Act and either "(1) conduct within the United States that constitutes significant steps in furtherance of the violation, even if the securities transaction occurs outside the United States and involves only foreign investors; or (2) conduct occurring outside the United States that has a foreseeable substantial effect within the United States." Similar provisions were adopted with respect to jurisdiction over actions under the Securities and Investment Advisors Acts. Congress also directed the Commission to study whether the same approach should be taken for actions brought by private plaintiffs. The Commission released its report in April 2012, noting various options and concluding that "[a]bsent legislation, lower federal courts in particular will likely be called upon to resolve myriad novel and difficult issues regarding the application of the new transactional test."

Ironically, given the Supreme Court's framing of extraterritorial applicability of section 10(b) as something other than a question of subject matter jurisdiction, section 27 as amended arguably does nothing to reverse *Morrison*'s holding with respect to transactional coverage; it merely confirms the Court's holding with respect to jurisdiction. Still, there is no doubt that Congress intended to restore

---

[3]   130 S.Ct. 2869 (2010).

what was generally the state of pre-*Morrison* law for government enforcement purposes, and the courts presumably will give effect to that intent.

Other Requirements of United States Law

Section 30(b) of the Exchange Act generally exempts from that Act's coverage any person transacting a business in securities outside the United States. Although section 30(b) authorizes the Commission to regulate such persons, the Commission has declined to do so. Accordingly, foreign broker-dealers usually need not comply with the complicated regime to which domestic broker-dealers are subject.

This does not mean, however, that the other provisions of the Exchange Act do not apply to foreign persons. For instance, foreign security holders are required to file reports of their holdings as called for under sections 13(d) and 16(a). Moreover, in *Roth v. Fund of Funds*,[4] the Second Circuit found a foreign mutual fund liable for short-swing trading profits under section 16(b).

Enforcement Matters

The Commission does actively enforce the United States securities laws against foreign nationals. Its power to do so is, of course, subject to the difficulties of establishing subject matter and personal jurisdiction. According to section 22(a) of the Securities Act and section 27 of the Exchange Act, process may be served "wherever the defendant may be found." This breadth is limited by the due process requirement that the person to be charged must have good reason to know that his conduct will have an effect in the locale seeking jurisdiction.

As a practical matter, investigations involving foreign nationals can be hampered by foreign laws. In *SEC v. Banca Della Svissera Italiana*,[5] the court considered whether to compel a response to answer Commission interrogatories in a situation in which disclosure might subject the resisting party to criminal liability in its home country (under Swiss bank secrecy laws). After balancing the interests at stake and the good faith of the resisting party, the court ordered disclosure.

In some instances, enforcement difficulties are eased by international treaty. For instance, the United States and Switzerland have a treaty calling for mutual assistance in the investigation of activity that is criminal in both countries. Such treaties are, of course, limited in their terms and subject to the constitutional constraint of approval by the United States Senate. More frequently,

---

[4] 405 F.2d 421 (2d Cir.1968).

[5] 92 F.R.D. 111 (S.D.N.Y.1981).

the Commission enters into non-binding Memoranda of Understanding, or "MOUs," with its counterparts in other countries. These MOUs typically call for inter-agency sharing of information.

The International Securities Enforcement Cooperation Act of 1990 gave the Commission a partial exemption from the United States Freedom of Information Act for information received from a foreign authority under an MOU. This legislation also permits the Commission to sanction securities professionals for activities illegal under foreign law. Moreover, the Commission generally is authorized (under the Securities Fraud Enforcement Act of 1988) to cooperate in foreign investigations, even where no violation of United States law has occurred.

TABLE OF CASES

223

INDEX